GOTHIC PATHOLOGIES

Also by David Punter

ASLEEP AT THE WHEEL

BLAKE, HEGEL AND DIALECTIC

CHINA AND GLASS

INTRODUCTION TO CONTEMPORARY CULTURAL STUDIES
(*editor*)

LOST IN THE SUPERMARKET

ROMANTICISM AND IDEOLOGY (*with David Aers and
Jonathan Cook*)

SELECTED POEMS OF PHILIP LARKIN

THE HIDDEN SCRIPT: Writing and the Unconscious

THE LITERATURE OF TERROR: A History of Gothic Fictions from
1765 to the Present Day

Vol. I: The Gothic Tradition
Vol. II: The Modern Gothic

THE ROMANTIC UNCONSCIOUS: A Study in Narcissism and
Patriarchy

WILLIAM BLAKE: The New Casebook (*editor*)

WILLIAM BLAKE: Selected Poetry and Prose (*editor*)

Gothic Pathologies

The Text, the Body and the Law

David Punter
Professor of English
University of Stirling

First published in Great Britain 1998 by
MACMILLAN PRESS LTD
Houndmills, Basingstoke, Hampshire RG21 6XS and London
Companies and representatives throughout the world

A catalogue record for this book is available from the British Library.

ISBN 0–333–65801–9 hardcover
ISBN 0–333–65802–7 paperback

First published in the United States of America 1998 by
ST. MARTIN'S PRESS, INC.,
Scholarly and Reference Division,
175 Fifth Avenue, New York, N.Y. 10010

ISBN 0–312–21260–7

Library of Congress Cataloging-in-Publication Data
Punter, David.
Gothic pathologies : the text, the body, and the law / David
Punter.
p. cm.
Includes bibliographical references and index.
ISBN 0–312–21260–7 (cloth)
1. Horror tales, English—History and criticism. 2. King,
Stephen, 1947– —Criticism and interpretation. 3. Horror tales,
American—History and criticism. 4. Literature—History and
criticism—Theory, etc. 5. Literature, Comparative—English and
Chinese. 6. Literature, Comparative—Chinese and English.
7. Gothic revival (Literature)—Great Britain. 8. Chinese fiction-
-History and criticism. 9. Body, Human, in literature. 10. Law in
literature. I. Title.
PR830.T3P86 1998
823'.0872909—dc21   97–38767
                                                            CIP

For Caroline

Contents

Preface and Acknowledgements

Is this a book about Gothic? It is that, of course; but I would like to think that it is also something more, an attempt to explore the implications of a theory of literature. That theory of literature is built upon textuality and loss, on textuality *as* loss. My principal debts in the elaboration of this theory are to psychoanalysis. To Freud, naturally; but not so much, the reader may find, to Lacan, by whose work I remain largely unimpressed, although I accept that some of his perceptions have sunk into everyday usage. I think there are two reasons for my scepticism: first, that the idea of the name-of-the-father, and the extensive superstructure which follows from that idea, is, in my view, fundamentally flawed; and second, that Lacan's work provides no evidence that he understood the power of dream.

Since my notion of literature is at all points connected to dream, it will therefore probably come as no surprise that Jung is extensively present in what follows, particularly as mediated through the major contemporary figure in neo-Jungian thinking, James Hillman. My revision of the category of the name-of-the-father flows in part from these sources; but is also, as I see it, in tune with thinkers as diverse as Bettelheim and Baudrillard.

A colleague of mine disarmingly said to me recently that when I was appointed to my current post I was advertised to the department as being not really a literary critic at all, but something to do with cultural studies. I am not sure how true that is, but it does appear to be the case that the material in this book could be, again in my view, regarded as cultural psychology or, perhaps better, cultural pathology. I would like to think that this focus is a matter of some political urgency, for reasons which I hope will become clear to the reader in the final chapter.

The chapters in the book are diverse. Chapter 2, for example, is pretty much historical; Chapters 3 and 7 might be seen, on the other hand, as primarily 'mythopoeic', if that term still retains any meaning. The first and last chapters consist in large part of general reflections, although in the latter case these reflections are anchored to a specific body of contemporary writing. Other chapters take up different stances, some more, some perhaps less, easily describable.

Parts of the book rely on material I have already published elsewhere. An earlier version of Chapter 2 was published in *Eighteenth-Century Studies* as long ago as 1982. Chapter 3 derives from work published in *Les Cahiers FORELL* in 1994, and from an article published in Italian in 1995, in *Romanticismo Europeo e Traduzione*, edited by Lilla Crisafulli Jones and others. Chapter 5 develops from a piece published in 1991 in *Tropes of Revolution*, edited by C.C. Barfoot and Theo D'Haen, and Chapter 6 from an article published in 1994 in a special edition of *Women's Writing*. A version of Chapter 8 figured in *American Horror Fiction*, published in 1990 and edited by Brian Docherty, and a version of Chapter 9 in *LIT: Literature, Interpretation, Theory* from 1994. My first encounter with the material of Chapter 10 can be found in a 1988 issue of *Strawberry Fare*.

I wish also to make some acknowledgements, although I have never been very sure how to do this. I ought at least, though, to attempt some distinctions. First then, acknowledgements of intellectual discussion. These have, for me, never been very extensive; I have usually found myself, against my own apparent wishes, but for reasons that may be all too apparent to the reader, working outside critical trends. But in recent years I have found particularly rewarding contact in conversations with Nicholas Royle; and I should also like to acknowledge other members of my current department at Stirling, particularly Lance Butler, Glennis Byron and Rory Watson, and of my previous department at the Chinese University of Hong Kong, especially Louie Crew and Ying-hsiung Chou (the Chinese Oedipus), as well as members of the International Gothic Association, particularly Jerry Hogle and Allan Lloyd Smith. Psychoanalytically (which is quite different), and apart from those mentioned above, my main influences have been (perhaps inevitably) from the dead, for example Félix Guattari and Wilfred Bion. Between the two, in that difficult terrain which sits uneasily within the transference, my main debt, as always, is to my only mentor, John Broadbent; but now also, and in a measure impossible to quantify, to my wife Caroline Case, who is also psychoanalytically trained, and who is continually horrified at my cavalier use of analytic concepts; to whom also I owe an inexpressible personal debt, even though some of these chapters were conceived before we knew each other; which is, of course, no telepathic bar to her influence. In that other difficult terrain which is the literary, which to me also means the terrain of thinking, among my guides have been Brecht, Adorno and the good ol' boys of Central Europe; often as mediated to me by the brilliance of my colleagues at the University of Silesia, Tadeusz Sławek and Teddy Rachwał. In the closing stages of the book, I have been much helped by conversation with students currently writing dissertations under my direction, at undergraduate and postgraduate level: Christos Anthis, Vic Arrowsmith (who claims I taught her all she ever needed to know about violence), Alan Bissett, Claire Boydell, Judy Hendry, John Lund (who taught me more than I need to know about interference) and Sara Martin Alegre. I owe a debt too to several more or less phantasmagoric institutions: Foreign Body; Phantom fx; the Centre for Twenty-First Century Studies; and above all the Institute for Resistance to Contentment (IRC), whose work on loss and absence informs all these pages.

1
Gothic Origins: ↱ Introduction to the Gothic Lit.
The Haunting of the Text

– Dreams, a certain guard said –
were never designd so
to re-arrange an empire.[1]

To begin with what may appear a bold statement: in the context of the modern, Gothic is the paradigm of all fiction, all textuality. We have been used to such claims down the ages; they used to arise from, for instance, the drive of a national literature to discover in textuality something of 'essence' which could be rhetorically vaunted; more recently, we have seen romantic claims for the fragment, postmodern claims for the narrative of self-consciousness.

What would it be like to inhabit a world, one of many possible ones, in which Gothic were seen 'at the centre'? It would, first of all, entail a radical decentring; for Gothic is always that which is *Gothic* other than itself. The term itself challenges history: it enters us *novel* upon a terrain on which we might have to ask, who were the Goths? And thus it brings us face to face with an origin which is no origin; for Gothic fiction, Gothic culture, as all the accounts tell us, began only in the later half of the eighteenth century.[2]

This origin, however, took the form of an imaginary recapture. The shared gesture of these 'original' Gothic writers (who have since been castigated all too frequently for their lack of 'originality') was to reach beyond, and behind, their perceived predecessors and to discover there, 'exhibited by candlelight', a previous ghostly shape.[3] This shape, we might say, took from the start the form of a haunting, of a spectre.

These spectres arise, we may hypothesise, on the site of vanished cultural territory. Or we could say that the form of haunting itself, which is the form of all textuality, is brought to a certain pitch in Gothic writing. What might it mean to say that haunting is the form of all textuality? One route through that maze would be to say that

1

all writing is 'haunted' by the shapes of all that it is not. Gothic is 'forever' caught in the act; caught in the act of creating, or recreating, other books. When even a pulp writer like H.P. Lovecraft speaks obsessively of the Necronomicon of the mad Arab Abdul Alhazred, then we must read these last three syllables for precisely what they say: 'all has read', that which has been read by everybody, although nobody will admit to having read 'it', whatever 'it' might be, because of a danger; the danger of contamination.[4] Just as people prefer not to admit to having 'read' Lovecraft.

The notion of haunting exists in this curious space between realisation and its opposite. By the body we may be all too easily contaminated, as, for example, the Restoration dramatists were no less aware than we are now; but if we are to admit to an originary infection, to see that in the end our myths of origin are flawed, that there are areas through which the unknown and the unsolicited may none the less stray, then we need to find a form of being which carries all the terrifying weight of infection while eschewing the bodily; thus the haunting, thus the nature of the ghost. The ghost comes to menace the bodily with its limitations; but it also comes to celebrate the loss of the body, just as, in all textuality, we are invited to be in the presence of simultaneous celebration and mourning of loss, the loss, we might say, of the 'text instead', the text, always more perfect, more preserved from arbitrary incursion than the text we have, in any 'reasonable' or daylight scenario, succeeded in writing or reading ourselves;[5] or, therefore, any 'selves' we may have succeeded in producing, reproducing, 'reading' under these curiously limited conditions in which dreams and ghosts, therefore the forms of our memories themselves, are disavowed.

But in this curious imbrication – and it involves also all readers, as we hover, like ghosts, over the terrain of the text while suspecting that it is our very shadow as we overfly which gives this terrain its striations, its folds and crevices, its mountain ranges and valleys[6] – in this imbrication we have also always to do with the law. What is the law? We might hazard an initial answer: it is the mass, specific to a particular society, of the supposedly unhaunted textual materials which it knows.[7] In other words, the law is the imposition of certainty, the rhetorical summation of the absence, or the loss, of doubt; which means in turn that the law is a purified abstract whole, perfected according to the processes of taboo, which can find no purchase on the doubled, creviced, folded world of the real; by which it in turn is destined to be haunted. The law is thus there to will away the body; where the law is, bodies cannot exist or plead. Similarly, the law can have no cognisance of ghosts; it can exist and function only on a radically thinned terrain, where the deeps and crests of imaginary geographies have no being; it takes its sights along a single trajectory, and in doing so it seeks to exile haunting, seeks to find a pure line of explanation.[8]

The contemporary manifestation of this shadow battle, to which I shall allude later in this book, will bring onto the stage the rival forces of the law and psychology (therapeutic and psychoanalytic), the rival regimes, if you prefer, of surveillance and the imaginary. But we might better begin, if such a beginning is possible, by considering the abstract forms of Gothic: the text, the body and the law.

Let us put it this way: the law is not absolute, it is a way of seeing things. Ways of seeing things, as Hegel and John Berger in their different ways have pointed out, have their own armies; indeed, armies exist to promulgate ways of seeing things, under, perhaps, a 'normal "regime" of hallucination', as Derrida puts it.[9] This might seem a grotesque statement, especially to those who have suffered or seen others suffer under the impact of armies, who have seen the vapour from the barrels of guns, who have heard the shell-shocked hills. But it remains true, or as close to the true as we can get. We can think of the rival mythic instances: guns surrounded in Prague by roses, or further back, football matches under the shadow of the military advance. Terror goes so far: it goes as far as the dismemberment of the mind and the dismemberment of the body. All of this it does; and yet, in its most everyday and hideous forms, it remains haunted by something other than itself.

As an aside, let us remember that ghosts too have – are – their armies; and fatally skewed armies they are, as they come lurching out of the ground to reproduce the night of the living dead. But precisely their disorganisation, their impossibility of success or even of recall, marks them out for the fate Slavoj Žižek talks of, the fate of forever 'looking awry',[10] which means both seeing through a curious perspective and at the same time appearing odd, athwart; the perspective of the ghost is always wrong, it always exists in distortion and thus, as we shall see later, it is the essence, the distillation of the wish where no residue whatever of the conventional real remains to re-contaminate a discourse of power and desire.

Sometimes, as in these mythic examples, terror is haunted by shades of its own dealings with the world, like an arch hung about with climbing flowers, metal none the less. Always, though, it is haunted, shadowed by textuality; for the very existence of the text is testament, witness to a limitation on the power of terror. We have this, again mythically, in so many forms: the survival of the impossible diary, the legacy of humanity in a scenario where all might seem burned away; Primo Levi, Solzhenitsyn, Ballard, for example.

Is there, then, a literature of terror; or, more significantly, what might this 'of' in the literature 'of' terror really mean? There are literatures about terror; there are literatures which survive terror. But with the Gothic, and especially with its more modern forms – and here we should not shrink from looking at the most repulsive filmic examples of perversion and mutilation – we have a more complex dealing with terror.[11] One thing is clear: it is certainly not seen as cathartic. We may worry about whether children are damaged by watching certain videos; we rarely pause to wonder whether such watching might, by some ostensibly purgative means, make them better people. Yet perhaps we have to do here with subtler dealings than that: dealings with the haunting.

Sometimes, textually, it turns out that ghosts, or rather their own (textual) messages, can be understood. But more usually, ghosts remain as the shape of the unintelligible. They may frighten the marrow of our bones, but that does not mean that they bring to us a message which can ever be simply reduced to blood and guts. On the contrary, the possibility that we are haunted, as war poets seem, for good reason, to know very well and as the story of the Angel of Mons conveys to us above, perhaps, all other similar legendary manifestations, can be seen to convey to us hope: hope that whatever the shackled body may endure on the 'hellcrown',[12] none the less it has still been intimate with intimations – not their direct recipient, of course, for bodies can never be that – of some other sphere, which moves us beyond the disintegration of the physical.

Let us backtrack and reassert that all of these reflections should, properly, be confined to the sphere of the textual; for after all, as Derrida reminds us, there is nothing else. Yet even, and perhaps especially, here we encounter precisely the paradox which Derrida no doubt intended: which is that outside text there is indeed... Nothing.[13] Gothic fiction is haunted by this: it is haunted by Nothing, and even my insistence on the 'capitalisation of Nothing' to endeavour to drive the poles of this paradox apart are of no avail when we read that 'sentence' to ourselves, when we know the 'sentence', in all the bizarre forking of its meaning, which has befallen us.

I therefore now mean 'sentence' to remind us again of the judicial process, of the law. Of the many instances of textual haunting in legal rhetoric one could pick, let us take the most obvious, the most prevalent and at the same time the most powerful in its effects ... upon other texts, upon lives, upon bodies. Let us take the notion of 'guilty'. What an extraordinary fiction this is.[14] One might say, in more commonplace terms, that a jury's, or even less probably a judge's, verdict might determine a balance of probabilities that the accused committed the crime, might thus even seal a fate, or more than one fate, for life; but does this imply that somebody (who?) is 'guilty'? Of course, the law is more supple than this, and will admit defences of diminished responsibility and so forth; yet that term 'guilty' remains enshrined. It is frequently the case, for example, in British and US courts that it is 'advantageous' to 'plead' guilty. What can this mean?

It generally means that it seems more advantageous to the accused to claim (not admit, but claim) that s/he committed the crime than to contest the allegation, on financial grounds or on the more controversial grounds that to claim a lack of guilt might involve the court itself in more work and expense. None of this has any bearing on guilt; the law, as Derrida says, is mad.[15] It is mad, however, also for a broader and more interesting reason: it is mad because it has grown old in a regime of self-supporting falsities.

In saying that, I am of course not (merely) reflecting my own opinion; I am also reflecting the opinion, such as we can find it, of a number of Gothic texts – Maturin's *Melmoth the Wanderer* (1820) would be an example, as it is also an example of any kind of growing old amid an uncomprehending world, and as it also takes its trajectory from the ambiguous dealings with the human law which, to my mind, frame the 'emergence' of the Gothic and which will be the subject of the next chapter.[16] We might offer this as a provisional hypothesis about Gothic fiction: it deals with those moments when we find it impossible, with any degree of hope, for our 'case to be put'.

We touch here upon the all-important rhetoric of the 'case'.[17] What (but how can we say, or frame, this without multiple ambiguities) is the case? The case is the compound of rule and singularity. When we talk of 'case law', when we talk of the importance of the individual case, even when we talk about the linguistic notion of case, then in all these instances we are discussing the exception which proves the rule, or, and undecidably, the rule which brooks no exception. Thus the notion of the case.[18] The case is also the suitcase, the briefcase, the container – and here I mean deliberately to verge upon terms from psychoanalysis in the tradition of Wilfred Bion – in which our claim on life – or continued life, or at any rate non-incarceration – can be placed to ensure its security, against contamination, against haunting.[19]

What Gothic shows is that this case always falls open (and, as it were, things fall out). Perhaps the emblematic text here is Godwin's *Caleb Williams* (1794); but more familiarly we might point to *Frankenstein* (1818) and to the ways in which the monster is continually trying to find a site on which his case might be heard, a site on which his illusion of a sane human law might be enacted. This is, of course, a fantasy but it is a strong and powerful one, and the reason why it is so is that it is one with which we live most of our lives. In other words, the wish that our case be heard is an infantile wish; which is by no means to contest the claim that it finds its true emergence in writing. We might, for example, consider that eminently infantile novel, Jane Austen's *Pride and Prejudice* (1813), in which the 'adolescent' hero Darcy, confronted with the impossibility of placing what is within him outside by any spoken or physical means, decides that the only solution is a letter.[20]

This calls to mind two relevant reflections: one is on the use and importance of performatives, the other is on the nature of adolescence. Both are integral to Gothic. Let me begin with the second first. Adolescence might usefully be seen as a time when there is fantasised inversion of boundaries. To put it very simply: we exist on a terrain where what is inside finds itself outside (acne, menstrual blood, rage) and what we think should be visibly outside (heroic dreams, attractiveness, sexual organs) remain resolutely inside and hidden.[21] All carnival, therefore, is adolescent; it is the return of this inverted world, and thus it is all a series of attempts to go through the rites of passage again – possibly with the hope that, this time, things might come out right (or come right out; or perhaps, just come out – the increasingly cant term 'exfoliate' comes to mind).

Performatives are crucial to the law; they are the very means by which the law retains its tenacious hold on the body of which otherwise it can know nothing. But also the performative is in a curious and undecidable situation between speech and writing. The law has to do with all manner of wills, testaments, written evidences, but it also countenances all manner of spoken simulacra, of appeals, lamentations, excuses and pleas. Where is the performative here? It has been said that the performative consists in (and exemplifies) the power of language alone;[22] the donning of the black cap comes to refute that, as to refute all final purchase against death, in a gesture which we can only call, by a singular turn among these terms with which we are trying to deal, 'Gothic'.

Performatives – and the speech-act theory which has been built around them – attempt to stabilise a turning world. Alternatively, we might say that they attempt to produce (directly) a world which is free from distortion, in which there is no intervention between cup and lip. Gothic heroes, from Montoni to Freddy Kruger, are strong on performatives, they are strong on commands 'which brook no opposition'; but this strength usually turns out to be a laughably misplaced one. Gothic heroes share a tendency to think that, if there is distortion in the world, it is they themselves who are producing and controlling it; what is revealed in the texts is all too frequently that in fact we can only view even their actions through a violently distorting prism, a prism composed of intervening manuscripts, perversions which are not always *père-versions*.

If we are here looking, then, at a world where distortion that initially appears to be local turns out to be general, and in which therefore there is no solid ground on which to place our feet, then we are in the world of desire;[23] and here again we might stake our claim for the paradoxical centrality of Gothic. This is not at all to say that Gothic is free from the iron law of disavowal (the plea of not guilty); it is rather to say that Gothic provides the site on which disavowal must fight for its life, on which it is engaged to the utmost with forces that rise up from a field beyond its comprehension and threaten it to continue in its 'habit'.

And Gothic is also about habit. It is about points where the movement towards humanisation, or in Jungian terms towards individuation, runs into a siding. It is side-tracked. It is placed upon alternative tracks. These tracks, which lead nowhere even if they are also perfectly marshalled – we are not here in a wilderness, but in a curiously ordered universe – we may call by the name of habit; or better, addiction. We may think of Victor Frankenstein's addiction to his scientific researches and experiments, in the course of which the emotional tie disappears;[24] or of the addiction signalled by the gradual but general takeover of the body which we find in, for example, Hogg's *Confessions of a Justified Sinner* (1824).

We may here hazard an illicit thought: which is that the body of the addict is not under the control of the law. Further: the body of the addict represents, perhaps incarnates, a limit of the law, a point at which, as William Burroughs' texts are aware, the whole process of law meets its redoubled opposite, the point where two iron necessities meet and collide; we can find a Gothic representation of this lumbering, armoured conflict in Japanese Gothic movies like Shinya Tsukamoto's *Tetsuo: The Iron Man* (1991). Framed, as it were, in this world where two impossible enemies battle, discoverable only by bending apart the prison bars, lies the terrain of the Gothic, where the body and the law discover their capacity for mutual self-destruction.

Or rather, there is, and can be, no 'discovery' here, but perhaps a 'recovery': a recovery of the sense that *rule*, the operation of a regime (and *contra* Foucault, we may hypothesise that there are two quintessentially modern regimes, law and addiction), takes its form as a defensive strategy, a type of fabulation. We might suggest that this possibility of recovery, which necessarily encodes within it the thought that recovery is only possible on the terrain of loss, is what constitutes textuality, or perhaps better, textualisation; and this again we can say brings us back to the question of Gothic as a marker of the pure form of textualisation, in which the residual traces of the rule, those traces which require us, for instance, to assent to some role for cosmic justice, divine order, have been burnt away; or in which such a burning away is, indeed, enacted.

What is left is the howling: the manic yearnings of a Melmoth, a Hyde or a were-wolf. And in these cases, we can also begin to trace another source of the power of Gothic. Deleuze and Guattari speak, in their books on capitalism and schizophrenia, of the relation between writing and the animal, a relation which Deleuze curiously finds at its strongest in the Anglo-American tradition.[25] They offer eloquent thoughts on how writing resembles, or can resemble (or perhaps re-assemble), the physical movements of animals: here, perhaps, we might sense writing at its furthest point from Heideggerian *Dichtung* or Derridean *littérature*.[26]

Let us pause for a moment to inspect this thought. *Dichtung,*
littérature, the whole field traversed by Heidegger, Derrida, Blanchot, implies a series of removes. These removes are colossal in
their stature: they go way beyond the bracketing of phenomenology, they threaten us with the possibility that the only 'pure word'
will indeed be an empty word, that the 'space of literature' will
have no content and will certainly have nothing to do with narrative. The emblems here are Mallarmé and Beckett.

Mallarmé and Beckett are perhaps not Gothic, although at least
in Beckett's case there is more to be said.[27] Gothic is, on the whole,
proliferative, it is not intrigued by the minimal: in its trajectory
away from right reason and from the rule of law it does not choose
to purify itself but rather to express itself with maximum – perhaps
magnum – force, even if on many occasions this also involves
considerable ineptitude. It tells stories, it tells stories within stories,
it repeats itself, it forgets where it left off, it goes on and on; it 'loses
the place'. Endlessly it seeks for excess after excess, and does not
draw a textual line under this.

What does this have to do with Deleuze and Guattari on the
animal? Not much, I think, with the cats and rats who are their
mainstay; but then, rather like their use of the nomad, I think it can
be shown that they are themselves romanticising this animal construct. They are ignoring the mess, the shit, the refusal of confinement, the pacing tiger and its face of fury. But Gothic does not
ignore that; it is beyond certain kinds of law.

When Don Aliaga says, in a memorable moment in *Melmoth the*
Wanderer,[28] that it is inconceivable to him how Melmoth can go on
and on boring him with his stories, we sense a certain grim
and delicate irony. Can animals bore us? Can they be bored? In
asking such questions, we are of course engaging in a metaphori-
city of which (one hopes) Deleuze and Guattari are fully aware;
never the less, animals come (and so do pets, for children) to
remind us of the body, and of death, the point beyond explanation
on which law and addiction converge in their parallel strategies of
disavowal.

We might suggest that Gothic knows the body (and thus the
animal) well. It knows about physical fragility, about vulnerability,
about the point where, according to all human reason, Little Nell
should bend and break before the massed might of Quilp (and the
haunting 'dream-of-Quilp'); and it also knows the value of stretching this confrontation to its limit. Dickens's audience, as we can

recall, felt profoundly discomfited by Nell's death; we are supposed to believe that the human will can survive all this.[29]

Of course, in Gothic, it is also true that the human will can survive everything; or is it? The emblematic case here would be Poe's 'Ligeia' (1838), with its memorably intertextual epigraph;[30] but the thrust of the story is all the other way, towards showing how such fantasised transcendences meet their mortal oblivion, encounter the limitations of the body. There is a certain enervation to many modern and contemporary Gothic heroes – Frank in Iain Banks's *The Wasp Factory* (1984) comes to mind – which invariably gainsays textually their claims to the status of the *Übermensch*.

For Gothic fiction will not make superheroes of us; if we want to find fiction which will feed our fantasies of aggrandisement, variously gendered as we are, where better than Austen or Lawrence with their resolute introspection, their emphasis on the possibility of an at least momentarily true perspective. Gothic by contrast deals in dizzying heights and depths – the painter John Martin still remains one of the surest exemplars – and in vertigo, the sense that there is indeed nowhere to go, not up, not down, and also that staying where you are has its own imponderable but tangible dangers.

To mention Martin is to bring on stage the vexed question of the relation between the Gothic and the sublime; and indeed the discourse of the sublime is now grown so enormous as to make comment upon it very difficult.[31] Perhaps we may put it this way: the Gothic and the sublime best encounter each other on the terrain of memory and forgetting. To stand upon one of John Martin's bridges across hell it is necessary, the official story goes, to remember: to remember, for example, the supporting arms of God, or of the human community in which one might comfortably reside if one were ever to reach the other side – a trajectory which, of course, the physical activity of painting in fact prohibits with its own iron law of the present. However: one might also say that to stand upon such a brink – and this brink may now be expanded to include, for example, the brink of madness which is skirted in recent novels such as Will Self's *My Idea of Fun* (1993) among many others – is to employ, or at least to be employed by, a forgetting; a forgetting of the law which will make you topple, the law which says that such things are impossible.

What, however, if you remember and forget at the same time, as Eliot has it in 'Marina' (1930),[32] in the magical, post-*Tempest* world he there displays? Then you are in the midst of the trembling, the shivering, the uncertainty beloved of so many Gothic writers; you are no longer protected by imaginary railings, but neither are you controlled by the iron law which would have you plunge into the deep. It is, however, also not as though you are thereby freed into some exceptionally human sphere by virtue of this apparent privilege; rather, you are returned to the body, the animal, which knows not which way to turn.

In other words, you are reduced to, or produced in, the position of terror: not horror, for horror requires you to stand aghast, it proclaims the impossibility of any action as the monster crawls towards you down the tunnel; but terror, which allows your eyes to flicker every which way, ceaselessly looking for an alternative, searching for a 'version' in which either this is not happening or there is a way out. But from the customary distortion of perspective in which we live, the universe of desire, it is impossible to see such an exit clearly; as Bret Easton Ellis says at the conclusion of *American Psycho* (1991), 'this is not an exit';[33] any more than Norman Bates could find, or have found, a way out of the closed system of addiction which had usurped in him the vestige of the human.[34]

Vestige, vestment: Gothic questions how we are 'clothed' in the human. Such putative enrobings and disrobings are of the very stuff of Gothic, for at heart it is also true to claim that Gothic is ceremonial.[35] This is immediately to put it on a collision course with the law, for the law claims that all ceremonial is its own, while also knowing that the vestments of the state within the state – Rosicrucianism, Freemasonry – have already fatally polluted these apparently pristine garments. Everything is soiled: the judge's wig, as Gothic has known from the late eighteenth century on, is already a body of corruption; it is, again, impossible for 'the case' to be heard.

And if the case cannot be heard, then it must continue, perhaps endlessly, to utter itself in private, in the personal spaces, under the cover of crypt, vault, castle, suburban home. I hope that nothing I have said above, although I have been talking in terms of textuality, or rather of rival textualities, has prohibited the notion that Gothic is all around us: it erupts on the streets from time to time, causing a kind of mayhem which, while abhorred at the time, turns out to have done little real damage to the social fabric.[36] Perhaps, on this basis, one might argue that Gothic, even with the worst will in the world, is weak; but there is other evidence to suggest that this is not so.

For Gothic is able, because of its freedom from the law, to play; and when play happens (anywhere, and at any age) then powerful feelings are mobilised; the mechanical syndromes, which have an ear always cocked for a game, are alerted. Textually, they often come to us in the form of monsters or machines; but really we are talking here about the mechanised bits of the psyche, the ones on tracks, down the sidings, the addicted parts of the self, the parts where no law can run because they are already clogged with traffic and the work of explanation is lagging far behind.[37]

And so we return again to these compounded myths of origins; and we notice that, just as Gothic manifests a fascination with such myths, so also they function in different ways to structure and authenticate each of our chosen systems: the text, the body and the law. But in the Gothic, particularly, something is not merely lagging behind, it is known to be so, it is known to be following our footsteps, we can hear its dragging tread, sounding slow but mysteriously well able to keep up with us, not fading out of sight – or more usually hearing – but continually reminding us to look over our shoulder.

We might refer this to a historical construct, and say that we have here the continual reminder that we should learn from history lest it repeat itself; but the operation of the repetition compulsion is perhaps not so easily to be rhetorically cowed. What Gothic might say about this is that the lessons of history do indeed perpetually follow us; but also that we are locked in a position where it is virtually impossible for us to turn our head and stare the deliverer of these lessons in the eye (if it has an eye). For the particular remains which drag themselves around after Gothic are not to be obviously or readily learnt from; for they are the remains of the body, they are the imaginary products of vulnerability and fragility, they are the 'remains' of that which still 'remains to us'; or not.

For an emblem of Gothic would be this: it is already ruined.[38] And behind this thought stand the forms of obsession, compulsion. We might say that obsessive actions – Melmoth's quest for souls, Pat Bateman's serial murders – are the ruin of action; in so far as action may be designed to produce an effect, then obsession denies the possibility of that effect ever escaping from a closed circle, ever moving beyond square one.[39] For the obsessive, the world is already ruined; only through massive efforts of propitiation can it be kept in being at all, so obsessive action takes place 'before' the world, as a site of meaning or explanation, can begin.

Obsession, ceremonial: these are terms I suggest to be descriptive of Gothic even though they perhaps seem to stand in stark contrast to a more familiar critical rhetoric of transgression. In Gothic we can see a series of propitiatory acts to ward off the worst; such a view would precede the old and vexed question of Gothic's political affiliations. But the question of the political, of course, remains all-important, as it has ever since de Sade found in the Gothic a measure of responses to the travails of the French Revolution; or, as he might alternatively have put it, a set of reactions to a world where bodies had been made markedly vulnerable at the same time as the writ of law appeared, at least for a time, to have failed.[40]

Under such circumstances, all manner of otherwise prohibited gestures become possible; those gestures, to return to the topic of adolescence and its link with Gothic – strongly evidenced at the moment in the audience for horror videos – envisage a certain temporary freedom, perhaps a quasi-transitional space, in which it is no longer necessary, or at times even possible, to 'measure' the power of the world. Gothic heroes are 'incommensurate'. Their relation to the world is posited on a pure trajectory of desire, with no appreciation of limits; the limits are for later, for an unimaginable maturity which will be marked by the ever-impending rule of law, when our bodies will bow down to the rule of 'that which is', still under the sign of a marked thinning of the notion of the real.

Thus Gothic will always appear to have to do with a kind of madness, an inexplicability: as Stephen King puts it in *Christine* (1983), the assemblages are 'teenage car songs', 'teenage love songs', 'teenage death songs', all with the lyrics never quite intelligible to the concerned adult.[41] But there is therefore also a further shadow; as Gothic eludes the sliding under the sign of social normalcy, so also it carries with it tremulous memories of a past childhood (another 'point of origin') in which freedom did not have to be defended so vigorously, in which self-consciousness had not reared its head. Thus another 'case' of the 'in-between' status of Gothic, just as sociologically its roots can be traced to the 'in-between' class, the emergent bourgeoisie; and we might ask what a bourgeoisie can ever be but emergent, prone always to states of emergency.[42]

I am trying in these remarks to draw some kind of boundary around Gothic, to isolate a topic for discussion, even with the attendant risk of setting up a master-narrative; but in any case, Gothic persists in eluding this notion of 'rule'. What haunts Gothic, we might provisionally say, and more especially in contemporary contexts, is Gothic: a ghost haunted by another ghost, almost as eighteenth-century Gothic was haunted by Jacobean tragedy, and Jacobean tragedy by the horrors of Greek drama; and as all these textual manifestations are themselves further haunted by a world which comes prior to text yet which we can know only in and through text, a world of oral tradition, of more primal hauntings by word of mouth. Yet we can readily see that there is no way out, this is not an exit; for in order for the haunting to occur at all there must always have been something prior, yet that 'prior' is always one which will elude clear sight, will always move beyond the bright world of the law.

Gothic, then, provides an image language for bodies and their terrors, inhabits a point of undecidability in the area of the growth of self-awareness. One exemplary locus here would be the threat of premature burial, which returns us again to the fear that the case will not be heard; who will hear the clawing on the inside of the coffin? In *Wuthering Heights* (1847) a complex solution to this problem is essayed; but for it to work it requires a double burial, and it also requires a multiplicity of narrators and listeners within the text, all attending to the case, all supplying different pieces of evidence, all tainted by personal and vested interests.[43] As is well known, Gothic deals therefore with unreliable narrators: Dickens's narrator, for example, in 'The Signalman' (1866), or Poe's in 'The Fall of the House of Usher' (1839), both of whom hint, as it were despite themselves, that they may in some unimaginable way have provoked the very events they seek to describe; as we might see the author as that which has indeed provoked the text and which/who, as we see perhaps particularly clearly in the conclusion of Martin Amis's *London Fields* (1989), is the only one who at the end of the day can commit the promised murder; 'end of story'.[44]

Those bodily terrors will naturally be cathected onto social groups which are most exposed to their memory; this seems 'to go without saying', and is one starting-point for the discussion of the 'female Gothic'. We can also, of course, go further and state that the maternal body is an emblem for all vulnerability, for the animal as much as for the human, and thus in the animal layers of the psyche. It is in our dealings with this fantasised maternal body that the formations of sadism and masochism appear, in projected and introjected torture of the mother, which is bound back into the circle 'of fear and desire' by the inseparability of this body from all our hopes of nurture and thus of having a 'hearing', a receptacle for our point of view.[45]

And so the body of the mother cannot be killed off without also involving our own doom; but it can be manipulated, harmed mercilessly, and in these obsessive and repetitive actions we find also a surrogate working out of our own tolerances. How much damage can we stand? This is another way of putting the crucial question of censorship: a society which is incapable of providing adolescents with sensible or reasonable tests of their increasing physical abilities will be forced to provide or endure surrogates – hunting camps, horror movies, road rages – which enable the acting out of the growing body but necessarily involve it in collision courses with larger powers, which we may again state to be the powers of the law, in so far as they perpetuate within us 'in-between' states of impotence and incomprehension.

Hareton Earnshaw hangs small animals;[46] he does not appear to derive any particular pleasure from this, neither are his actions particularly foregrounded in the text, but we need to see in this minor (?) obsession a memory, a memory of how he has himself been treated, how he is even now being treated: by his parents, by Heathcliff, by the text/author. And so we also confront in Gothic and its traces glimpses of the hidden narrative of abuse; and perhaps that should be a major contemporary focus for a critique of the Gothic. For abuse has become the stage on which a mighty battle is being played out; it is a battle for the nature of memory, and it is also a battle in which we can see defined two opposing notions of culture, which I will call the culture of horror and the culture of therapy.

These two cultures are neatly encapsulated in Greg Bear's *Queen of Angels* (1990), where the daytime world of law and order, financial success, is marked off by the fact that all its citizens have been 'therapied', and this becomes also the only answer to crime. The alternative is sponsored by the regime of Hispaniola, which occupies the site once occupied by the island of Haiti and which practises a primitivism which is partly serviced by the export of 'hellcrowns', torture devices which have a closer relation to the law of retribution than does therapy.

But we can see the battle going on not only in such texts, but also, and emblematically, in courts of law. Where are the limits of

individual responsibility? Since the individual has no origin, how
can we find a way to isolate the individual as a legal entity and
thus begin questions about blame, guilt and innocence? All we do,
no doubt, we do because of what has been done to us; and if it was
done to us effectively, then we have no memory of it – for which
very reason among others, as John Forrester puts it, psychoanalysis
can have only an oblique relation to legal argument.[47]

Yet sooner or later, if we are to be in any way efficacious, then
we must have to do with legal argument, for only there can power
be traced. Gothic, I suggest, has known this from the beginning; has
known the problem of the thin line between justice and persecution, has known the moments when the state order is stretched to
breaking point and the law appears either as naked force or as
weakened beyond recall. We all need law: not because it has anything to do with what is right and wrong, but because law and law
alone serves to validate memory, continuity; without law, no matter what the time, we shall be in a postmodern space – and in that
space, of course, it is true that our case can be heard, but nothing
will flow from that hearing because there is no line of authority by
which it may be transmuted into action and decision; as with
Kafka.

If the individual fully takes on board – enrobes him/herself in –
the pressures of the personal and cultural past, then, Gothic says,
something strange happens; it is not that the individual becomes
mysteriously rich and full, but rather the other way round: because
such knowledge is so weighty, so intrusive, the boundaries around
the self implode and the result is a blankness, the kind of blankness
we can find running through, for example, the writings collected in
the emblematic anthology called *The New Gothic* (1991).[48] Feeling,
emotion, we may hypothesise, can only exist at all while there is a
space around the self; if the self is crowded in on, then we become
automata, and are again in a different and dangerous part of the
world, a part of the world that has frequently been referred to as
the uncanny.[49]

These are hypotheses which Gothic tests. Gothic tests what it
might be like to be a shell; perhaps, as Derrida says, a shell which
always 'faces on two fronts',[50] but at any rate a shell which has
been filled to the brim with something that looks like ourselves but
is irremediably other, to the point that we are driven out, exiled
from our own home, removed from the body. Thus it is we ourselves who are cast as the ghost, the spectre, the 'revenant' who can

in fact never return, but who can only watch this mysterious body performing actions below – like Hogg's Robert Wringhim – which he/she will never be able to understand or love.

None of this will prevent the law from punishing that body; and here it might be preferable to see the law less as an external institution but more in terms of the superego, as the legislator within. Superego and id; to use one of Freud's older and simpler formulations, when these conspire together then the self is beleaguered indeed and has no place to call its own. Gothic is thus a fiction of exile, of bodies separated from minds, of minds without a physical place to inhabit, cast adrift on seas of space and time which appear to bear no relation to the moral life.

If Gothic therefore has to do with the barbaric, then this is not a matter of an external pressure; rather, it is a matter of looking at the pressures which turn us into barbarians within, barbarians in relation precisely to the society and the body in which we were born.[51] Thus we find tales of self-mutilation, self-torture, in the end self-destruction, the incarnation of the Satan myth; and thus we loop back again to abuse, to satanic abuse, in which the body is the site for a struggle which can end only in death or in the blankness which results most effectively from trauma.

Gothic enacts an introjection of the destruction of the body, and thus it introjects death; in so doing it attains sublimity because it is necessary for there to be a circling, hovering, transcendent self which can enact the survival and supersession of physical difficulties, the 'last man', the wanderer, the ancient mariner. These figures are the marks of what is left after the fantasised destruction has taken place; as such they have to do with guilt, legal guilt, and terror. As they watch their own bodies collapsing, they are faced with an eminently Gothic question: how shall I get home – or must I attain to a perpetual exile, tramping amid the Arctic snows or on an unending orbit through cold space?[52]

Gothic is therefore all about supersession, about the will to transcend, and about the fate of the body as we strive for a fantasy of total control, or better, total exemption – from the rule of law. Gothic enables us to consider our options, in a wider space than is usual: we may contemplate what it would be like to be a devil or an angel, what it would be like if the domestic space were simultaneously freighted with the extremes of passion, what it would be like to have at one's service a double for whose actions we are not responsible and who, we know, might at any moment proclaim him- or herself ruler of the house which we had imagined our own. In such dreams as Gothic gives and incarnates, we are no longer in control of this house; we are tenants of an unimaginable landlord whose return is weighted with expectation, hope, fear, terror; as I said above, there is after all more to be said about Beckett as a Gothic writer, and perhaps more to be said in general about the minimalist, reductive component of Gothic which stands over against its manic, self-justifying, self-doubting proliferations.

But what follows in this book will never succeed in being a general account of Gothic, although this text is haunted by my former attempt at just such a thing;[53] rather, it will take the form of a series of incursions into uncanny territory, from which one can return with knowledge, but a knowledge which will always be compounded of previous excursions, previous hauntings, previous lives which crowd in upon the present, surround it, like the gallery of grotesques which surrounds Little Nell, with the imagery of persecution, obsession, violence which marks Gothic dealings with the text, the body and the law.

2
The Gothic and the Law: Limits of the Permissible

The law is cryptic. There is no pure space of the family, or of textual genealogy, or of presenting and passing judgment on 'textual evidence'.[1]

Eighteenth-century fiction, the 'site' of the Gothic, is obsessed with the law, with its operations, justifications, limits. Where the universe of the seventeenth-century romance was bounded and controlled by cosmic justice, reflected in already-given quasi-mythic structure, the universes of Defoe, Fielding, Radcliffe, Godwin are limited by various manifestations of human law. Legal characters and legal processes are key 'figures' in the fiction, and we can use an exploration of these figures as a beginning for the search for the elusive 'beginning-in-continuity' of Gothic.

We may cite, for example, the frequency with which legal devices are used to bring fictional worlds into being. Captain Singleton's path through life is set when his 'Gypsey Mother' is hanged;[2] Moll Flanders begins her 'history' with a complaint against the inadequacy of the social provision for the children of convicted criminals, her mother having been transported for a petty property crime.[3] Smollett's Roderick Random is effectively despatched on his travels by his grandfather, the 'hard-hearted judge' who 'was remarkable for his abilities in the law, which he exercised with great success... particularly against beggars, for whom he had a singular aversion'.[4] Goldsmith's major device for reducing the Vicar of Wakefield to the extremes of indigence which he requires for his moralising is not natural disaster, though this ensues, but a 'statute of bankruptcy';[5] the action of Fanny Burney's *Evelina* (1778) hinges on an unpleasant legal trick by Sir John Belmont;[6] thus it comes as little surprise that the introductory material to Radcliffe's *The Italian* (1797) operates against the background of the law of sanctuary, which then becomes a key figure in the polarities of the text.[7]

This insistence on the law as origin requires a matching series of legal termini. Poor Singleton's fictional career ends amid the creation of an unexpected series of new legal problems centring on the intriguing issue of how pirates are to take their goods safely back to Britain. The marriage settlement which effectively if not actually ends *Pamela* (1740) is given to us in full legal detail, thus counteracting the equally legalistic argument earlier in the book by which Pamela is called upon to respond to a series of articles drawn up by her Master.[8] Roderick Random's return to grace has an eminently practical tinge:

> If there be such a thing as true happiness on earth, I enjoy it.... Fortune seems determined to make ample amends for her former cruelty; for my proctor writes, that, notwithstanding the clause in my father's will, on which the squire founds his claim, I shall certainly recover my wife's fortune, in consequence of a codicil annexed...
>
> (p. 435)

On the one hand, the forceful discourse of foundation and recovery, on the other, the wiles suggested by the 'codicil annexed', the haunting supplement which always calls into question the massive body of the law; texts as far apart as *Tom Jones* (1749), *Vathek* (1786) and *Caleb Williams* bring themselves to resolutions couched in terms of the law.[9]

Between origin and resolution, legal considerations serve a variety of narrative functions. In *Joseph Andrews* (1742) scenes 'staged' before the Justices of the Peace virtually act as extra punctuation, so regularly do they occur. In *Tom Jones* Fielding authoritatively and ironically plays with the possibility that Tom will end up hanged.[10] That Smollett could interpolate into *Peregrine Pickle* (1751) the notorious *Memoirs of a Lady of Quality* is particularly strong evidence for the appetite of the contemporary audience, and even in *Humphry Clinker* (1771), where a generalised comic benevolence tends to swamp legal conflict, we have Lismahago's reflections on the jury system to satisfy our interest.[11] In both *Evelina* and *Mysteries of Udolpho* (1794) much of the tension of the action turns on the law: on whether Evelina and her friends will go to court to seek restitution, on whether Montoni can manage to manipulate the law so as to relieve first Madame Cheron and then Emily of their estates.

I suggest that in these representations we find a key factor in the constitution of the Gothic; in describing this we would need to come across the law's presumed antiquity, its imperviousness to reason, its status as a discourse of mystery, its ability to mortify the body. To trace this 'prehistory of Gothic', to sense the twists of this recapitulation of a presumed former power, we can look to four principal areas of representation. The first is the figure of the attorney, which is portrayed through, and intimately bound up with, questions of legal language and thus of language and duplicity in general. Moll Flanders, in an emblematic situation, finds it necessary to hire an attorney not to reveal truth but to avoid recognition: even to this end her 'governess' must distinguish between a 'very creditable sort of a man to manage it, being an attorney of very good business and of good reputation' and 'a pettifogging hedge solicitor or a man not known'.[12] In *Tom Jones* these two types meet each other at the Bell in Gloucester, the first personified as Mr Dowling of Salisbury, the second 'unrecognised', not dignified with a name, but referred to throughout as Petty-fogger, 'one of those who may be termed train-bearers to the law; a sort of supernumeraries in the profession, who are the hackneys of attornies, and will ride more miles for half a crown than a post-boy' (p. 388); clearly the body of the law, such as it is, has its own excrescences and parasites.

Yet even this measured and undeceived view is rare in eighteenth-century fiction outside the already compromised Fielding. Moll's lawyer should be considered largely as an aspect of her perennial good fortune; more to the point is the statement that the Younger Brother is 'bred to the law' (p. 31), and Swift puts a more extreme case into the mouth of Gulliver when he describes attorneys to his Houyhnhnm master as:

> usually the most ignorant and stupid generation among us, the most despicable in common conversation, avowed enemies to all knowledge and learning, and equally disposed to pervert the general reason of mankind in every other subject of discourse, as in that of their own profession.[13]

Attorneys, then, are a prime source of discursive contamination; anywhere within their purview there is dereliction, disturbance, a textuality of the unreliable which suffers all manner of bodily damage without being able to grasp its origins or effects.

Often the ignorance of these attorneys is merely comic, as in *Joseph Andrews* where Mr Barnabas and the surgeon, 'the two doctors, spiritual and physical', those who might work for the betterment of body and soul, divide the legal work of the parish between them:

> They had consumed the whole night in debating what measures they should take to produce the piece of gold in evidence against [the thief]; for they were both extremely zealous in the business, though neither of them were in the least interested in the prosecution; neither of them had ever received any private injury from the fellow, nor had either of them ever been suspected of loving the public well enough to give them a sermon or a dose of physic for nothing.[14]

Perhaps, then, the law is a form of ministry; but if so it is one uncertain in its motivations and its effects. When we turn to trained practitioners the situation with regard to justice and common sense is all the more tenuous: Fielding and Smollett present us with a gallery of lawyers destroyed by Latin and wine, one sufficient example being the one on whom Squire Western calls to give a view on the legality of setting Sophia's pet bird (the Owl of Minerva?) free:

> The lawyer, with great gravity, delivered himself as follows:
> 'If the case be put of a partridge, there can be no doubt but an action would lie: for though this be *ferae naturae*, yet being reclaimed, property vests; but being the case of a singing bird, though reclaimed, as it is a thing of base nature, it must be considered as *nullius in bonis*. In this case, therefore, I conceive the plaintiff must be nonsuited; and I should disadvise the bringing any such action.'[15]

Lying, in its many meanings, and sexual innuendo form the ground of this and the many other passages like it in Fielding and Smollett; attorneys, we might say, are those without functioning bodies, in whom discourse can only serve to fill up these empty, impotent spaces, and indeed in the figures of Roger Ravine in *Peregrine Pickle* and Micklewhimmen in *Humphry Clinker* we cannot but detect the lineaments of an unaccommodated sexual and familial revenge.[16]

But this constellation of fools should not blind us to the danger represented by such as Lawyer Scout who, according to Fielding, is 'one of those fellows who, without any knowledge of the law, or being bred to it, take upon them, in defiance of an act of Parliament, to act as lawyers in the country, and are called so. They are the pests of society, and a scandal to [the] profession...'[17] Peregrine Pickle attends the trial of an attorney who has been 'doubling', presumably indistinguishably, as a pickpocket, an episode recounted with the brevity of the conventional.[18] The evil Thornhill in *The Vicar of Wakefield* (1766) brings in a lawyer to do his dirty work, while in Bage's *Hermsprong* (1796) both 'law and divinity... applaud' the appalling Lord Grondale's intentions when he announces his determination to drive the harmless Hermsprong out of the country.[19] Perhaps Grondale's pet lawyer Corrow should stand as the archetype:

> Mr Corrow had a prodigious respect for Lord Grondale, and for money, and would have done for one, or both of them, any thing, or every thing, that the law, in any of its latitudes, would have enabled him to do. To press down to the earth, and under it, a poor man, is easy – it is the work of every day; but to make a man, with money in his purse, guilty of crimes he never committed, requires a superior fund of knowledge of the more tortuous parts of law, and superior intrepidity.
>
> (p. 147)

An associated image here is of the labyrinth, and in this labyrinth, as I have suggested above, it is possible to distort the notion of 'guilty' until it comes to stand for nothing but an enforced passivity of the body under the rule of law, just such a passivity as we shall shortly find operating in the bodies of Gothic victims from Frankenstein's monster onwards; admittedly in this case Corrow does not succeed in his attempts and convolutions, but this is explicitly because the wealthy Hermsprong has resources foreign to the common man, is himself an unassimilable 'foreign body'.[20]

The indictment laid against Gulliver in Lilliput, the many parodies of legal language in *Joseph Andrews*, the parodic Latinisms of Sterne, all three of these examples represent a significant attitude and a significant fear, but they also serve as extremes in the representation of language, and especially performative language, as power over the body. Swift's version, of course, is complicated by its reference to specific contemporary events, and it thus constitutes a double bluff: those who have drawn up the document are convicted of obscurity, while the author himself shelters behind the opacity of the text. The case of Sterne is particularly complex: when Tristram Shandy quotes 'the article in my mother's marriage settlement', we slide at once from parody into accurate – but bizarre – representation.[21] Legal discourse fulfils the function assigned to it in *Ferdinand Count Fathom* (1753):

> His council behaved like men of consummate abilities in their profession; they exerted themselves with equal industry, eloquence and erudition, in their endeavours to perplex the truth, browbeat the evidence, puzzle the judge, and mislead the jury…[22]

Fathom, as has been said before, is one of the border-works which leads directly into the Gothic;[23] we shall find this condemnation of the senseless violence of the law writ large in settings from monastery to London street to small-town USA as we continue our trajectory through Gothic writing up to the present day.

We touch here, we have to say, on real problems with the eighteenth-century legal profession. When Fielding says that Scout is 'in defiance of an act of Parliament', he presumably refers to those Acts of 1729 and 1731 by which an attempt was made to regulate admission to the status of attorney. One of the witnesses before the Strickland Committee, which conducted the background investigation, was typical in claiming that 'several broken tradesmen and bailiffs, do practise as attorneys and often set the people at variance, and have got £10 or £20 of each party, by being concerned, and, before the matter comes to trial, make the affair up between their clients for a bottle of wine and a treat.'[24] The Acts failed badly in their main purpose: Robert Robson is perhaps exaggerating when he claims that they 'merely detracted from the dignity of the profession, and made it easier than ever before for illiterate and unprincipled men to become attorneys' (p. 13), but certainly they did nothing to establish control or registration. When the Society of Gentlemen Practisers in the Courts of Law and Equity was founded in 1739 it found itself in its efforts to cleanse the profession 'continuously occupied' with 'the attempt to remove from the Rolls the names of solicitors who had been found guilty of misconduct'.[25]

Yet these historical details do not go far enough in explaining the
burden of anxieties with which representations of the attorney are
fraught; nor do they entirely explain the complex of attitudes
which we discover when we turn to that other staple of the eighteenth-century legal system, the Justice of the Peace. Again it is
Fielding, with his concern for demonstrating at least the *eventual*
justice of the English legal system, who sets out for us a balanced
fictional debate, between the Squires Allworthy and Western. Western, obviously, is a terrible magistrate, arrogant, partial and ignorant, and it is only the intervention of his clerk which prevents him
from dangerous mistakes.[26] 'The day-to-day government of the
country', we need to remember, 'was in the hands of the Justices
of the Peace...in the counties and the corporations and justices in
the Boroughs'; 'virtually the only way of controlling such local
authorities...was through the prerogative writs...issued by the
common law courts'.[27] Western, we may note, 'had already had
two informations exhibited against him in the King's-Bench', one of
the common law courts, 'and had no curiosity to try a third'.[28]

Allworthy's legal performance is less straightforward. In the
case, for instance, of Partridge, it seems that Fielding is suggesting
that the good squire has not properly thought through the consequences of his judgment and sentence, since the unfortunate criminal is forced to leave 'the country, where he was in danger of
starving with the universal compassion of all his neighbours';[29]
here the dictates of the law stand in stark opposition to the needs
of the body, which are seen, if at all, as working in a realm
completely separated from the realm of judicial decision. Again in
the case of Molly Seagrim, Allworthy 'exceeded his authority a
little in this instance'; Fielding only excuses him on the grounds
that 'so many arbitrary acts are daily committed by magistrates'.[30]
And in a third example of damaging judicial incompetence, the
apparently reasonable justice meted out by Justice Willoughby of
Noyle is overturned by the evil Lord Justice Page.[31]

The system administered and promulgated by the Justices is
irrational at its heart; it conduces to a sense of justice alienated
from the common man and from any sense of right and wrong, it
supports a discourse of arbitrary power. Moll Flanders gets away
with attempted theft simply because a JP sees that she has enough
money to support her character; Matthew Bramble in *Humphry
Clinker* is a benevolent JP, as he is a benevolent landlord, but only
because he is a crusty old amateur with a heart of gold, not because

of any legal knowledge or even experience he might possess. One of the vilest portrayals of a JP in eighteenth-century literature, apart from Justice Gobble in *Sir Launcelot Greaves* (1760), the most hideous caricature of them all, is Pimpernel, also in *Humphry Clinker*, but the significant fact about Pimpernel is that before he became a JP he was also an attorney, and thus it is asserted that it is his acquaintance with the hidden recesses, the crypts and labyrinths, of the legal profession which stains his judgment.[32]

In a keynote episode about the arbitrariness of the law and about extremes of anxiety on the part of those who may fall into its clutches, we find in *Roderick Random* (1748) that a highwayman called Rifle has been captured; Random and Strap, to their annoyance, are detained as evidence and set out to look for a JP:

> About the twilight we arrived at the place of our destination, but as the justice was gone to visit a gentleman in the country, with whom (we understood) he would probably stay all night, the robber was confined in an empty garret, three stories high, from which it seemed impossible for him to escape...
>
> (p. 43)

Nevertheless he does, before the magistrate returns.

We have here, then, a picture of the law largely during the first half of the eighteenth century; but what needs to concern us is the change which affects this picture as the century progresses, and as the realist novel gives way to Gothic. As a crude summary, we may say that the unreliable and amateur figure of the JP vanishes and is replaced by figures of more consistent and autocratic power. Attitudes towards the day-to-day running of the legal system darken and shadow; there is clearly here a reference to a more general 'organisation' of legal power and discourse which acts as spur to the development of the Gothic vision, a deepened awareness of the bodily suffering entailed by being kept indefinitely in a garret 'three stories high', which as the century goes on becomes a tower from which escape indeed becomes impossible.

When Manfred pronounces his dreadful sentence on Theodore in *The Castle of Otranto* (1765) we are being exposed to early melodrama,[33] but it is nevertheless worth keeping in mind what the actual relation is between this discourse and the practice of the law. JPs in the eighteenth century had the right to try even the most serious of crimes – treason, murder, forgery and bigamy. They 'had the right to order the death penalty even though by the eighteenth century they did not exercise this right. They did, on the other hand, make full use of their discretionary powers to order transportation, flogging and imprisonment.'[34] Although it is notable that Manfred chooses to hand down his judgment in pseudo-Shakespearean language, there is nothing else to differentiate him, depending on the question of perspective, to which we shall return, from any other authority of the time.

Sir William Thornhill in *The Vicar of Wakefield* is just as much an angel as Manfred is a devil, and clearly represents an individual force for good which can only operate outside the complicated and corrupt system. In Reeve's *Old English Baron* (1777), legal problems are resolved by the appointment of a group of 'commissioners', a harkback to a more primitive period of legal history;[35] they have the ambiguous merit of speedy and active interrogation. In *The Monk* (1795) justice is emblematically achieved by the Cardinal-Duke, not through invoking the due process of law but through invoking the might of the Inquisition in a purely arbitrary fashion.

The Justices, the legal historians tell us, declined in 'public favour' during the century;[36] what is certainly noticeable is that by the closing decades there is no hope in the literature of getting any kind of 'justice' out of them. In *Caleb Williams* they are in the pockets of the wealthy and influential, which, because of stipendiary problems, they were indeed increasingly becoming; in *Hermsprong* they are politically motivated and merely serve the interests of Grondale; and Brockden Brown provides a fitting coda to this array of despair in *Wieland* (1798), a book built round the failure of the heroine to find any human means of achieving justice, and in which she can only end by invoking the divine power of the 'righteous Judge' to provide the succour and redress which human means cannot guarantee,[37] and here we begin to glimpse the darker lineaments of the 'case which cannot be put' and its psychological and political ramifications, as well as a signal point of origin for the 'paranoid Gothic'.[38]

In different ways, then, the attorney and the JP represent the law as forked between authority and caprice, and the emergence of autocrats in the fiction of the later part of the century can be seen as a simultaneous evasion of and submission to this caprice. The attorney – perhaps – understands the system to which he ministers, but has no interest in communicating it to his client; the JP does not even understand it in the first place. A Manfred or a Montoni solves this problem at a stroke by not keeping to the system at all; thus they manifest the direct privilege which was, after all, in any case substantially enshrined in the magistracy, with its property and wealth requirements. Later in the century we also find a strengthening interest in two other important areas of legal process: in the prison, and in the trial itself. I put them that way round because that is the way round they usually occur in the fiction; characters rarely *end up* in gaol, but they often have to spend time there before justice is achieved. And this, in turn, reflects a truth about the eighteenth-century penal system, for through most of the century prisons were to only a very minor extent a place for convicted criminals, but 'more a place of confinement for debtors and those passing through the mills of justice',[39] satanic mills indeed as they are generally represented. Imprisonment was an uncommon form of punishment for those convicted: of sentences handed down at the Old Bailey in the years 1760–4, only 1.2 per cent involved imprisonment, far more popular being the pillory or the stocks, whipping, transportation or hanging.

The pictures that Defoe, Fielding and Smollett give us of prison life are not as eccentric as they may now appear to us, in that we have come to expect gaols to be places of confinement, whereas during the eighteenth century they were not. The few convicted felons in them were usually chained down, precisely because the majority of debtors and people awaiting trial possessed so-called privileges of free movement, which account for much of the internal social life which these novelists depict. This, however, is by no means to claim that these novelists were always striving for a 'realistic' picture: in *Moll Flanders* (1721) the principal mode in which Newgate is described is clearly symbolic – in itself an interesting rarity for Defoe:

> the hellish noise, the roaring, swearing, and clamour, the stench and nastiness, and all the dreadful afflicting things that I saw there joined to make the place seem an emblem of hell itself, and a kind of an entrance into it.
>
> (p. 242)

A hell, a bestiary, a jungle: in *Roderick Random* Miss Williams, committed to the London Bridewell, believes herself 'in hell, tormented by fiends: Indeed, there needs not a very extravagant imagination to form that idea; for of all the scenes on earth, that

of Bridewell approaches nearest the notion I had always entertained of the infernal regions' (p. 131). Roderick himself later
ends up in the Marshalsea, but this is a rather different matter:
whereas the Bridewell was at least nominally a house of correction
and Newgate a common gaol, the largest in the country, the Marshalsea was specifically a debtors' gaol, and Random is accordingly
able to carry on his everyday life virtually as if nothing had happened. Similarly, when Peregrine Pickle is gaoled, he makes an
immediate point of getting transferred to the Fleet, another debtors'
gaol which enjoyed a contemporary reputation as London's largest
brothel.

But it is also in *Peregrine Pickle* that a naval lieutenant, indicted
for riot, is brought before the Bench but acts with 'defiance against
the authority of the court'. He wounds one of the constables in
attendance:

> This outrage was such an aggravation of his crime, that the court
> would not venture to decide upon it, but remitted him to the
> sentence of the warden; who, by virtue of his dictatorial power,
> ordered the rioter to be loaded with irons, and confined in the
> strong-room, which is a dismal dungeon, situated upon the side
> of the ditch, infested with toads and vermin, surcharged with
> noisome damps, and impervious to the least ray of light.
>
> (pp. 684–5)

The final part of this description can be paralleled, word for
word, in the later Gothic works of Radcliffe and Lewis, who are
often accused of sensationalism, yet it is far from clear how far
either Smollett or the Gothic writers were diverging from actual
reportage. There is on record the case of a Bristol man, placed in
gaol for suspected firebombing, of which he was later acquitted.
Due to shortage of accommodation he was put in the 'pit' and
chained down with convicted felons for fourteen weeks before his
case came up.[40] And he was one of the lucky ones, in that he
emerged from prison at all; John Howard, the prison reformer,
'discovered that many prisoners were punished after acquittal.
They languished in jail because they could not pay the discharge
fees that the jailer required before he would knock off their fetters'.[41] Nominally, the prisons were under the supervision of outside bodies and officials – the sheriff, the magistrate, the grand jury
– but in practice there were no established systems of control and

inspection, with the result that the wardens ran their prisons for
their own profit: 'no one was more helpless in the face of extortion
than the prisoner, and no institution was more chronically under-
financed than the prison. This, however, suited the magistracy. The
ruinous condition of so many of the prisons can be explained
largely by the JPs' unwillingness to pump money into a system
that lurched along mostly paying for itself.'[42]

The earlier novelists are intent on portraying the social life of the
prisons, and especially on using it as an inverted image of the
outside world, but in doing so they also make it seem as though
the boundaries between prison and the wider world are not very
strong. Fielding's and Smollett's characters wander in and out of
gaol with the insouciance of men of fashion going slumming. What
is not emphasised is that, for a very high proportion of inmates,
gaol was a terminal experience; we know that it usually was in the
hulks, and Newgate would have been little better. Quite apart from
gaol fever and other diseases, there was little incentive for the
keeper to keep alive prisoners who never stood any chance of
paying their way out. It might be that such a situation could
occasionally produce the effects Goldsmith describes, when Dr
Primrose arrives in gaol to find that 'the prisoners seemed all
employed in . . . forgetting thought in merriment or clamour', but
this seems too light-hearted for real credibility.[43]

What happens in the last years of the century is that the image of
the prison as organically linked with the city, as a painful, even
hellish, but essentially social experience, disappears; it is replaced
by the recurrent images of the solitary dungeon on the one hand,
and on the other the ubiquitous convent, social but silent, the home
not of bluff and desperate honesty but of midnight intrigue, and
there are obvious connections here with the evolution of psychology and with portrayals of the boundaries between inner and
outer psychic worlds.[44] In the earlier fiction, escape is not really
an issue: the convicted cannot escape, short of the miraculous
appearance of a large chainsaw, those awaiting trial do not dare
to try, and the large population of debtors is unimpressed with
thoughts of freedom. The first escape described in any detail is that
of an officer from a bailiff's house in *Peregrine Pickle*, but it is in the
1790s, with Godwin, Radcliffe and Lewis, that the mechanics of
escape take the front of the stage, in a constellation of imaginings to
which the 'fall' of the Bastille also obviously belongs. It would be
fair to say that Emily in *Mysteries of Udolpho* spends the whole of

her time imprisoned: occasionally in 'vile' and 'noisome' dungeons, more often in the castles of her oppressors, always inside her own restricted psychic outlook. And it is this reticulated structure of imprisonment which Lewis mocks by taking to extremes the fears about social restriction which Radcliffe so delicately lays before us.

A principal reason for this shift of emphasis lies in the agential status of the various protagonists. Characters like Tom Jones and Roderick Random, no matter how adverse their temporary circumstances, are given to us as essentially in command of their own lives; they have choices, they make decisions, and sometimes, when they are lucky, their choices and decisions bear the fruit they had intended and the law relaxes its physical grip. This is the case neither with Emily nor with Caleb Williams: they never manage to get to a position outside prison, so it is small wonder that their confinement thickens in intensity. The very conviviality of eighteenth-century prisons may have been for some a source of their horror, but in the 1790s solitude, even when, as in *The Italian*, initially entertained as sanctuary or escape, becomes the most potent emblem of fear. The settings of the Gothic writers may not at first glance appear to resemble what we know of eighteenth-century prisons at all, but when one remembers that at the Gate House in London there was 'no dietary provision whatsoever for the six hundred to seven hundred prisoners annually committed';[45] that in the Bridewells there was continuous danger of starvation; that the number of prisoners during the American war increased dramatically as a consequence of the non-feasibility of transportation, with a concomitant worsening of conditions; that Newgate, calculated to hold 427 prisoners, was at one time holding 1200;[46] and that many contemporary observers noted a sickening increase in levels of punishment in the last two decades of the century, then one realises that the writers of terror were carrying a significant aspect of real social anxiety, one which the earlier writers had not chosen or been able to emphasise.

Trial scenes of one kind or another occur in virtually all the texts so far mentioned, and there is an increasing tendency for them to occupy crucial points in the narrative. There are interesting passages in *Moll Flanders* on the public disclosure of crime;[47] *Roderick Random* contains a parody trial on shipboard; *Tom Jones* abounds with scenes, in the houses of Allworthy and Western, wherein a traditional setting for social resolution is transformed into a temporary courtroom. *Peregrine Pickle* and *Humphry Clinker* both

contain trial scenes; in *The Old English Baron* the trial is replaced by
a ritualised duel which serves the same narrative function. *Caleb
Williams* presents us with no less than six trial scenes and hearings
of assorted kinds, *The Monk* with two more; both *Hermsprong* and
The Italian culminate in courtroom scenes, the latter of immense
length; while in *Wieland*, although the trial scene occurs rather early
and is recounted secondhand, the final confession comes replete
with legal metaphors.[48] For a picture of the features on which the
literary representations tended to dwell, I shall look here at the
relevant material in *Pickle, Clinker, Caleb Williams, Hermsprong* and
The Italian.

The trial in Chapter CVI of *Pickle* is not, in fact, an imagined
proceeding but Smollett's partisan version of the hearing of the
celebrated Annesley case. What is remarkable is that the hearing
goes very well; the poor but, according to Smollett, honourable
claimant of the title and estate acquits himself soundly, brings on
satisfactory witnesses, impresses the jury far more than his wealthy
Establishment opponent, and in due course is vindicated by that jury
who, almost uniquely in eighteenth-century fiction, are both honest
and perceptive. This, however, is only the beginning of the legal
battle. The defendant, Lord Anglesea, proceeds to take out a 'writ of
error' in order to hold up proceedings, and then sets about stripping
the claimant and his party of such money as they have managed to
acquire in order to prevent them from continuing the case:[49]

> For that end, all the oppressive arts and dilatory expensive con-
> trivances that the fertile invention of the lowest pettifoggers of the
> law could possibly devise, have with great dexterity been played
> off against them in fruitless, quibbling, and malicious suits,
> intirely foreign to the merits of the cause. Not to mention num-
> berless other acts of oppression, the most extraordinary and
> unprecedented proceedings, by means whereof this sham writ
> of error hath been kept on foot ever since November 1743, is to me
> (said the doctor) a most flagrant instance, not only of the preva-
> lency of power and money, (when employed, as in the present
> case, against an unfortunate, helpless man, disabled, as he is, of
> the means of ascertaining his right) but of the badness of a cause,
> that hath recourse to so many iniquitous expedients to support it.

The episode ends with Smollett (the 'doctor' in the above passage)
and his hearers, including Pickle, all hoping for a satisfactory

outcome, which they were in fact to be denied: the actual claimant died before the case was settled.

The impression given here by Smollett is of two sets of legal process: a public one operating through the courts, but below it a more secretive one operating through the solicitors and attorneys. Public judicial decision could be overset by tortuous legal gerrymandering, and by the inability of the courts themselves to achieve the executive power to make their writs run, especially where powerful vested interests sought to impede them. And this, of course, was precisely what the Fielding brothers, in their capacity as stipendiary magistrates, were also saying at the time: that judicial correctness was pointless without some sort of power, some way in which decisions could be mediated to particular parties and to the public in general.

In *Clinker*, Humphry himself is accused by a postillion of a robbery which he did not commit and brought before a JP; the ensuing scene is designed to bring out the difference between what the courts know and what they are able to prove, and the dire consequences which flow from this difference.[50] Clinker runs into trouble and is unable properly to 'put his case' because his extreme Methodist convictions prevent him from giving a simple answer to questions like, 'In the name of God, if you are innocent, say so', to which he can only muster, in a further twist of the problem of the definition of guilt mentioned above, 'No...God forbid that I should call myself innocent, while my conscience is burthened with sin.' The postillion's testimony is inexorable; the JP commits Clinker although it turns out that he knows the identity of the real thief; this thief is, furthermore, present in court, and is indeed the only person who pleads in Clinker's favour:

> He was a young man, well dressed, and, from the manner in which he cross-examined the evidence, we took it for granted, that he was a student in one of the inns of court. – He freely checked the justice for some uncharitable inferences he made to the prejudice of the prisoner, and even ventured to dispute with his worship on certain points of law.

Both justice and systematic lawbreaker know the rules of the game, whereas everybody else is liable to get squeezed between them; the point is underlined by the presence in court of thief-takers, who much appreciate the little dramatic spectacle being staged for them.

Trial scenes are perhaps incidentals for Smollett; his fury with the law is part of his wider fury with the Establishment.[51] For Godwin, thinking at least of the primary Gothic text *Caleb Williams*, the law is the primary means of social oppression. The entire book is Caleb's plea to the reader in a simulated trial: 'I have not deserved this treatment', he says at the beginning, 'my own conscience witnesses in behalf of that innocence, my pretensions to which are regarded in the world as incredible' (p. 1). His attempts at self-justification are consistently disbelieved by the people around him, and he spends much of the book in gaol or escaping from it, and yet, as he says, the blame is partly his own for daring to tamper with the secrets of power:

> I had made myself a prisoner, in the most intolerable sense of that term, for years – perhaps for the rest of my life. Though my prudence and discretion should be invariable, I must remember that I should have an overseer, vigilant from conscious guilt, full of resentment at the unjustifiable means by which I had extorted from him a confession, and whose lightest caprice [*sic*] might at any time decide upon everything that was dear to me. The vigilance even of a public and systematical despotism is poor, compared with a vigilance which is thus goaded by the most anxious passions of the soul.
>
> (p. 151)

The rhetoric here of secrets and confession is crucial to the development of the relations between the text, the body and the law, and I shall return to it below;[52] for the moment we may note that despite what Caleb says, 'public and systematical despotism' is also rather effective in keeping him oppressed; or, to put it more clearly, in the status and position of victim.

In the first of the six major trial scenes in the text Hawkins is arraigned by Tyrrel under the Black Act, which Godwin quotes, and wrongly found guilty. In the second Falkland is accused of the murder of Tyrrel and wrongly found innocent. In the third, informal hearing, Caleb is brought up before Falkland and Forester on a trumped-up robbery charge and committed to gaol. In the fourth, Caleb is arrested on suspicion of being a felon, and his demonstration that he is not makes little difference to the outcome:

When I had finished, [the JP] told me it was all to no purpose, and that it might have been better for me, if I had shown myself less insolent. It was clear that I was a vagabond and a suspicious person. The more earnest I showed myself to get off, the more reason there was he should keep me fast. Perhaps, after all, I should turn out to be the felon in question. But, if I was not that, he had no doubt I was worse; a poacher [sic], or, for what he knew, a murderer.

(p. 268)

This hierarchy of crimes takes us back to the history of enclosure, to the myth of Robin Hood, to the Green Man; in this particular instance, however, the evil inclinations of the law are thwarted by the still more evil inclinations of the thief-takers, since when the JP appoints them to take Caleb to gaol and having failed to extort money from him, they get bored with their commission and let him go.

The fifth of these trials is Godwin's *tour de force*. Caleb is at last tired of Falkland's persecutions and determines to end it all by laying information against him before the magistrates. He has been saving up this final resort throughout the book, convinced that nobody can avoid concluding Falkland's guilt from his evidence. This is the reply he receives from the magistrate:

First, I have to tell you, as a magistrate, that I can have nothing to do with your declaration. If you had been concerned in the murder you talk of, that would alter the case. But it is out of all reasonable rule for a magistrate to take an information from a felon, except against his accomplices. Next, I think it right to observe to you, in my own proper person, that you appear to me to be the most impudent rascal I ever saw. Why, are you such an ass as to suppose, that the sort of story you have been telling, can be of any service to you, either here or at the assizes, or anywhere else? A fine time of it indeed it would be, if, when gentlemen of six thousand a year take up their servants for robbing them, those servants could trump up such accusations as these, and could get any magistrate or court of justice to listen to them!

(p. 304)

The narrative shock here is surprisingly great, due to the care with which Godwin has built up the likelihood of success: the sixth and last court scene, in which Falkland at last – and largely only out of fatigue – confesses his guilt, is comparatively insignificant.

Godwin's courts are nightmares; they are places where all our expectations that our case might be heard are reduced to rubble; they represent the law in ruins, and at the same time able to inflict ruin on the body of the victim, and here we find the seeds of the most persistent of all Gothic themes. The Sessions which concludes Bage's *Hermsprong* constitutes the necessary antithesis to this, functioning as wish-fulfilment;[53] where Godwin uses trials to demonstrate the power of the aristocracy, Bage uses them to achieve vengeance for their multifarious misdemeanours and to humiliate them in the process. His Lord Grondale enters the court 'attended by a numerous suite, amongst whom were half the bench of justices'; Corrow's opening address is a masterpiece of political innuendo. The magistrates are divided among themselves: Blick, Grondale's man, is balanced by Saxby, a member of the Quorum and thus 'a gentleman of the greatest weight upon the bench'. The arguments advanced against Hermsprong are various: he is accused of radicalism; of purchasing a property which Grondale has coveted – a purchase which, according to Corrow, 'I presume to think, we shall shortly set aside in the Court of King's Bench, by proving the purchaser an alien'; of seducing Grondale's daughter; and finally of assault and battery on one of Grondale's henchmen.

In fashioning Hermsprong's reply, Bage has a difficult task. He has on the one hand to acquit him of the charges, while on the other maintaining his character as an instinctual radical; he largely betrays this difficulty by converting Hermsprong into a relative of Grondale and a thoroughgoing member of the gentry. Again, these legal scenes reflect the differences between Godwin's and Bage's general approach: Caleb Williams is supposed to be a figure with no particular hold on the law and thus continuously overwhelmed by it, while Hermsprong is largely exempted by virtue of a fantasised panoply of wealth, freedom and intelligence, and thus exposes the shortcomings in the legal system not by personal example but by demonstration from the outside.

But it is the Godwinian tradition which flows into Gothic, although with the long trial scene in *The Italian* we detect a distinct shift occurring in representation.[54] The scenes I have so far mentioned take place for the most part in the bright light of day; the discourse is often clear in ways which suggest an improbable composure on the part of many of the participants. In *The Italian*

this clarity disappears: the whole scene takes place in semi-dark-
ness, the discourse is broken, imperfectly grasped, often not even
fully heard. In Godwin, JPs terrify by virtue of their combination of
power and ignorance; in Radcliffe it is the court itself, impersonal
and clever, which terrifies, whatever the justice it metes out – and it
is interesting to note that both Radcliffe and Lewis rely on the
Inquisition to right wrongs.

The scene in *The Italian* is an early attempt to represent a trial
from the point of view of persons unversed in the ways of the law
and highly uncertain about either the potential outcome or the
physical limit of the court's powers. Our heroes are not always
ostensibly on trial, but it is perfectly clear that this trivial legalism
would matter not a whit to the Inquisition if its purposes were
better served by reversing the positions of prisoner and plaintiff.
Undoubtedly part of what is happening here is a representation of
women's experience of a very foreign and powerful male-dominated world, although Burney's response to that situation is
exactly the opposite: to reside in an absolute faith in the justice of
legal process.[55] Radcliffe has merged courtroom and gaol into one
symbol of horror, or rather she has suggested continuities in the
psychic state produced by the 'majesty' of the law, no matter what
its apparent purposes. What she has also done is construct a
powerful realisation of the legal power of the word; there are few
other examples in eighteenth-century fiction of a dialogue so closely worked and full of verbal tricks. What we are seeing is an
inversion of many of the characteristics already noted: an imaginative leap, for example, from the imputed stupidity of the English JP
to the imputed diabolical cleverness of continental and Catholic
systems of justice. But we are also seeing an exploration of ways in
which fiction can match courtroom experience in general, how
words can be made to figure forth doubts, uncertainties, terrors
which inhere in life-or-death situations. Radcliffe is talking about
the limits of reason; yet put another way she is also talking about
the administration of a judicial system in which, at the Black Assize
of 1750, two prisoners were brought on trial so infected with
typhus after their lengthy stay in gaol that, after they had been
somewhat pointlessly sentenced to death, fifty other people died as
well, including judge, jury and legal officers.[56]

We can then identify a set of problems which arise in eighteenth-
century representations of the law and which we can trace right
through the century until they begin a slow transformation into the

materials of Gothic textuality. The first concerns the ambivalence of expressed attitudes towards legality. There is, for instance, a marked emphasis, especially in Defoe and Smollett, on ways of cheating or eluding the law. The paradigm here is again *Moll Flanders*, in the Preface to which Defoe makes a claim which has since become famous:

> Throughout the infinite variety of this book, this fundamental is most strictly adhered to; there is not a wicked action in any part of it but is first or last rendered unhappy and unfortunate; there is not a superlative villain brought upon the stage but either he is brought to an unhappy end or brought to be a penitent; there is not an ill thing mentioned but it is condemned, even in the relation, nor a virtuous, just thing but it carries its praise along with it.
>
> (p. vii)

This, of course, is not true, the most outstanding example of an 'ill thing' which is not 'condemned' being Moll herself. Defoe goes on to claim that one of the purposes of the book is to warn the citizenry against criminal devices. Occasionally, it is true, Moll does this, as when she gives her advice about how to seize a pickpocket, but these episodes are outweighed in number and attraction by those wherefrom only the criminal could feasibly derive any instruction. It is, on the other hand, true that Moll feels little more sympathy for her criminal colleagues than she does for the people she robs; as far as she is concerned almost any other person or institution is significant principally as an impediment to her own progress and wellbeing, and the law is merely another of the hurdles which an unsympathetic society places between her and prosperity.

There is little to distinguish the lawyer from the criminal in much eighteenth-century fiction; and hence comes the profusion of thief-takers and Jonathan Wilds who straddle both sides of the fence. Where the criminal robs without legal sanction, the lawyer robs with it; Swift relishes his life among the Houyhnhnms because (in a catalogue of extraordinarily resonant conjunctions):

> here was neither physician to destroy my body, nor lawyer to ruin my fortune; no informer to watch my words and actions, or forge accusations against me for hire: here were no gibers,

censurers, backbiters, pickpockets, highwaymen, housebreakers, attorneys, bawds, buffoons, gamesters, politicians, wits, splenetics, tedious talkers, controvertists, ravishers, murderers, robbers, virtuosos...[57]

Both Swift and Bage, among many others, describe England as a nation of litigants,[58] although clearly the blame for this must be shared between the avarice of attorneys and the gullibility of the populace.

The problem of how the criminal can be distinguished from the wielder of unjust but legalised power absorbed the Gothic writers. Lewis in particular delights in giving extra twists to this already contradictory situation: when his characters fall prey to various vices, the implication is nearly always that they had been trying to live under a system of laws too stringent for human wellbeing. When Agnes suffers her hideous punishment, it is not because the nuns are transgressing the law; the prioress points out that on the contrary it is the laws of the order themselves which 'are strict and severe; they have fallen into disuse of late; but the crime of Agnes shows me the necessity of their revival'.[59] Not surprisingly, the people who suffer under these deadly systems become deeply confused about their own legality: Agnes, again, feels herself criminalised regardless of the innocence of her actions.

From this problem of the legal and the criminal derives a second, to do with the circumstantial justification of crime. 'Both in France and in England', we may well agree, 'at that period of low wages and casual employment, the criminal was the necessary consequence and victim of the country's social organisation',[60] and it is easily possible to substantiate the view that it would have been almost impossible for anybody living in the country or the town *not* to transgress the law, and that prosecution was thus allowed to depend on the whim of the powerful. The excuse for arrest was always there and, perhaps more to the point, so was the motivation for crime, both in financial terms and in terms of natural justice.

This was clearly a difficulty which the novelists saw and about which they agonised. When Moll Flanders at last gets to America she finds there not the slightest circumstantial inducement to crime, and is *therefore* a reformed person.[61] Even in *Journal of the Plague Year* (1722) Defoe sees no explicit contradiction in allowing his characters a little justified criminality when their circumstances seem truly to demand it. Goldsmith performs a small arabesque on this theme in the character of Jenkinson who, we are told, becomes a criminal because he has such a naturally cunning face that nobody has ever believed a word he says, a career path more usually associated with politicians.[62]

The effect of these two areas of uncertainty is, despite individual portrayals of benevolence, justice and charity, substantially to discredit legal *mechanisms*, and this is of course a political point. As Smollett puts it in *Sir Launcelot Greaves*, 'that which is acknowledged to be truth in fact is construed falshood in law; and great reason we have to boast of a constitution founded on the basis of absurdity' (p. 204). It should therefore be hardly surprising to find a great deal of play made in the novels of alternatives to the dominant English mode of legality: from Defoe to Godwin, we find speculations about whether there could exist, or perhaps does exist, in some foreign country or in some alien or suppressed way of life, a form of democratically just society, and about what forms of law it would possess.

The justice, for instance, of actual foreign states, whatever the historical justification, is often suggested to be less stringent and/or less arbitrary than our own. The French legal and military officials whom Peregrine Pickle encounters are curiously compassionate about his strange behaviour, and although arrests are made to seem regular occurrences on the other side of the Channel, they are never followed with the dire consequences which beset him in Britain. In *Udolpho*, Radcliffe has cause to refer to Venetian justice, and again is content to treat it without criticism.[63] In Swift the same theme exists: his account of the Lilliputian legal system is clearly intended in part, despite its eccentricities, as a corrective to the English system, and the questions the King of Brobdingnag asks are designed to expose home weaknesses.

More important, however, and usually more graphically described, are the frequent episodes in which the dominant legal system is compared unfavourably with that system which supposedly obtains in some criminalised social subgroup. Captain Singleton's pirate band sets the tone:

Being now...a considerable Number of us, and in Condition to defend our selves, the first thing we did was to give every one his Hand, that we would not separate from one another upon any Occasion whatsoever, but that we would live and die together; that we would kill no Food, but that we would

distribute it in publick; and that we would be in all things guided
by the Majority, and not insist upon our own Resolutions in any
thing, if the Majority were against it ... [64]

The first thing with which the pirates dispense is *secrecy;* they also
tackle the commercial withholding of essential supplies and unde-
mocratic forms of government (although admittedly they then
proceed to appoint a 'Captain'). In *Tom Jones,* the gypsies are the
sociological testing-ground, although here there is considerably
more irony: Fielding points out that gypsy society is an absolute
monarchy, and adds that, although the gypsies in question appear
to be all too happy, there remains 'one solid objection to absolute
monarchy', which is 'the difficulty of finding any man adequate to
the office of an absolute monarch' (p. 597). In gaol the Vicar of
Wakefield performs the remarkable feat of transforming the prisoners themselves into a decent and legal society: 'in less than a fort-
night', we learn of this exceptional worker priest, 'I had formed
them into something social and humane, and had the pleasure of
regarding myself as a legislator, who had brought men from their
native ferocity into friendship and obedience' (p. 243).

Defoe, Fielding and Goldsmith are clearly thinking of three very
different versions of an improved society, but each of them allows
a vision of these possibilities to flourish in the underworld, a
tradition which continues into much British and German Gothic
writing, although this cannot be found in Radcliffe, who uses
banditti for largely landscaping purposes. In *Caleb Williams,* however, we find a band of brigands very similar to those in Schiller or
Francis Lathom;[65] they are not quite the exiled and curiously clad
metaphysicians of German tradition, but Caleb is 'by no means
inclined to believe them worse men, or more hostile in their dis-
positions to the welfare of their species, than the generality of those
that look down upon them with most censure' (p. 248).

As a prelude to thinking through issues to do with the Gothic
and its dealings with the text, the body and the law, we may say
that the novelists of the earlier eighteenth century see and portray
individual legal instances very clearly, but we may reasonably ask
to what extent they demonstrate awareness of an overall *system*,
imbricated as they emblematically are within it. The more specu-
lative, general discussion of the law comes not from Fielding but
later in the century: we may think, for example, of the surprisingly
serious reflections which Dr Primrose offers on the purpose of the

law while he is himself interned; of Godwin's ceaseless and prob-
ing speculations on the extent to which laws which may be
betrayed into becoming oppressive are necessary in the first
place; of the sometimes detailed criticism which Bage offers of
English law with respect to property, privilege and sexual discrimination; of the speculations in *The Italian* about the occluded,
secret connections between crime and the law.[66]

It is in these later years of the eighteenth century, around the
origin of the Gothic novel, that the strains of the legal system and
its inadequacy to changing social circumstances become most
obvious: 'the three quarters of a century after 1750... from the
point of view of the development of the English legal system...
were years of repression and retreat'.[67] But the matter is more
complex than this, because it is in these years that the emphasis
of the fiction moves more substantially into the realm of private
experience, and indeed into the confrontation between such experience and the 'outer world', often perceived as a single oppressive
system devoted to the repression, criminalisation and incarceration
of the body. Defoe, Fielding and others present us with a reasoned
and 'experienced' view of the detailed operations of the law; Godwin and Radcliffe insist on representing the face – or mask – of
terror which the law wears to those enmeshed in its toils, and thus
begin the process of entertaining the reader as victim, as oppressed
and desperate body, which will prove to be a mainspring of Gothic
textuality.

3

Laws which Bind the Body: The Case of the Monster

Our walls, our bodies, are no problem to them.
Their hungers are homing elsewhere.
We cannot see them or turn our minds from them.
Their bubbling mouths, their eyes
In a slow mineral fury
Press through our nothingness where we sprawl on beds,
Or sit in rooms.[1]

It might be fair to ask, on the basis of the comments made in the previous chapter, the apparently simple question: what is the law? But to this essentialist question there is, of course, no answer. Despite all its social and historical complexity, the law is the law; and it is so because that is the law. As we look at formations of the law, however, we may begin to glimpse attempts to link, or to neutralise, significant opposites: one would be the opposition between the baroque and unintelligible forms of distant history and a principle of contemporaneous order.[2] As we look at the panoply of the law we see a pretension to the most minute accuracy imbricated with a reliance on archaism and a point of origin which is always beyond current recall. The voice in which the law speaks to us is the voice of absolute authority; but it is simultaneously the voice of a caprice which we readily re-interpret as mystery.

That the law, for these reasons, exerts fascination cannot be denied; but at the same time I would want to insist that in the relation between the law and the novel there lies a curious historical fold, and one which continues to reverberate through the history of representation. One way of looking at this relation would be by focusing on the novel's specific claim to represent the variety of social life: to move away from and beyond the more restricted class orientations of previous fictions and to provide a capacious home for multitudes. In opposition to this, the law

43

stands for unity. There are, of course, *laws*; there are also changes in
the law, accretions and occasionally reductions, twists and turns as
the attempt to retain a fix on emergent multiplicity necessitates the
introduction of new statutes, the repeal of those which are out of
date. Nevertheless, my concern now will not be directly with these
laws, although I have provided examples of several of them in the
previous chapter, but with *the law*, that law which we find, for
example, in *The Island of Doctor Moreau* (1896) to be that which
stands between the human and the beast, that which provides the
single 'bounding line', to quote Blake, which will contain the world
of order and consign the rest of experience to the dark places and
the wilderness.[3] I am concerned now – as is Gothic – with the law
as physical and discursive limit.

Looked at in this way, we can see the process of textualisation I
am describing as a process of contamination. Since the law functions as a set of border posts, as a guardian against encroachment
by the night, then it is always peculiarly open to being re-coloured
by precisely those forces which it seeks to repress, and its discourse, while it strains toward clarity, must also undergo the
opposite process, which is a continual obfuscation. It is in the
novel that this process begins to be uncovered; and we can say
that as the eighteenth century progresses it becomes increasingly
difficult to represent the law without finding oneself directly impli-
cated in its ambiguous status.

One response to this, particularly clearly emblematised in Smollett, is fury, or outrage; but outrage is only possible while one
clings on to a notion of how things could be otherwise, while one
continues to measure the law by some idealised version of itself
according to which purification would be possible. This is the
rhetoric of reform, of improvement. But Gothic can be identified –
as it can, of course, in many other ways – as a point at which this
idealised other fades away and we are left confronting the stark-
ness of the law; this then becomes the stance of the victim, the
realm of terror, or in the case of, for example, Kafka, the realm of
the agonisingly absurd. At this point it also becomes clear that
dealings with the law are always also dealings with text, dealings
with a discursive body but a discursive body which is imbued with
the utmost power; before this power, the character loses progres-
sively his or her agential status, becomes a victim, enters into the
vault. A new textuality has to be constructed, but at the same time
it is obvious that this new textuality will be perpetually haunted by

its own other, by its own opposite, by the theoretically clear, unhaunted textuality of the law.[4]

There is also another way of looking at this process, which is through the body.[5] The law is the performative taken to the highest degree, that version of the word which has immediate physical effects, of incarceration, for example, of pain, of death. Thus the law forms a frame or grid through which all bodies must pass; at the same time, and inevitably, it serves to standardise those bodies. For the law to function at all, there must be an assumed undifferentiation – of the pain threshold, for example, or of the endurance of solitary confinement. That the law can make 'allowances' – can, for example, occasionally enact pleas for mercy, or can, at some times and in some places, produce a differentiated penal scenario for children – only emphasises this construction of a standardised body, some of the effects of which have been charted for us by Foucault.[6]

What the law cannot permit is the exceptional body; before the law, therefore, there cannot be monsters.[7] To take the matter the other way round, the existence of a monster therefore poses the utmost threat to the law; and our readerly pleasure in the situation of the monster has its origins, I suggest, in our apprehension of the dismantling, if only for a certain time, of the discourse of the law. The monster thus takes on some of the contours of carnival, as we can still sense in audiences when King Kong bends the bars of society, when Dracula announces that he is above all regulation. As spectators in this scenario, we are split, and the two sides of this divide stand in a relation of fascination to one another; on the one hand we have the spectator, or reader, as freed, as participating in a process of exemption before which the law might quail; on the other we have the residual feeling of potential victimisation, the knowledge that this freedom may not in the end be ours, that we may ourselves share in the role of, in the case of *Frankenstein*, the terrified peasant – in which posture, as we shamefully sense, we may ourselves also need to call the law to our aid.

And yet, in another way, this relation is more contorted; for to be the monster is also to be the monster's victim, to be the monster as victim. Gothic, if we may hazard yet another description, enacts those complicated, often confused moments in which the rhetoric and practice of power seem for a moment to shimmer before our eyes, when the uncanny seeps in and boundaries which had once seemed stable appear permeable. Through these mists, we see the shapes of the terrifying; but these shapes are also reassuring, because they promise us that prison is not forever; the monster comes to rescue us, even if that rescue implies our death. This dialectic of monstrosity, then, has been within Gothic from the beginning, and it focuses on the body, on what we might call the 'case' of the body, in the redoubled sense which we might give to that vexed term: the 'case' as casing, as protective 'shell' which is always on the verge of dissolution; or 'case' as individual example, the unrepeatability of the body, precisely that unrepeatability which renders the body, even while it suffers most, perpetually unamenable to the rule of law. The battle between the monster and the law is at all points an attempt to exceed or encompass the other; Gothic labyrinths are metaphors for this process, and for the absence of communication which this presupposes.[8] The monster resists even the strongest of performatives, we might even say it is that shape which psyche projects in order to resist performatives, that shape which will have that perpetual exemption from obedience which at once returns us ambivalently to the omnipotence and powerlessness of the infant, and also to a time before words, a time which precedes even a putative consciousness of undifferentiation, wherein performatives had no purpose or purchase.

It should go without saying that the law returns us to this position, which is inseparable from a certain impotence; but in doing so it renders us at the same time free. A crucial instance here is that of Cholly Breedlove in Toni Morrison's *The Bluest Eye* (1970). Cholly is a rapist of his own daughter, a despicable and hopeless father and husband; but, Morrison puzzlingly tells us, he is free.[9] In what sense is he free? Free from what, or free for what? Free, we may surmise, because he has recognised – not necessarily consciously – his own powerlessness; he knows at some level which can neither be brought to consciousness nor eradicated that he is beyond the bounds of the law and therefore he is uncontained. Whether this can ever be considered a moral virtue is something which continues to vex readers and critics of *The Bluest Eye*; what it certainly is, though, is a condition, a state, and it represents the state which the law finds most slippery.

Before the law, then, there is always the possibility of being childed; but once we have been childed, there is nothing more that can be done with or to us; thus the law's victims are always in danger of sliding between its stretching fingers, of reducing the law to a merely sonorous rhetoric which resounds in our ears but signifies nothing. Here is where our imaginings of the non-standardised body, of the monster, attain their greatest power; and of all the emblems of the non-standardised body, it remains Frankenstein's monster which has the most force.

It is with the greatest trepidation that I return yet again to a text which itself has become genuinely monstrous,[10] a thing of display and exhibition, de-monstrable precisely because it is well-nigh submerged in a sea of critical writing, a fit inhabitant for the watery arctic wastes which are the monster's destiny. Those wastes are the scenario for an endlessly adjunctive process, such as one can also not fail to see in the destiny of Mary Shelley the author, adjoined to the career and signature, the very name of her husband. *Frankenstein* is an emblematic text here, a cardinal 'case', a 'legend' in the sense of that word which means that which is 'readable', but inscribed in this 'case' on the body.

But *Frankenstein* is also, crucially, a text; and in dealing with such a text we have also to encounter the very different rhetorics which we might need to deploy on text and body. We need, for example, to consider in this context the question of ways beyond the critical impasse between deconstruction and materialism, or, to put it another way, of working at the *aporia* of the symbolic and the Real. I want to look at the text as precisely – now – containing within itself a refraction of a critical battle, and one in which we can see precisely the lineaments of the law, specifically here as further refracted through the childing process and thus as to do with the construction of the father. To try to work *Frankenstein* through as a *critical* motif: it might be considered, for example, surprising that deconstruction, with its rigorous eschewal of the author and its quasi-analytic questioning of the authority of the father, should have continual recourse precisely to named fathers, fathers who, it would not be going too far to say, are worshipped and endlessly 'deferred' to: one such, an icon around whom all the anxieties of influence congregate and whose name would not be foreign to the incarnators of a 'modern Prometheus', is Nietzsche, shown to us by Derrida, for example, as the ultimate sceptic, as the thinker who above all puts into question the naivety of our assumptions about the relationships between discourse and world, text and body, and who can also serve us as a primary questioner of the law.[11]

Let us, in response to this increasingly hegemonic interpretation, bring forward one or two statements by Nietzsche. In *Beyond Good and Evil* (1886) he tells us that every great philosophy is 'a confession on the part of its author and a kind of involuntary and unconscious memoir'.[12] This is a difficult statement to square with many current approaches to Nietzsche. Here we have the 'author', as it were, in full flight. If the 'author' is a fictive construct of text, it is hard to see in what sense we can ascertain the nature of a 'personal confession'; if discourse unpacks itself only in relation to preceding discourses, then there would be no possibility of discussing such movements, which I would want to call crucially movements, swayings, bendings of psyche.

Or again:

> The function of reason is to allow expression of certain passions at the expense of others. A morality is a set of principles which restricts passions; a successful morality is one which restricts only the life-stultifying passions, which may be fatal, where they drag their victim down with the weight of their stupidity.[13]

Reason and morality are, of course, relative and pragmatic matters in Nietzschean thought; what is not relative here, and what is not amenable to an all-encompassing pragmatism, appears to be the level of the passions, a level familiar to the practice and criticism of the Gothic. In pursuit of this we might also turn to a more recent philosophical formulation by Jerome Kagan:

> Construction of a persuasive rational basis for behaving morally has been the problem on which most moral philosophers have stubbed their toes. I believe they will continue to do so until they recognise what Chinese philosophers have appreciated for a long time; namely, feeling, not logic, sustains the superego.[14]

We may make several interpretative moves in the context of this formulation. First, we may rewrite the passage not only as a comment on the difficulty of finding a rational basis for moral behaviour, but also as about the difficulty of finding a rational basis for *reading*, for the process of legend; for reading is, of course, a form of behaviour, undertaken by men and women, and can hardly be exempt from the difficulty Kagan identifies. Second, we may note that he names this difficulty as specifically Western: I do not know why he restricts himself to the Chinese philosophers, for the centrality of feeling, the passions, and the endless conflict between their claim and the other claims which occur in the course of life

have been the 'experiential' substance with which Hindu and Buddhist philosophy over a wide swathe of Asia have dealt for millennia; but the point remains. Thirdly, in suggesting a different
constellation for the superego he is rehearsing arguments which
have taken place within psychoanalysis over, again, many long
years, and these arguments will enter again into the substance of
succeeding chapters. They find still their most appropriate expression in Sandor Ferenczi's analyses of the reliance on rationality as a
key neurosis, the source of madness in so far as it is left
untreated;[15] and it is left untreated while arguments among ration-
alists and anti-rationalists continue to be conducted on a shared
terrain,[16] precisely that terrain which, like the law, refuses the
difficulty of the non-standardised body; which is intimately related
to the discourse of the passions, for the passions should be considered here not as matters which occur 'within' psyche and body,
but rather as states, conditions through which the self passes. The
passions have the power even to distort the body: we know this
from the whole history of masks, from the ways in which from
earliest times a person in the 'grip' – resonant phrase – of a passion
has been portrayed as dehumanised, as removed, that is, from
assumptions and standardisations, whether that removal has
found its natural emblem in a certain kind of animalisation, a
type of rapprochement with the expressive faciality of the beast,
or not.

What might any of this have to do with *Frankenstein*? One connection is paramount, and it is that the point of the intellectual
suppression of the passions is to be found psychoanalytically in
one place and one place only: namely, the disavowal of the body.
The work of interpretation, which is the work we are engaged upon
for much of our lives, can be expressed in a simple trope: it is the
conversion of *matter* into *what matters*. As such it is modelled on the
dreamwork, and about these connections between dream and interpretation there is much to say, but I shall leave that aside for the
moment. Matter, matters, matrix: I am aware also of the manifold
connections here with the womb, and thus with women's writing,
inscriptions on women's bodies; the point can also be made according to a different politics, in the sense that the disenfranchisement
of bodies is what intellectual work in the West is revealing itself
increasingly as being about. Bodies, especially starving, suffering
bodies, are too tough to deal with naked, or too naked to deal
with anything but toughly: within this lacuna, this absence, we

downgrade and insult the Real in the hope that it – the starving millions, the growing western underclass, the terrifying body of Africa – will go away. And *Frankenstein* is a text which, crucially, is about the body; and, like the other locations I have pointed to above, it therefore deals in, and at the same time fosters, that which is beyond the law.

It is about the body in many different ways; indeed, it is more obviously about the body than any other *novel* in the Western tradition, the most immediate connection being with myth, not the stated myth of Prometheus, in which the body is merely an adjunctive site of pain and punishment, but the Christian myth and the suffering body of Christ on the cross. Like the Christian myth, *Frankenstein* is a work of torment and torture, distortion and gro-tesquerie, the tender passions hung on the cross of pride and reason. More precisely *Frankenstein* is about, first, the cannibalisa-tion of the body, the work of the charnel house, and thus about the threat of decay and of what happens after decay; there is a sense in which the novel cheers us up because it assures us that even our remains might be of use some day, that we might all become, if you like, brain donors. For the monster is not merely 'born'; he is reborn, of course as 'a thing of shreds and patches', but never-theless as a living reincarnation, thus a living Buddha in some sense of that term, but with the crucial difference that the material of his rebirth is body-stuff, not soul-stuff: he is put together from the detritus of the organic, and he thus stands for the resurrection of the *body* which is to come.

Second, it is about the physicality of birth. We know, of course, that this is a male birth, that it is birth from a father/mother who has rigorously eschewed nature, who has cast himself adrift, like the Herculean ego descending to Hades, from all laws of family and reproduction.[17] The image of the Herculean ego, I suggest, is significant here, as these mythic images are in general crucial to the Gothic, in ways which I shall hope to amplify below. It is clear that Frankenstein, searching, though not very attractively, for a world beyond the law, makes a symbolic descent to the underworld, he tears aside the boundary which the law constructs to separate the living from the dead: it is in the forbidden realm of graves, tombs and crypts that he discovers the material for his task. This work with crypts is also work with secrets,[18] as we have already seen in eighteenth-century dealings with the 'underside' of the law, and in so far as it is work with secrets it is womb-work, it is delving into primal, birth-giving matter, into the originary matrix, an unimaginable return to a hypothesised primal scene, be that scene the stuff of recollection or construction; but it is at the same time and inevitably a masculist attempt to bring back that which cannot be brought back. The relevant myths here are those of Orpheus, or of Persephone, 'the bringer of destruction'; but for our purposes it is also important to point out that this delving into a world of secrets is precisely a recapitulation of the kind of work which needs to be done psychically if one is to find – or rather, recapture from childhood – a position for oneself outside the law, a position prior to the submission to the name-of-the-father.[19] For before the law every secret must be told; to turn the matter into a more narrative channel, we may now see the law again as the opposite of the novel in that it provides only the end of any story, the uncovering of all difference, which the novel in its original forms was concerned above all things to preserve.

But here there is a further problem. In this patchwork of myth there are crossed threads, dropped stitches, *aporia*; especially in the assumptions I have so far made about relationships between the world of Hades and the world of the womb. The neo-Jungian thinker James Hillman tells us, in *The Dream and the Underworld* (1979) and elsewhere, that there is nothing in common between these worlds, that the dead underworld and the fertile underground are 'worlds apart'.[20] Yet I would want to argue that in *Frankenstein* they are precisely crossed and slatted together; and the same might be said for Gothic fiction as a genre, where the neat distinction between fertility and sterility, between the organic and the inorganic, is continually 'crossed'; as, emblematically, in the case of the monster. This leads us to two possible hypotheses.

The first would be that these realms are psychically less distinct than Hillman claims – in other words, that the analysis of dream which underpins his thinking and which, I am now suggesting, provides a suitable framework for consideration of the Gothic, needs further reticulation. We would need to suggest that within the dead cold of Hades where all bodies seem disanimated, where all animations are disembodied, something nevertheless stirs, there is some hint of the organic which provides the slightest flutter of saving grace from which rebirth might be possible. And this of course is true in the myths themselves: not everybody who comes down to Hades is enveloped, there is always the exception that proves the rule, just as Yama, the Buddhist Lord of the Dead, can

sometimes be prevailed upon to return the soul which he has
captured in his net if only the loving survivor can persist for long
enough in her or his pursuit and entreaty. We would need also to
suggest that within the world of fertility and reproduction there is
something deadly, something which will never 'return' in all the
senses of that word, something, if you like, beyond recall or reconstruction, some ineluctable but undecidable primal scene which
lurks like cold steel or like the biting snake at the heart of sexuality;
the thing Blake saw as the invisible worm in the sick rose, and the
thing which haunts our recollections of the mother, the terror and
the secret which make the body forever irreducible. Heights and
depths, strainings upwards and returns downwards, these are the
topographies which structure *Frankenstein* as they continue to
structure the Gothic in general.

On mythic and psychological grounds this sounds a plausible
hypothesis; indeed, put in this way it is the alternative which
would sound implausible, for to keep these realms totally separate
would be to assert that the psychopathy of the one depth and the
jouissance of the other were somehow held in different compart-
ments of the psyche, as though one could sink wells in different
places without the ever-present threat of unknown underground
contact, hold secrets without the danger of their mutual contamination; whereas we in fact know that everything in the psyche – as
in *Frankenstein* – is flow, seepage, mutual implication. This, perhaps, we may see as the unconscious content of Freud's own over-
cleanly hydraulic metaphors.

The second hypothesis would be that there is that in Mary
Shelley, in the bodily, pressured shape of Mary Shelley, which
causes, or becomes the specific site for, this cross-hatching, this
mysterious interlocking of birth and death. And this, I think, is
also the 'case'. We may put it this way: that the dropped stitches,
the crossed threads, the lines in *Frankenstein* which run nowhere, all
this is the work of the mythic spider; it is, to use the most resonant
symbol, knitting, but it is the knitting of a beginner, it is knitting at
the threshold; and in the shape of Mary Shelley, as we peer into the
gloom, we see a series of thresholds which intervene between us
and the descent of *Frankenstein* into the depths. The most important of these takes us back to Mary Shelley as a woman writer, and
we need to remind ourselves of the importance of not falling into
the trap of gender symmetry. In order for a woman to become a
writer, thresholds have to be crossed; each one has its ritual, and

usually, as we know, this ritual involves naming or re-naming, woman into man as the female body dons the cloak of the 'author' and enters into the realm of the permitted, the lawful, but the main point about crossing thresholds in the mythic or psychic realms is the more general one that in any case you are not the same person on the other side of them as you were when you approached; these thresholds, in offering you an alias, at the same time condemn you to functioning as the dominant and approved other and allow you, in some sense of that term, to be free. The liminal change, which is a subtle or blatant reordering of power structures, of dominances and submissions, of stoopings and growings into fantasised 'spaces beyond' (for in one sense there is never a space 'beyond' the threshold, only 'within' it) involves inner and outer: and so the 'writer Mary' becomes a textual person bearing the marks of a different insertion into the patriarchal order, bearing them for example in a set of readerly and critical assumptions, standardisations, as to what 'she', the physically gendered person, does, or should, know or not know, to what 'scientific' knowledge, for example, she should have access; and in that mere set comes the whole train of the logomorph. Just so the text of *Frankenstein* reflects in its hesitancies, in its narrative labyrinths, the threshold of its own historical becoming, a particular moment in the arrival of a new discourse: the moment of scientistic and productive utopianism, or whatever else, in the slipping and sliding terms of Foucauldian historiography, we might like to call it. But the point is, of course, that all these thresholds are represented in the convoluted structures of confusion, form themselves precisely into the impossibility of weaving a coherent cloak for change, symbolised, to take just one example, in the substitution of alchemy for science, an investigative realm which does not obey the law as it is known for one which might, as this particular threshold threatens us with inner and outer changes which are too powerful, too threatening to be represented direct.

Two hypotheses: one that claims a theoretical and analytic conflation of fertility and sterility, of reproduction and death, which the text cannot help but reinstate; the other that sees in the shapings of the text the pressure, the negative image, as it were, of Mary Shelley, of a historically located woman in whom access and taboo are inextricably cross-hatched; a hypothesis of psyche and a hypothesis of the body. What we have to say is that these hypotheses are unassimilable and at the same time experientially

inseparable. If we say that in the conversion into textuality these
realms are always cross-hatching, we may interpret this phrase as
also referring to the constant production of monsters, bodies without souls, souls without bodies, hybrids of animation and de-
animation, 'cases' indeed for the case history or cases as outer
clothings for the inherently contaminated, limping and indetermin-
able gods, bird-boys and coughing ghosts, fantasy and Gothic.
Thus the dream, thus the inherent and exultant unclassifiability
which we might know as soul, which is formed where psyche
and body share a primal childbed; and thus the importance,
which the text negatively underlines, of soul-work.[21] Yet those
cross-hatchings are themselves only incarnated, only renewed,
only called into imaginal being from a differently natured realm
by the specificity of circumstance; they are precisely called, or *recalled*, by the passions, by the sound of voices from above which are
uttering strongly enough for some answer to be unavoidable, even
though these things of the below have no wish, as we know from
the unease which pervades *Frankenstein*, to be disturbed. Hindu
myth typically reverses this process; there we find a constant
emphasis on the way excessive righteousness in the world heats
up the throne of the king of the gods and he then needs to descend
to the earth to discover what is going on: once here he may engage
in a variety of actions, from rewarding the saint for his ascetic
endeavours to punishing him out of jealousy that the saint himself
might come to compete for the throne of the gods. What we find
here is the other way around: the way in which excessive bodily
suffering – is this suffering Mary Shelley's or the young Frankenstein's, or is it the suffering of identification, where the coat of the
textual character irritates the withheld body of the female writer? –
in the wide, 'passionate' sense which might simply be reducible to
the term 'excessive experience' might call out downwards and
prompt an answering, and answerable, movement in the realms
below, where the writ of the law cannot run. This, I think, is one
view of the narrative of *Frankenstein*, not the narrative within the
text but the narrative of conversion into authorship within which
the text occurs.

What does seem clear is that in whatever underworld it is he
goes to Frankenstein behaves with true Herculean force: in
other words he behaves, as do so many men roaming about, law-
fully or unlawfully, in a world to which women's bodies are
intimately connected, 'cruizing o'er the ocean woman', as Byron

so ingloriously puts it,[22] like an oaf, a lout. He has no sense of
natural rhythm, no sense of the organic: he instead settles for a
panicky climax, a mechanical putting together of bits and pieces.
He goes down, we might say, to the all-important depths with his
mind clouded: it is clouded precisely by the notion of a simply
conceived linear or lawful task, for he is venturing into realms
where such linearity is irrelevant and obscuring, where the writ
of the law does not run. He goes to Hades with it in mind, like
Hercules, to perform a 'labour'.

But in the world of Hades, as we are given it in the myths, there
is no labour, and there is no lurching about in search of a goal;
although one rhetoric would have it that the descent spells the end
of differentiation, another would argue that it is only when confronted with the spell-binding which is Hades' mode of dicourse
that the individual finds her- or himself with the 'freedom' to
differentiate; although, or because, it is too late. The world of
Hades, although it is not women's world, the world neither of
Gaia nor of Hecate, and also despite its subsequent demonisation
by Christianity, is nevertheless a world of subtlety. Hades, we need
to recall, is the god not only of death but also of riches and wisdom:
we are told in the myths that once we have heard the least hint of
Hades' wisdom we will no longer yearn for anything else. Hercules, of course, would have none of this, but contented himself
with a quick in and out, and with killing a dog while he was at it.
So much for the male version of sexuality.[23]

This kind of awareness of the point where Gothic might go
seems to me emblematic of the realms beyond the law with
which it has to do; and this is where, we might argue, the deconstructionist crux looms once again. As we try to make these interpretations, is it, after all, of no consequence that we are here
looking at a text written by a woman?[24] Is it not precisely because
of this fact that the Herculean ego, which never in any circumstances doubts the law, can stand exposed in such nakedness, can
be subjected to such implicit ridicule; or are we incapable of sensing the irony in the equation of Frankenstein to the modern
Prometheus? In *Frankenstein* we need, as it were, to read *through*
the text to see the shape of the motivating passion behind it; this is,
of course, a metaphorical procedure, but so are all critical strategies. Scepticism is itself a metaphor, as Nietzsche knew well.

We are speaking now, as Gothic so frequently does, of passion;
and when we speak of passion, we need again to stress that the

passions are crucially dealings with the body: when we think of lust, envy, greed, hate, we are immediately on the terrain of the body, with its inherent confusions about what is remembered and what is forgotten, what is legal and what is not, and this is where we find ourselves as we follow the interactions between Franken-stein and the monster. In the exclusion of the female body from this dialectic we run the risk also of the exclusion of passion, so we must read parts of the text negatively: the discussions between the creator and the created, fraught as they are with rage, are none the less curiously disembodied, as, of course, are all such intra-male arguments, while in the background the real action is going on – between bodies which are speaking quite a different language, acting on quite another scene, which is what makes *Frankenstein* a text so amenable to treatment in terms of the expressionist cinema, which is after all a theatre of bodies.

So *Frankenstein* is a text about cannibalisation, and also about birth. It is therefore about birth through death; and I would say that it is thus a text which enacts a cultural displacement of that very early form of legal enactment, the sacrificial feast. But what it lacks in this sense – or rather, the lack which it represents – is a clear manifestation of accepted, or of acceptable, hierarchy. One central aspect of the myths and rituals we would normally describe under the heading of the sacrificial feast is that they take place in the presence of, and under the aegis of, a clearly defined set of laws. Anything else is blasphemy and travesty; indeed, the sacrificial feast itself is also blasphemy and travesty, but it is precisely sacra-lised by its acceptance into a religion, a culture, a legal system, and it is the difference between this feast and the bloodshed and car-nage it replaces which marks 'civilisation', it is the transformation of blood into wine, or of the brute and savage stuff of inter-tribal warfare into a sacred repetition of, for example, the seasons – the harvests and wine-presses of Blake are a cardinal exploration of this liminal mythic and psychic territory.[25]

Frankenstein the scientist is not sacred; his secularity, which might be better renamed profanity, is emphasised by his desperate attempt to gather the ragged sacerdotalism of alchemy around him, just as, at another level, the nakedness of the emperor/patriarch seems to be evident to Mary Shelley, at some level at least, despite the attempt to clothe the disavowal and torture of the body in the raiment of intellectual argument and respectability – and here lies one major reason for the text's fruitful incoherence. We continue to

wonder how it is that the 'myth', as we like, for no doubt our own
reasons and because of the inferiority complex of this 'civilisation',
to call it, of *Frankenstein* lives on, and this is surely one root of its
longevity: that it enacts a drama on a stage on which rituals might
be supposed to happen, but in this case without real legal sanction;
it is a tragic drama without stage direction, and thus poses us a
continual problem. It signifies a point of instability, perhaps one of
Barthes' *points de capiton*; we could say that it implicitly and symbolically queries the point at which murder becomes legalised as
warfare or cannibalism by the belief in the greater good, the point
at which this greater good – of the state, or of the species – over-
rules more simple ordinances of respect and duty, or that endlessly
contestable point, which the law cannot resolve, at which passion
becomes obsession.

But its *différance*, the *différance* of *Frankenstein*, is that it does not
represent this set of doubts, this overbalancing of dominance,
through the apparatus of masculist argument, it succumbs to the
work of no pettifogging attorneys; it cannot do it through the work
of the wakened consciousness, which is in any case always inferior
to and threatened by that work which proceeds without the intervention of the will, which takes place in secret and which could
only occupy an ambiguous, vestigial, haunted presence if called
upon as evidence. It does it through the body and thus it has to do
with the dreamwork, with the inexorable, pointless, bizarre procedure – procedure which we fruitlessly try to recuperate through a
distinction between different 'logics' – which the body *espouses*
(and the impossibility of 'espousal' is a further subtext which we
cannot take the space to trace here). What further complicates the
situation is that patriarchy sufficiently invades Mary Shelley's
image system to make it necessary for the monster to become
articulate, to move beyond its own childedness before a system of
laws whose existence and operation it barely but evidently suspects, and it is here, of course, that many of the contradictions
really focus. Does the articulacy of the monster signify a coming
to consciousness of the primordial matricial body, or does it signify
an imperialist takeover by language of a state of bodily innocence?

The answer can only be that the two are inseparable; they are
haunted by each other, and this inseparability is itself not fully to
be distinguished from the inseparability of universal and temporal
'cross-hatching' I spoke of above; and this is a revelation to which
the text of *Frankenstein*, in all its many reincarnations, can uniquely

bring us – and of course the brute material fact of the many
incarnations of *Frankenstein*, its endless making over into the social
substance of different epochs, its amenability to changes of mood,
tone, temper, is crucial to our attempt to apprehend the text,
whether we are concerned with its phenomenology or with its
never dismissable relation to an historic or mythic *noumenon*. But
it seems also important that this revelation, which *is* an image
for the inherent ambivalence of the gift of articulacy, puts an
implicit question to one of deconstruction's main cornerstones,
its appropriation of Lacanian analysis,[26] for one of the main
distinguishing features of such analysis is its unequivocality in
'naming' the name-of-the-father, as we saw above, as the 'name'
of the law, the gift and the oppression; in this univocality it betrays
precisely, as does all univocality and in precise symmetry with the
law's need to utter only with a unified voice, the fear which
motivates it. For with Lacan we see again the formation we have
seen in previous generations of analysis; and below I shall try to
gather some textual examples which point in quite a different
analytic direction.

What we might learn from *Frankenstein* is that the Lacanian (and
Bloomian) efflorescence of concern with the patriarchal lineage is a
deflection, and one which Mary Shelley well understood, provided
one can accept that the unconscious has its own understandings –
and after all it is only the unconscious which *under*stands. To
illustrate this point we might turn to the 'case' of Otto Rank, who
broke with Freudian orthodoxy over a question of interpretation
of that classic instance of haunting, the Don Juan legend.[27] To
'recall' the original substance of the Don Juan legend is to remember that the force of retribution, the personification of the inexorable law, is the Commendatore, whose daughter Juan has seduced
and who reappears as a stone statue to beckon, or drag, Juan down
to the underworld.[28] Rank's analysis of this legend calls attention
to the mismatch between the implications of Juan's actual behaviour, which is clearly born of a desire to revenge himself on
women – to avenge, in other words, his birth – and the masculised
figure of the Commendatore. Rank's understanding of Freud's
version of the phallic was that this power of the male interdict,
the formation of the superego through reason, was by Freud taken
literally, through the construct of penis-envy; whereas for Rank it
was clearly a disavowal, and the stone statue, the figure of inexorability which defeated time and preceded and succeeded the

'dramatic' action of life, was a displaced representation, which we might see as linked to many other Gothic representations, of the female, specifically of the mother; which is also to name it as an exiled, refugee version of the passions and to put the primacy of castration through a further twist.[29]

To return from Rank to Lacan, just so we might say that the name-of-the-father, the source of all law, is open to further interpretation, and *Frankenstein* is especially emblematic in this sense because behind the narrative position we know that there is a secret, perhaps even an illegality; and that secret is a hidden female. The hiddenness is itself important, because it figures as both the Heraclitean hiddenness of nature, *physis kryptesthai philei*,[30] precisely that hiddenness which Frankenstein invades and brings to light when light is not its element, and the hiddenness of the woman behind the façade of masculist strife; this motif of the secret is one we shall continue to trace through the Gothic. Christine Berthin has asserted that the 'magic word' in *Frankenstein* is 'hideous';[31] I would say that the text *appears* (if it 'appears' at all from under its carapace, from its dealings with secrets away from the light or gaze of the law) to be about the 'hideous' because it is really about the 'hidden', which is so much simpler and yet, of course, entirely impossible. So we return to the question of the author, and to the question of the body in the text (we know from a different but related genre that there is *always* a body 'hidden' somewhere) from a different – perhaps non-Herculean – perspective: not armed with the super-oracular question of where the author *is* in the text, nor of where we can situate the text in the context of the vanishing of the author, but with the decrypting message which addresses the question of where the author might be *hidden*, where she or he might be waiting to spring out and play her androgynous hermetic tricks, waiting to manifest a body which is, precisely, dis-articulated. We are here again in the presence of the maze, the labyrinth, with the monster, the Minotaur, at its heart; masculist myth will hold to the Ariadne version, to the notion of the compliant female who will save the Herculean hero from the consequences of his folly, but there are surely other versions, in which the Minotaur is itself the woman, waiting patiently at the end of all things, beyond the thread, consorting with violence and slow time while the hero is trying still to fumble his way along the linear narrative which is, from beginning to end, a lie and a disavowal, merely the story repeated to Walton, who is, in any case, a lost solitary engaged on the exploration of other worlds still further removed from the human, from the passions which provide the deeper level to which all scepticism about narrative must still remain responsive; or be silenced.

If we are to follow through for a moment the issue of the passions as locations, occurrences, icons in which the ordinary limits of the body are distorted and (as in the emblematic figure of the *crime passionnel*) move beyond the bounding lines of legal responsibility, then we might say that one of the many questions which remain is that of what passion *Frankenstein* itself incarnates. If, as I have tried to suggest, the connection with passion underlies and underscores the restrictions of textually-based scepticism, and exposes that scepticism as a reticulated form of disavowal, then how can we further structure the dealings with passion which constitute, on this view, the primary process of the text? We need to recall that the word 'passion' comes from the same common Greek root as 'pathology', and so in approaching the passions one is simultaneously approaching a pathology; thus the figure of the court pathologist, trying to extrapolate a narrative from a dead body, will haunt us here. The crucial difference is one of emphasis: where pathology emphasises precisely the *logos*, seeks truth through mechanism and reason, the word and the law, passion stands for an approach through the organic. The pathology of the text of *Frankenstein*, as I have tried to outline it through the myth of Hercules and Hades, is about narcissism, about the ego's determination to reconstruct the world in its own image, to convert the unamenable into the intelligible; but the passion, I think, lies one layer deeper than that, in that from which narcissism psychically springs: the sense of loss. This loss structures *Frankenstein* on many levels. It is loss of a sense of home, family, community, imaged in the scientist's rejection of domestic ties, in the monster's transcendental homelessness. It is loss of name, which is the clue to the monster's namelessness but is also redolent of the experience of women down the centuries. Behind all this lies loss of the inner world: in the part of the textual psyche represented by Frankenstein himself the imagination has been drained outward, fantasy made real; which is, paradoxically, to kill off the inner life as that life is also killed off in our psychical and physical reductions before the outer might and majesty of the law. In that part of the textual psyche represented by the monster there are clear signs of this imagination coming to life again; but the rage of the ego cannot allow this to happen, and thus the internal duel to the death which the text becomes.

We may have here a more inward root of Gothic; in psychic terms we are confronting the loss of the body, the making over of the body into the control and power of another; again we are looking here in particular at women's experience. Yet again: this sense of loss goes beyond scepticism but it may be true that scepticism and its contemporary critical forms are in general a further series of strategies to accommodate and countermand loss.[32] At all events, *Frankenstein* contains *and* hides that which resists reduction to the free play of discourse: bulkier things than words loom out of the shadows. We may then go back full circle, to Mary Shelley and her husband, to a life lived in the shadow of another, which is another way of referring to loss of self, a real-life constellation without consideration of which criticism is doomed to a collusive circularity in which words speak only to words and we repeat Frankenstein's own mistake, which is to suppose that he can create something external when he has destroyed, ignored, disavowed the greater reality inside him, a reality which Mary Shelley, with a prescience which we can truly classify as uncanny, knew to be under threat and pressure of loss in herself and her time, and which she was able to, or perhaps we should say forced to, articulate and incarnate in a speaking image which still haunts us today, which we seem endlessly to need to recall; and which perhaps also, from some other place where the products of the cross-hatching breed and merge, is always recalling us.

What we are now talking about is a legend which is in a sense unreadable and nameless; lawless. Or, perhaps better, unnameable and illegal: as the body is itself unnameable and illegal, as its naming dissolves in the charnel house and what is born from it is beyond the realm of names and bears the mark of a nameless goddess – perhaps we might be tempted to refer to her as the great mother – who presides in so many myths over the activities of her lesser, named and differentiated underlings. What is crucial is that the not naming is also to do with the not giving birth: with the character who is never allowed to appear in the novel, and yet who might, were there time enough and space, provide the key to these mysteries: the unborn bride of the monster, the solution to all taboos, the incarnation of that incest anxiety against which so much of the law is designed to protect us, the resolution to the text which is – at least in this text itself if not in some of the later films –

always postponed, always delayed; woman as the gift which cannot be given, that which is withheld by the father to keep the son in
a state of perpetual submission. But to see woman as gift is once
again, of course, to enter into the hall of mirrors, for it is, after all,
she who gives, who makes a life of shreds and patches into an
organic whole, a whole which persists in the imaginary long past
the intricate severances and dealings of our subjugation to the law.
The 'monster', we need to remind ourselves again, is etymolog-
ically 'that which is shown'; the feminine quality of writing, in
Frankenstein and the female Gothic as elsewhere, is 'that which is
hidden'; perhaps in that dialectic lies the route towards a further
dealing with myth and the psyche, with the mutual pressure of
body and mind which gives rise to soul; or which is endlessly
prevented, in the textual labyrinth of which *Frankenstein* is one
cardinal example, from doing so.

4

Re-enactments of the Primal Scene:
The Example of *Zastrozzi*

The law . . . must be written; but it must be written ideally, so that its spirit and its letter are absolutely congruent – which means that it in fact cannot be written at all.[1]

In so far as the monster places us back behind the law, we might begin to see it as a figure of primal undifferentiation, as a myth in itself of origins. On this terrain, we cannot but come up against the further figure of the primal scene, and thus the whole question of memory, which is crucial, in different ways, to text, to the body and to the law.[2] It is central also to Gothic, with its ceaseless questionings of memory, its recastings of received history, its tentative assertions of a different history, a history in difference, where the shadows that conceal the approaching monster may also shade into the shadows that hide the primal scene from our eyes; or, perhaps, suggest the existence of such a scene, even where of other evidence there is none.

I want in this chapter to approach these issues by focusing on *Zastrozzi*, one of the two pieces of prose fiction – perhaps 'romance' is a polite word for them – which Percy Shelley wrote while still a schoolboy at Eton, and which was originally published in 1810. *Zastrozzi* is not frequently written about, and this is hardly surprising: very few claims could be made for its literary quality, and none at all for its originality, for it follows assiduously in paths already carved out by an older generation of Gothic novelists – the very name 'Zastrozzi' appears to be a modified version of 'Strozzi', which appears, for example, in Charlotte Dacre's *Zofloya, or The Moor* (1806).

No text, however, is without its interest, and the version of the text I have used in preparing this chapter is curious; for if you look for a modern edition of *Zastrozzi*, one of those which you will find is, complete, in a book called *Shelley and Zastrozzi: Self-Revelation of a Neurotic*, written by a psychologist and therapist called Eustace Chesser and published in 1965. The book contains a long essay by Chesser which purports to construe *Zastrozzi* as a psychological document, followed by the text itself, followed, rather oddly, by a reprint of 'The Necessity of Atheism' (1811), the inclusion of which is nowhere fully explained.

I do not want to go into Chesser's interpretation in detail; instead, I want to lay out the bare lines of an argument which will rest upon a necessarily sketchy analysis of some aspects of the text of *Zastrozzi*; it will attempt a reinterpretation of some of the ways in which we might look at the text in psychoanalytic terms; it will invoke the notion of the 'primal scene'; it will explore what we might loosely call a Gothic 'Italian connection'; it will attend to the questions already raised in the preceding chapters about the relations between text, body and law; and it will, finally, turn to some possibilities about the 'haunted text', and refer to Dickens's *Mystery of Edwin Drood* (1870).

I shall, however, begin by loosely following Chesser's interpretation of *Zastrozzi*, as a narrative of the split personality. I do not mean this, as Chesser appears to, as a premature judgment on Shelley's psyche but as a statement about the characterology of the text. We have a split masculine force, split between the protagonist figure of Verezzi and the classic Gothic villain Zastrozzi; and we have a split feminine force, split between the desired but already lost object, Julia, who is separated from Verezzi for the entire length of the book, and the figure of commanding and destructive desire, Matilda, who partly unwittingly brings about Verezzi's death. In Jungian terms we might say that here we are talking about 'partial systems', parts of the personality split off and projected as independent beings. Zastrozzi has many aspects of the Jungian Shadow: a comparison with Blake's Spectres would be illuminating here, as would a more general comparison with the Zoas.[3] As Chesser says, it is as though we are watching a single actor playing four parts, albeit some of the changes of costume are somewhat breathless and incompetent.[4] Zastrozzi's aggression is clearly directed inward as well as outward; he is one of a long line of self-haters and thus represents all that Verezzi cannot own to in himself.[5]

It is interesting to note that Zastrozzi and Verezzi can, in textual terms, hardly be on the same scene at the same time; if they are, they seem to cause an implosion of psychic impossibility, and the same is true of Julia and Matilda, whom we can see as incompatible representations of anima. We may speak, in very obvious terms, of Julia and Matilda as madonna and whore; what is perhaps more interesting is to see them as figures who represent entirely different subject positions, as do the masculine 'parts' we have already mentioned. Matilda represents only outflow, Julia only inflow: Matilda needs to people with desire an empty space (the empty space is Verezzi); Julia exists only as that which is itself populated with desire through projection, for it would be unmaidenly for her to admit any of her own. We may go further and say that Zastrozzi and Matilda represent energy overflow: a desire to people the world with images so strong that it is in danger of shaking their bodily frames to pieces. Verezzi and Julia represent energy starvation, twin 'chaoses' as Donne might have put it,[6] who can only come to life in and as they are peopled by the imagination of others. It follows, of course, that if they try to people, to concretise, *each other's* void nothing can come of it for they have not the substance, the wherewithal which would propel character into life. It might also follow, and this is relevant to some things I shall have to say later, that the entire text is inverted. Whereas it purports to tell the story of the separation of Verezzi and Julia, the real story, and certainly the only one with a possibility of fruitfulness and thus continuance, would be of a mating between Matilda and Zastrozzi, despite or because of the explosive consequences; but it is precisely this possibility, which would be beyond the law in several different ways, that the text is designed to avoid, as it insistently tells its story, as does all fiction, through what is *not* on the page, as again do we all when confronted with the explosive possibilities which would follow from true, de-fictionalised recall – or reconstruction – of the primal scene, that scene before the truth or otherwise of which the law can only shrug its shoulders.

And so the classic primal scene of parental coupling is, I believe, relevant here,[7] but we can also trace a further line back through Jung and remember that we are, however, here in the presence of the mandala, and in a particular aspect: a mandala where two of the points represent all heaviness, all weight and constriction, and the two others represent lightness to the point of absence, an inherently unstable constellation in which all bodily presence is captured by a legally inadmissible pairing while the absence extends to any bodily fullness.[8] Chesser tries to assimilate this to hermaphroditism (pp. 37–9); but it seems to me more complex than that, because precisely what is being *prevented* is hermaphroditism, or intersexual relationship of any type, however imploded. The fascination may be there, but the fear intercedes every time. The textual preference seems to me clear: Matilda is the scarlet woman, Julia represents unattainable purity, but when we read this description – 'He advanced along a lengthened corridor – a female in white robes stood at the other end – a lamp burnt near her on the balustrade. She was in a reclining attitude' (pp. 75–6) – it is in fact Matilda whom we are seeing, purity as garb rather than as essence. What it means to stand in a reclining attitude is not entirely clear, unless it is the very approach to the forbidden land of his dreams which causes Verezzi's perceptions to push the desired female backwards until she is on the point of toppling over.

Zastrozzi as monstrous Shadow, Matilda and Julia as split anima; where then is Verezzi? Empty space. Narcissus, says Chesser, but more revealingly he also says that 'it is as though a glass screen separates him from all other human beings, making it impossible for them to break through the shell of his ego' (pp. 24–5). Narcissus and again the shell, the egg which will not break, the egg of the skull, ego: all of that may well be the case, but the crucial question that remains is about the mechanism which converts this apparent, albeit inward-turned, energy of self-defence into the actual manifestation which characterises Verezzi throughout the text: which is of an extreme and extraordinary passivity. That glass screen is perhaps also 'life's dark veil'; and we could also say that at a psychobiographical level it relates to Trelawny's familiarly uncanny tale about the attempt to teach Shelley to swim which ended with him lying motionless at the bottom of (Narcissus') pool;[9] but there is something more peculiar about Verezzi than this. For a start, it is clear that he has effectively lost his wits before the beginning of the story – he begins already 'torn from the society of all he held dear on earth' (p. 59), he is already free from the 'emotional tie', and thus has placed himself beyond the bounds of accountable motivation – and that he never fully regains them. On the third page we learn that 'his mysterious removal from the inn near Munich...confused his ideas, and he never could bring his thoughts to any conclusion on the subject which occupied them' (p. 61). On another occasion, just before he performs one of his frequent lapses into insensibility, we learn that 'a thick film overspread his eye' (p. 94).

There is bodily sickness here, but interestingly it is displaced. It is Verezzi who suffers all the consequences of illness; but it is only Matilda who, at a crucial moment in the story, and as a result of her own hypocrisy, gets wounded:

> Matilda's snowy arm was tinged with purple gore: the wound was painful, but an expression of triumph flashed from her eyes, and excessive pleasure dilated her bosom: the blood streamed fast from her arm, and tinged the rock whereon they stood with a purple stain.
>
> Verezzi started from the ground, and seeing the blood which streamed down Matilda's garments, in accents of terror demanded where she was wounded.
>
> (p. 126)

This, I think, is the crucial wound, the one which concretises the body as sign within the text: it is a wound which the text produces on the body of Matilda, but really the reason why Verezzi starts from the ground amounts to an uncanny shock of recognition, for it is only some such wound, delivered primally, which could account for what we now find to be increasingly described as his 'Lethean torpor' (pp. 131, 159). His responses, under conditions of distress, are absolutely to fall to the bottom of the pool and refuse to re-surface: for example, when he realises that Julia has seen him in the company of the dreaded Matilda, that a law of taboo has been potentially violated, 'the extreme of horror seized his brain – a frigorific torpidity of despair chilled every sense, and his eyes, fixedly, gazed on vacancy' (p. 139).

Shock returns him to an inner void, where a bodiless drama goes on which consists mainly in a draining of action, a leaching of blood, an utter forgetfulness which measures an approach to Hades, a condition of life-in-death which is familiar to us through-out the Gothic;[10] something here, at all costs, *must not be seen*, something must remain invisible or, at best, shadowed to the point where it cannot be adduced as evidence in any possible 'trial scene' – and here perhaps we begin to glimpse the signific-ance of the relation between the primal scene and the 'scene of trial', which operates to expunge the uncertainties, the shadowings of the primal scene, to efface it under a patina of accuracy which none the less draws its strength from an alternative history, history as a matter of codes of law, statute books, regularities against the onset of chaos. In fact, most of the action of the text remains invisible to Verezzi because he spends a good half of the book unconscious. We find him 'still wrapped in deep sleep, from which all the movements he had undergone had been insufficient to rouse him' (p. 59); we find him 'insensible and stretched on the shoulders of Ugo' (p. 64), one of the villains; we virtually trip over him languishing 'in torpid insensibility, during which his soul seemed to have winged its way to happier regions' (p. 65); all this in the first few pages and in fact this plethora of unconsciousness seems to start to spread from Verezzi to his surroundings, for it is not long before even the two strong-arm men Ugo and Bernardo feel its effects and 'overcome by the extreme fatigue which they had undergone, and strong as the assassins were, fell fainting on the earth' (p. 74). Physical, even Herculean, strength is not proof against this cloud of unknowing, even when this involves us in observing behaviour which is not, we might feel, characteristic of the average assassin.

But although this lust to sleep, or for a kind of somnambulism to which we shall return below, this longing for absence which may also be an unconscious need not to give an account of oneself, does spread outwards beyond Verezzi until we wonder whether even any of the characters, let alone the readers, are still going to be awake by the end of the book, it is he who is undoubtedly the centre of it, the dreaming void which inculcates unconsciousness in all around it. All Verezzi wants is to close his eyes. To what? I do not want to follow Chesser into dubious speculations about Shelley's family background but to keep to the field of the text; within this field there is indeed a primal scene, a hidden source of energy, perhaps even of reproduction, which were it ever to be viewed might reveal who knows what nameless collusions and cohabitings: I refer again to the little-described relationship between Zastrozzi and Matilda, the only two potent figures in the text and the only two with access, however twisted, to power. It is from this that Verezzi's eyes must be averted, as it is from the possibility of their strategic cooperation that textual energy must be redirected – and thus indeed it is, since the text continually convicts them of working at cross-purposes in seeking the execution of their villainous designs, much as the law itself is continually thwarted in eighteenth-century fiction by the very machinations of those who wish to serve it most abjectly. But those designs are not after all so unusual: Zastrozzi wants Verezzi dead, Matilda wants him in bed.

If we reverse the projection we see an easy Oedipal unriddling: Zastrozzi has to be a dead father before Verezzi will be able to emerge from his cocoon of sleep, and Zastrozzi's secret, and the entire secret of the immortal Gothic villain, is thus unmasked; he wishes to stay alive long enough to outlive his son and to stop him from winning the mother;[11] or, to put it in other terms, he – or more usually she, but here again we touch upon issues, not of hermaphroditism but of gender-crossing – wishes to stay alive until a time when there is some chance of his case being heard in terms, and in a place, on a scene, which is not already contaminated by the ghosts of the farther past, whether we conceive those ghosts as past legal authorities or as the haunting presences of mother and father on the primal bed. A reasonable wish, but one from which Verezzi, naturally, can only avert his eyes and his soul.

From this enveloping realm of sleep, as one might expect, dreams are not absent, but here I want to mention only two of them: interestingly, they are both dreams of Matilda's, and so we should see them as re-projections of anima from a disincorporated psyche: in other words, they are dreams which refer back to the protagonist and which demonstrate mandala aspects of which he is purportedly unconscious. This is the first:

> Confused dreams floated in her imagination, in which she sometimes supposed that she had gained Verezzi; at others, that, snatched from her ardent embrace, he was carried by an invisible power over rocky mountains, or immense and untravelled heaths, and that, in vainly attempting to follow him, she had lost herself in the trackless desert.
>
> (p. 124)

The second:

> At one time she imagined that Verezzi, consenting to their union, presented her his hand: that at her touch the flesh crumbled from it, and, a shrieking spectre, he fled from her view: again, silvery clouds floated across her sight, and unconnected, disturbed visions occupied her imagination till the morning.
>
> (p. 127)

All dreams in fiction are of necessity complexly multivocal, but I wish to treat these as dreams fed by the narrator, through the

blocked and unconscious channel of Verezzi, to Matilda, and if we
see them in this way it is apparent that they are dreams of supernatural evasion. In the first we have Verezzi as Batman, able to
elude the most determined pursuit over the roughest terrain.
Maybe a better image would be the Wendigo with its burning
feet of fire.[12] In the second we have Verezzi as Houdini, the final
escape artist who will in the end escape his own body in order to
cheat the contamination which might come to it through any problematic contact with another. In this scenario, in this web of projections and re-projections, nothing can be brought down to earth,
because if it were it might have to submit to an authority which
might, in fact, supersede all fiction and provide a different kind of
'ending', not an ending within the text but the ending which
involves the judge's black cap, the final sentence.

Thus much, I think, should be obvious; the most interesting
image remaining is the 'silvery clouds'.[13] I am not sure what
these are, except that one might refer to them as objects about to
undergo, as clouds do, immediate dissolution, and in saying that I
use a phrase from the novel. When Verezzi is, as usual, ill, a helpful
doctor warns Matilda not to approach him because the sight of her
might cause his 'immediate dissolution' (p. 99); this reminds us of
the theme of suicide in the novel, the theme of voluntary shedding
of the body in circumstances where it is simply too difficult to hold
it together, but also of something else.

For there is a connection here between Matilda and the myth of
Medusa. It is after all Medusa who was the most potent mythic
cause of a different kind of 'immediate dissolution', and it is also
interesting that in, as it were, the Matilda context (Lewis's Matilda
as much as Shelley's[14]) the term 'dissolution' contains the different
connotations of 'dissolving' and 'dissolute' (perhaps this is the
conjunction of the 'silvery clouds'); Matilda causes, we are told,
destruction to any prospects of happiness, she is a blight and a
petrifaction of hope. She is also referred to as a siren.

In trying to think through these various inner mythic relations of
Gothic, I have had cause to refer to Hercules, Narcissus and
Medusa; I want to move for a moment to wonder what the function
is in this text of Hephaestus (whose contemporary earthly form
was, perhaps, Byron), who I take to be the presiding god of romantic fashioning. Interestingly, Chesser mentions him in the context of
hermaphroditism, reminding us of the passage in the *Symposium*
where Hephaestus appears to two lovers and offers to weld them

together into one (p. 39). But perhaps this is not really the subtext here; the reason I refer to Hephaestus is that we have it on record that Hephaestus and Medusa did mate, once; how they did it we do not know, we have nothing on record about how to make love to a Gorgon, although obviously there are ways one can think of. Anyway, we know of this mating because they had a child, and his name was Cacus; and we come across Cacus in the course of the labours of Hercules, when he was one of the many villains Hercules suppressed, in, as it happens, a particularly horrible fashion, and only because Cacus was a thief; as was Hercules.[15]

But Cacus' name signifies dirt and confusion; Cacus is shit and the Herculean ego, the ego of the enforcer or terminator, does not like that.[16] Hephaestus, the lame, and Medusa, the once-beautiful, must not be allowed to come together; because on them have been heaped the detritus, the blackness and unmanageability of the human body and the threat it presents to legal society, all that stands for the 'body impolitic', and that is very scary. We are back to Zastrozzi and Matilda again: displaced aristocrats – gods? – who have been offered mortal wrong but who must not be allowed their consolatory vengeance, because what is so often forgotten about Gothic fiction is that it is not usually about revenge but about revenge thwarted, about reinforcing the impossibility of being maimed by one's father and mother, which would not do at all in a brave new age, and which would certainly not do if we are to be offered a repertoire of consolatory fictions in which we can move beyond constraints and find our way to the stars, those stars which, in much science fiction, turn out to be populated by what else than monsters. If *that* were to happen, then the only way out would be suicide, the lying (lying?) at the bottom of the pool; here we have part of the drama which the text enacts – in blindness, in unconsciousness, in fainting and Lethean torpor.

'Now let us together solve the great mystery.' This phrase occurs, of course, not in *Zastrozzi* but in a different context from which Chesser quotes in his introductory essay (p. 55). These are supposed to have been the words Shelley said to Jane Williams while out rowing with her shortly before his death, and Jane Williams said afterwards that she knew that he meant them to refer to the mystery of death and thus to the possibility of a double suicide – a fate which she famously and bathetically avoided by replying, 'No thank you, not now; I should like my dinner first, and so would the children'.[17] Very possibly – and without deciding now whether we

are speaking literally or symbolically – the great mystery in that
context *was* death; but the words themselves can just as easily be
seen as referring to sexuality, reproduction, birth, the secrets of the
body-in-life, and there are several indications that this is indeed the
great mystery which *Zastrozzi* is seeking, on an adolescent plane, to
plumb. Verezzi's plight returns us to the womb early on in the text,
both through an escalation of lapses into unconsciousness and also
when, for example, he is 'precipitated...down [a] steep and nar-
row staircase' (p. 69). Matilda adds her strands to this fabric when
she eventually gets Verezzi to return with her to her castle, where
the text speaks of a feeling 'which is excited by a return to the place
where we have spent our days of infancy' (p. 111), and here again
we are speaking of a fantasy scene of childing.

Yet these attempts to return in image to a primal scene, certainly
on Verezzi's part, are constantly thwarted: whenever he is able to
rouse himself to make enquiries as to his location, or the reasons
for the mistreatment from which he is suffering, we find that all his
questions go unanswered, that there is no authority to solve the
riddle. The reason for this lies in the relationship between Verezzi
and Zastrozzi: where Verezzi is drained of action, Zastrozzi, the
denying father whose discourse is always inflected with the tones
of the judge, is all action; it is said at one point that he plays a
'double part' (p. 78), which literally refers to the way in which his
collusion with Matilda masks a deeper design but which psychologically, I believe, refers to the firmness of Zastrozzi's lock on
power, which is of the form of a double bind, the kind of double
bind known in Freud's depiction of the primal horde where,
loosely (and therefore not bindingly) speaking, the wish to do
away with the all-powerful presiding judge is in exact balance
with the countervailing wish to be protected by his strength.[18] It
would not be possible here to go into this in detail but there are
passages one could adduce from Freud's case history of Dora
which would take us further with this lock, because indeed Dora
experiences the textual power of the father/judge in a remarkably
complex way: not only 'tainted' by her father's syphilis and then
made the unwilling object of the affections of her father's friend,
she has her account further brought under the aegis of Freud
himself who, as the one with access to the codes of the master-
interpreter, proceeds to redouble the conflict about legality and
sexuality which is already wracking her psyche and, through the
symptomatic language of power and disease, her body.[19]

Let me try here to be a little clearer about some of the implications of the primal scene. True though it is that Freud frequently refers to this as the parental bed, and true though it also is that Verezzi spends large parts of the text avoiding the implications of this feared rememoration, we have also to look at the matter more symbolically; or more, if you like, deconstructively. We might, for example, call to mind another of Freud's case histories, that of Little Hans and the 'construction of the horse'. Little Hans conceived an irrational fear of being bitten by horses. Naturally Freud ascribed this to a castration anxiety, but he also makes some remarks which suggest a further ramification: namely, that we are mistaken from the outset if we embark upon a search for the *meaning* of the horse: what we should be looking for instead is the *meaning of Little Hans's fear*, a fear which antedates the construction of the horse image and which the horse in fact serves to make visible and intelligible.[20] Just so the issue of Verezzi's evasions is not to be 'solved' by looking to the terrifying relationship between Zastrozzi and Matilda, but rather to his experience of an *ungrounded* fear in respect of which the primal scene arises as an encapsulation, a housing, just as in Godwin we might see the unsuppressible recurrence, the repetition of the trial scene, as a way of finding a housing, an outer 'casing', for a series of primal anxieties which Gothic sets out to unpack. In *Primal Scenes: Literature, Philosophy, Psychoanalysis* (1990), Ned Lukacher has recently pointed out the continuity between this approach, the Heideggerian notion of the 'history of Being', and the general deconstructionist emphasis on myths of origin.[21]

'What right have I to pry into the secrets of another?' (p. 89), reflects Verezzi at one point; another way of putting the question would be by asking whence this sense of a secret comes, how it is that, to venture into the terms used by Abraham and Torok, we come across, in our dreams and in our intimations of the relation of soul between inner and outer, the notion of the crypt, the question of what lies buried inside us,[22] that which will not be drawn out of us even by 'inquisition', in prison or on the rack. The fear attached to this is indeed primal: all the rest – image, textuality, form – is conjured up, as Gothic so frequently sees, to give a shape to the darkness, just as Verezzi seeks explanation for his terror by seeking to explicate a relationship of which he knows nothing; or, failing that, by turning his face to the wall and dying continually in the course of the text in an attempt to return to and make sense of the

crypt which undergoes its own *unimaginable* processes of living
death within his mysteriously wounded body.

If we were to follow through the kind of analysis suggested by
Abraham and Torok's work on the case of the Wolf-Man, we might
expect to find a crypt in *Zastrozzi*; we would be looking for something excluded, something excised, the absence of which sends
continual ripples through the apparently substantial body of the
text and renders it in turn insubstantial, ghostlike; and we would
be looking for something which has also to do with encrypting,
with secrets and codes, with a message which cannot properly
worm its way through a blocked line, to take an image from
another text of the blocked body and the fear of the law, Sylvia
Plath's 'Daddy'.[23] Where might we find this in *Zastrozzi*? Perhaps it
is all too obvious. The text consists of seventeen chapters; but
Chapter Seven is missing. 'Seven' of all numbers, we might say,
noting the numerological significances of the number seven, its
association with magic and luck; or we might alternatively wonder
at the way in which this omission offers a half-parallel to so many
other so-called 'rediscovered manuscripts' in Gothic fiction, where
such omission is used precisely as a device to extend the problems
of textual origin or, we might say, to provide a break in the chain of
evidence in an effort to avoid 'conviction',[24] in at least one of its
many senses. Here we might well say that it is simply a mistake on
the part of the young Shelley; but from a more interpretative point
of view we would have to class this under the rare heading of a
literary parapraxis, and we should wonder whether we can get at
something about this omission, as Freud might have tried to do, by
examining the surrounding material, the tissue, as it were, out of
which this portion has been cut.

And here we come across something of interest. For at the end of
the previous chapter, Chapter Six, we have Verezzi slowly opening
his eyes. The following one, Chapter Eight, begins thus:

> His head reposed upon Matilda's bosom; he started from it
> violently, as if stung by a scorpion, and fell upon the floor. His
> eyes rolled horribly, and seemed as if starting from their sockets.
>
> (p. 93)

It certainly appears as though, just as for Verezzi to close his eyes
seems a necessary strategy for the evasion of knowledge, this rare
example of him opening his eyes is attended by the most

catastrophic results, imaged here in the scorpion, the archetypal image for the link between sexuality and self-destruction[25] and also, we might say, for self-incrimination, self-conviction, the kind of crucial lapse, at the end of the trial scene of so many television court dramas, in which all is revealed before the might of the law – or rather, the smug perspicacity of the investigating ego. It is the scorpion that here rears up as a replacement for the missing Chapter Seven, the scorpion that symbolises Verezzi's relationship with the breast and thus signifies the extreme danger of nurture in Verezzi's inner world, indeed in the inner world of the text. So challenging and so dangerous is this notion of the breast-which-bites that the evasion of the number seven leads us into a further numerological pitfall: we learn a few lines later on that we are waiting for eleven o'clock, but never have we been given a hint, nor will we be, of why. I do not wish to go into the numerological associations of the number eleven, but suffice to say that the omission of the chapter and the appearance of the scorpion have served the purpose of a kind of unhingeing: from now on even the certainty of times and dates, of the evidence which might be offered, becomes *un*certain, passes into the hall of distorting mirrors, and accuracy itself becomes complexly interwoven with secrecy, disappears into the crypt.

The bringing together of the breast and the scorpion signifies, if you like, a redoubled interminability of the search for origins: nurture and backbiting soldered together, with a sign over the door marked 'taboo'. If such confusion of nurture and murder thus becomes the keynote of the text after the textual trauma of the excised chapter, the missing organ, a 'textectomy', if I may coin a word, of evidently appalling brutality, then we will expect to find a further sign that all laws of contradiction remain suspended in this increasingly unconscious world where the writ of the law must not be allowed to run. There are many such, and I wish to mention only one. Much later on Matilda receives a summons to appear before the Inquisition, for narrative reasons which are intricate but of no particular importance, or alternatively because no such 'romance' can end without *someone* receiving a summons to appear before the Inquisition, the final court, the court of endings, the sense of being 'caught' in an ending; and the mood in which she conveys this information to Verezzi is described as one of 'serene horror' (p. 136). 'Serene horror', I think, is uncanny. Can we imagine it? Can we image for ourselves a state in which the worst excesses of fear would be met with a reaction which included both aghastness and serenity, composure? We are not talking here about bravery under adversity: the horror is still there, it is combined, as only dream could combine it, with serenity, there is some evidence of trauma here, of a trauma which would flow from revelation of the secret but which also in fact *precedes* such revelation as we proceed through its consequences in the interminably echoing chamber of fantasy.

And this brings me to a phrase which I find emblematic of the textual process of *Zastrozzi*, a phrase supposedly descriptive of Verezzi himself but also bearing a much fuller and more complex relation to the narrative, the phrase 'accents scarcely articulate'. For it is the repetition of this phrase, which occurs four times in the text in scarcely modified form, which rings like a heartbeat through the romance; if one were inclined to accept Abraham and Torok's account of the presence of a 'magic word' which can unlock discourse, an account which is itself interestingly suspect in what one might call quasi-legal terms, then this would be the 'magic phrase' of *Zastrozzi*. And this heartbeat – or tolling – starts precisely at the point I have just been discussing, the beginning of Chapter Eight, when Verezzi enquires of Matilda in 'accents scarcely articulate' (p. 93) whether Julia is dead, as she – Matilda – is trying to persuade him. A little later it is Matilda who enquires in 'accents almost inarticulate from terror' (p. 95) of the physician whether Verezzi is dying (as if, indeed, one could know the difference in a youth so febrile as Verezzi). We next have Verezzi accusing Matilda of murder 'in a hurried and almost inarticulate accent' (p. 101); and finally, when Matilda has overcome all Verezzi's scruples and has, as one might delicately say, gained him for her own, we have him, in 'accents almost inarticulate with passion', swearing to her 'eternal fidelity' (p. 131).

These 'accents scarcely articulate' can be viewed in a number of ways. They are, for example, no doubt a voice of adolescence, thus representing a trembling before the mighty thrones of sex and death which, in the forms of Matilda and Zastrozzi, dominate the text as no doubt they dominated Shelley's own adolescent imagination and constituted the twin forms of a putative criminalisation. They can also be seen in terms of the 'voice traumatised', the stutter which is all that is left of forbidden viewing, of the savage gaze which rends the inner world even as it shies away before the prodigiousness of the outer. They are all that is left as we approach closer to the primal scene, as we revert back to an undifferentiated world before word, which fascinates us yet of which we do not wish to be reminded lest all crumbles around us and we are precipitated into the dungeon; or crypt.

And inarticulacy, the world before the word, makes another interesting series of entrances into the text. For Verezzi, as the world becomes increasingly incomprehensible to him and as the forces of persecution mass ever more firmly outside his windows – like, perhaps, silvery clouds – turns to drawing. He comes to amuse himself with 'retracing with his pencil, from memory, scenes which, though in his Julia's society he had beheld unnoticed, yet were now hallowed by the remembrance of her' (p. 107). We should not, perhaps, make too much of the phallic connotations of Verezzi's pencil: more to the point is the implication that if there is a way of getting at the secret which is causing imminent anguish and doom it is by abandoning the word and by trying to 'trace' and 'retrace' the course of the past in a medium beyond and before discourse and thus before the encroachments and shapings of the law. It is by, if you like, establishing a supplement to the word, or by returning to a world of primal shapes, that the prohibitions which structure the text – as they structure all of Shelley's texts – can be bypassed or rendered into 'immediate dissolution'; and let us notice here that what Verezzi is doing is drawing forms which have been 'unnoticed', he is looking not outward, not to conscious or verifiable memory but to unconscious shaping beyond the possibility of evidence, seeking to replicate forms which his eye has never registered.

The text of *Zastrozzi* locates itself, of course, in Italy, as do many Gothic texts; and this is an aspect of Gothic which has been many times rehearsed and seen in ways geographical, religious and societal. Perhaps, however, we can now add something to this interpretative panoply, by suggesting that there is a connection between the psychic geography of *Zastrozzi*, the primal scene, and Italy, that Italy so beloved of and abused by North European Gothic writers. Verezzi in fact spends the first half of the story essentially unhoused: he does not know where he is, and as readers we are also frequently unsure where *we* are. In the grip of Matilda, the Comtessa di Laurentini, he is brought to Italy, to be precise to the countryside around Venice: but the crucial point is that he is not 'brought' there, he is brought *back*. It would be tedious to detail the many times in Freud's *Interpretation of Dreams* (1900) when he refers to dreams of his own in which he is *brought back* to Italy;[26] but these dreams obviously formed the substratum on which he produced the image of Rome as the situation of the unconscious in *Civilisation and its Discontents* (1930) – not Rome at any specific point in its history but Rome as we would see it 'now' were we able to view all of its historical phases at one and the same time, as if, that is, we were to be able to develop another sense, which we might characterise as 'historically unbounded seeing'.[27] And what would this historically unbounded seeing be? It would be a seeing from which there would be no secrets, in which all would be revealed, rather like the myth of the drowning person before whose eyes all flashes just once but in complete and appalling detail: it would be an end to forgetting, and thus best and inevitably forgotten: it would be a fantasy of habituation which would only be a prelude to death – and I have no wish to repeat the old maxim which connects the sight of an Italian city with death.

Yet this myth operated fast and freely in Northern Europe,[28] and we cannot of course dissociate it from Shelley, for the significance of Italy in this text is as a kind of displaced home, as the place to which one is brought back – to die (in either of its two most common senses), or to be devoured, or to have completed the work of the scorpion. It will be for other more historically-minded scholars to say to what extent this can be related to the outer circumstances of 'Shelley's life', if indeed we may speak of such a thing; but as data about the inner textual structure of *Zastrozzi* these inflections are inescapable.

And the sense of being 'brought back' haunts textual dealings with the law, from the repetitions of Godwin to the sense in Kafka that, 'in the end', the courtroom and the prison are our only home, the rest is a mere interlude between a series of inevitable confrontations with power, confrontations in which we are already stripped of our resource, in which we are already reduced to a way of being which prevents us from having recourse to inner depths and which will therefore invalidate whatever attempt we make to explain what it is that has been going on, whatever case we attempt to put.

So this itself, we can perhaps now see, is a reflection of a deeper and more prevalent scenario, whereby all of our 'appearances' will be doomed to failure; we shall not be able to make our voice heard. But this is not at all because we have a simple linear truth at our disposal which will somehow be repressed by a parallel and similarly linear version offered to us from on high; rather it is because the materials of 'our' truth are already contaminated at root, our individual motives and desires do not correspond to that which could be 'repeated' in a court of law, and therefore there is an inevitable entanglement. We are always guilty, always in possession of secrets. Because they are secrets, they have never been fully validated; therefore our state in relation to the evidence is always one of deficit, of loss.

What would it be like if we were to betray these secrets through the body; through, that is, expression, behaviour, deportment, or even through 'the lines of flight'?[29] Then we should have admitted to ourselves that the very notion of secrecy is no longer possible, that we can be read like an open book. Perhaps, therefore, we can now approach by a slightly different route the suggestion that there is something adolescent in Gothic fiction. For it is in adolescence that the need for secrecy is at its most acute, because much of what is happening to the body is secret even to ourselves, and certainly would not 'stand up' in a court of law. But to be an open book in adolescence, to have one's inmost desires seen, rendered visible, legible, is to strike at the very heart of desire. We might turn at this point to the notion of 'adolescent fiction', but even as we do so we sense that this psychological hypothesis has a material force; for it is very difficult to establish and market an 'adolescent fiction'. Where we can count the years of childhood in their twos and threes, and where the adult fiction market can remain relatively stable, the adolescent market remains unpredictable, inflected all the time by notions of what is that little bit too old or too young for the reader.

As adolescence is therefore the haven of hierarchy, and it is crucial to be one year, one class, older than the others, so we might similarly say that hierarchy is the haven of adolescence, and many of our institutions of that preeminent hierarchy of the law, their insistence on the single-sex, collegiate institutions of 'chambers', to take but one example, continue to reflect this notion that the law can only be properly administered by those who have – emblematically in the wearing of wigs – bypassed the ordinary processes of maturation and arrived at their power through *some other route*, a route which has not taken them through the usual processes of knowledge. Thus the dual stereotype of the judge as the most wise and the most ignorant; thus Brecht's celebrated attempt to conjure a judge whose wisdom resides precisely in undifferentiation, in being undistinguished from those to whom he would administer the law.[30]

I should like to conclude this chapter by trying to bring out what seems to me to be the 'force' of the Gothic considered in the context of the law. For the Gothic has always to do with that which goes beyond or behind; this has often been summarised as a dealing with the uncanny, and of course the Gothic and the uncanny are intimately related. Yet the textual field with which we are here dealing goes beyond this, and perhaps the example of Dickens's *Mystery of Edwin Drood* – a text which has a great deal to say about lawyers and their 'chambers' – might make this clearer. For *Edwin Drood*, a text totally unamenable to the law, brings us, like *Zastrozzi*, up short against what the law 'expects' as narrative. Such narrative must have a beginning (an origin), a middle and an ending. *Drood*, of course, has all of these things; and yet, hovering above its evidently completed textuality, if we are to take as the evidence of this completion its oft-repeated publication as a book, there is nevertheless the incompletion of the narrative, or the interruption of that narrative, if we prefer, by an extra-textual death, the death of the author.

It is possible to be tried for crimes *in absentia*, it may be theoretically possible to be tried for them posthumously; the law acts not only upon the bodies of living persons but also to continue to patrol its appointed boundaries to the general safeguarding of the living even if the perpetrators of specific crimes are not present before us. In – or rather, in some sense, after – *Drood*, we may continue the narrative in our own way; indeed, we have no option but to do so, for if we have read attentively, then we should be able as we put down the (incomplete) book to frame for ourselves a list of questions regarding that fantasised completion. Perhaps there are no books which end in this way – or in the way of Kafka's *Castle* (1926) – without there being a supervening, extra-textual reason for non-completion, whether fantasised or not; yet the question about *Drood* is not in the end about the many ways in which we might – and do – as individuals complete the narrative, it is about the uncanny effects set up when a discourse which looks like a narrative, with all the expectations that implies, does not carry out its allotted duty. It is this sudden crossing, this irruption of the extra-textual into text, which causes *Drood* to constitute an act of haunting; and yet one might say that earlier Gothic writers were often striving for precisely this effect, the effect of the broken manuscript: another aspect of *Drood*'s haunting is thus that it turns back on itself, and upon history, to haunt texts written before it was born. Judge Drood, we might say, comes to rewrite his own pre-history, but not towards a ritual culmination, rather towards an openness of the future, and an openness of history, which is where the law cannot in the end deal, because only living bodies can continue to form, to formulate the story.

And so, we might hypothesise, it is in these crevices, these interstices, that terror lies. It lies in the uncertainty of our entertainings as to where Dick Datchery might have come from, where he might be going; whether Drood is indeed dead, whether the drood has indeed been done, the way in which he and the text which he briefly inhabits is itself undead, as so many texts are now proving to be as they are rewritten, re-exhumed, made over into living zombies in the hands of new generations of literary grave-robbers.

And grave-robbing, as we now know, provides an essential context for *Frankenstein*,[31] as the 'night of the living dead' might be taken to be a true 'epitaph' for Verezzi, as a carelessness about bodies and their needs might be taken as the emblem for the anxieties expressed throughout the eighteenth century in regard to the 'legal profession'. All of these matters touch again on the question of whether our case can be heard; and this, I am now suggesting, is at least one root, and a strong one, of terror.

In *Drood* we know, of course, that John Jasper is the villain; this is not beyond our powers of reckoning, nor is it meant to be. Just so, it is not beyond our powers of understanding to identify the source of terror in individual human or demonised form; it is not beyond us to identify the figure of the terrorist, although when he or she has been thus identified there remains the question of where we are when the inevitable encounter between the law and the terrorist takes place, just as that question hangs over us when, textually, we try to entertain after the 'conclusion' of *Drood* the simultaneous possibilities of an ending within the law and an ending which will throw all into chaos. This is, of course, the threat of the terrorist; and although the very term was subject to an entirely different inflection during the heyday of Gothic fiction than at the end of the twentieth century, it remains true that Lewis and the others were known as 'terrorists' and that this placed them in a curious way aslant the law.[32] In order to pursue these issues, I want to turn now precisely to the question of the representation of the terrorist; a difficult history, and one which is, of course, without an ending.

5

Regimes of Terror: From Robespierre to Conrad

How good to stand again on terror firma...[1]

To broach the question of the terrorist is not an easy matter. In fact, this chapter might be considered as a fragment from a much longer work which, I suspect, may never be written; at all events, its writing could take place only outside the law, and would be in a permanent state of non-completion. That work would be a history of literary representations of terrorism, and there are at least three good reasons why such a book would be impossible to write or to publish.

The first is the extreme, defining difficulty of putting a meaning to the term 'terrorism' itself. The point may be made by saying that we do not refer to the activities of the French resistance during the Second World war as terroristic; on the other hand, whether we refer to the operations of the Stern Gang as terroristic is a decision which confronts us in starker and more demanding terms, as not only a bone of contention but also a political act in itself. For terrorism is not merely a set of activities, reducible to bombings, kidnappings and extortions, although at different historical periods it may appear to have expressed itself through particular means; rather, 'terrorism' depends on a location. This would not only be a physical or geographical location, but more a location in a legal, political or social space; such that, very frequently, terrorism is in fact defined by its own exclusions and negations – it is that which exceeds or combats the existence of a normative space within which society lives, moves and has its being.

The second difficulty is related to this, and is historical. As an excess or a negation, individual terroristic situations or movements cannot be understood beyond a highly immediate context. This is, of course, true of all historical event. But the *shadow* nature of terrorism, its monstrosity, its requirement of rapid and above all *secret* reaction to wider movements, means that to understand terrorism in the past requires an enormous wealth of detailed historical knowledge in itself; and without that it would be very difficult indeed to make sense of the various representational strategies which writers have used in connection with terrorism, as indeed of the strategic problems which they have encountered. But this very difficulty touches back on precisely the general difficulties of secrets and representation with which we have so far been dealing; in representing, in displaying that the very *scene* of which has been the way of its being held in secrecy, a secrecy which has been its most distinctive defining characteristic, then we automatically – in a realm indeed of automatism in which we feel the need, the desire to represent in the form of the simulacrum that which is otherwise inaccessible – distort that prior form of life and at the same time render its entire *raison d'être* valueless. There can be no sympathetic or value-free representation of terrorism for to represent terrorism is to commit an act of retributive violence against its own self-conception.

The third difficulty, however, is perhaps the most important of all, which is the extreme moral and political delicacy involved in talking or writing about terrorism at all. In Seamus Heaney's poem 'Punishment' the narrator, observing the disinterred corpse of a murdered woman from the neolithic age, muses on the nature of attraction: 'I am the artful voyeur', he says, 'of your brain's exposed/and darkened combs,/your muscles' webbing/and all your numbered bones'.[2] Not that Heaney remains content to reside in this position; but he still reminds us of a danger, that danger so well exemplified during the Romantic period, the period of the original Gothic, by Burke's fascination with the person of the French queen, this curious Ur-instance of futuristic necrophilia which will, whether I like it or not, inflect what else I have to say in this chapter;[3] or by Matilda's fascination with the body of the unconscious Verezzi.

The point from which I want to begin my trajectory is the Reign of Terror itself, with its multiple intersections with Gothic fiction and its myths of origins, its upsettings of the law, and thus with the notion of terror and the terroristic in writing. I then want to look at five literary loci for the terrorist: a passage from Blake's *Jerusalem* (1804–20); Dickens's *A Tale of Two Cities* (1859); Conrad's *The Secret Agent* (1907); H.G. Wells's *The Holy Terror* (1939); and finally Doris Lessing's *The Good Terrorist* (1985). This trajectory can of course in

no sense be a comprehensive one, but I hope that from a consideration of these texts certain common concerns may be seen to arise,
common ideological themes certainly but also common rhetorical
issues which I believe to have a bearing on the general issues of the
text, the body and the law. It is also my hope that these investigations at the margins of social space, on the borders of illegality, may
turn out to have a wider relevance to problems of representation,
especially in those areas which we might characterise as Gothic,
those areas in which the lines of the psychopathological, the legal
and the sociological are so thoroughly crossed.

But I would like to begin with a brief consideration of a critical,
or rather historical, text: Stanley Loomis's *Paris in the Terror, June
1793 to July 1794*, which was published in 1965. I have chosen it
because it is in itself a representative of a curiously involuted genre
of multiple historical biography, centring on three episodes, the
murder of Marat, the trial of Danton and what Loomis, perhaps
somewhat evasively, calls the 'end' of Robespierre. In this curiously
slantwise version of history perhaps the delineations of the Gothic
already begin to appear before us. Some comments Loomis makes
near the beginning illustrate the difficulties he encounters in getting to grips with the events within his purview. The September
Massacres, he says, 'have been viewed, and properly so, as an
example of the phenomenon called "revolutionary neurosis", in
which there occurs a complete breakdown of those instincts and
restraints that keep at a deep and usually harmless level the mani-
acal forces that flow beneath human consciousness.' Yet, he adds,
'though the roots of this outbreak of savagery may be found in
certain obscure elements within the human personality, the error
should not be made of dismissing the September Massacres as
some accidental outburst of passion. They were coldly and carefully organised.'[4]

We should not in this context, perhaps, take too far the issue of
Loomis's judgment on the causes of the Terror, and perhaps we
should also not pause for too long on the odd terms in which he
phrases an argument which one can only term psychologistic. But
it is perhaps germane to point to the swaying here between a
concept of anarchy, lawlessness, and a concept of over-much
order, of a regime extended to a point where chaos can have no
place; because this monstrous swaying is the result of what Loomis
clearly conceives to be an inevitable inability to conceive the
mind and practice of the terrorist. The terrorist is, in a sense, the

summation of those agencies which are already, and incomprehensibly, beyond the law; and thus their manifestation in text will always be the site of problems which cannot be expunged. Indeed, in Loomis's textualising we are brought to wonder whether terrorism is a human activity at all, despite the unavoidable fact that this is indeed *all* that it is or ever can be. He describes St Just, for instance, in relation to Robespierre, in these terms:

Like his master, St Just was a fanatic. For all Robespierre's faults – indeed *because* of his all too human faults – Robespierre belongs well within the pale of recognisable humankind. St Just does not. There is a frigidity about him, an inhumanity, a profound strangeness that makes him seem as alien as some species of reptile or insect.

(p. 284)

One way of trying to deal with violence, then, is to exile it beyond the human species, to colour its body with the colours of the monstrous; to treat it as a bestial abnormality which is simply the weird product of an ahistorical pathology; but here Loomis also uses a further rhetorical device which is even better exemplified in another passage:

To the left of Robespierre, to the left even of Marat, loomed the obscure and fearsome faces of the criminally insane, creatures such as Hébert, or Carrier who in a paroxysm of blood lust once [sic] raced about the room, foaming at the mouth and screaming, 'Kill! Kill!'

(p. 213)

The device of dehumanisation so familiar in the Gothic is applied across the board: St Just is inhuman compared with Robespierre, but we have learned a few pages earlier that Robespierre is inhuman compared with Danton. It seems that, in order to bring terror within our orbit at all, we have to set up ever further sets of boundaries, sets of boundaries which are, perhaps, 'endless', as we shade off further from historical and political activity and arrive increasingly at a kind of eternal madhouse of the soul, where there are always worse and worse exhibits on view.

'I am the rage of the people,' said Marat; and this notion finds its way in troubling, perhaps uncanny fashion into Blake's attempts to deal with the problems of revolution and terror. Blake, working under the constantly present impress of the French Revolution and its aftermaths and wedded to a professedly Gothic interpretation of history – Blake feeling himself, also, in various ways and for many reasons, to be outside the law – is not evasive about terror. In some of his 'prophetic' works he develops the mythological figure of Orc precisely as an attempt to come to grips, in characterological and narrative terms, with terror, with the unassimilable desiring and raging residue which forms a constant reservoir of savagery and which can only be released, held down or moulded into some sort of shape by the varying events of history.[5]

Blake's mythology is sophisticated, perhaps one of the most sophisticated in the English-language literatures; and Orc, like Blake's other mythological figures, emerges on several stages at once, as a historical energy, as a psychological force or, perhaps, drive, and as the 'fallen' form of a kind of passionate involvement with the world, known in Blake by the different name of Luvah, which has in the end a task of salvation to perform. In other words, what appears to us now or then as terror is only a harbinger, bent or distorted into a shape of evil by other pressures – principally in Blake by the usurpations of reason which we can also characterise as the 'monstrous' operations of the law. In an over-ordered society, according to Blake, in a society which comes to vaunt itself as mechanically organised – as, to his way of thinking, Enlightenment society did – there is no place for passion, or for intensity. Thus this passion or intensity is forced underground, to bubble up elsewhere, shorn of the loving restraint which should have been exercised so much earlier in its life – for there is here a myth of maturation and its vicissitudes as well, a myth of the abusive torture of the infant body – and accoutred now in the bloody robes and rags of an avenging fury.[6]

One of the thematically crucial passages in Blake, however, does not concern Orc. It comes from *Jerusalem*, Plate 31, and its principal actor is the character Los, who represents poetic inspiration and acts as the guarantor of future integration in a world given over to competition and the violent suppression of true energy. In this passage, Los has become aware of a series of social ills afflicting the body of Albion, in other words, the state of Britain. He embarks on a search for the origin of these ills, but breaks off this search to make the following speech:

What shall I do? what could I do if I could find these Criminals?
I could not dare to take vengeance, for all things are so
  constructed
And builded by the Divine hand that the sinner shall always
  escape,
And he who takes vengeance alone is the criminal of
  Providence.
If I should dare to lay my finger on a grain of sand
In way of vengeance, I punish the already punish'd. O whom
Should I pity if I pity not the sinner who is gone astray?
O Albion, if thou takest vengeance, if thou revengest thy
  wrongs,
Thou art for ever lost! What can I do to hinder the Sons
Of Albion from taking vengeance? or how shall I them
  perswade? [7]

Los is involved here in a highly concrete task. He has inspected the situation of the State, and he has discovered 'all the tendernesses of the soul cast forth as filth & mire'; in other words, he has detected the peculiar place that an internalised State terrorism has usurped in the soul. Another image Blake uses here is of individual souls being baked into bricks, hardened around with the exigencies of State power until all shreds of human feeling have disappeared. And now he has a problem with what his reply to this situation can be, for there is only one feeling plucking at his soul, and that is the desire for vengeance, Marat's extra-legal 'rage of the people'. So here Los is trying to argue himself out of the need for counter-terrorism, but his argument is curiously constructed. In the first five lines he appears to be advancing a view which is based simply on despair in the face of the power of the law: saying, in effect, that whoever you vote for, the government always wins; and the further response this evokes in him is simply one of cowardice. But later his argument becomes more clear, for it demonstrates that cowardice may in fact be part of the correct answer; for the *wrong* answer – of this Los appears quite sure – is counter-terrorism, vengeance. The whole enterprise of Blake's prophetic books may be considered in terms of the extension of this notion that, on the one hand, a revolution is possible; while, on the other, there is a constant urging that for it to be a revolution at all it must from the outset eschew the principles and methods of those forces which have provoked it in the first place, for otherwise terror will simply beget terror.

In the service of this familiar argument, Blake uses the controlling motif of Albion, but it is clear that his arguments are being
advanced at a more than nationalistic level. Such might not be said
of Dickens's celebrated portrayal of the Terror in *A Tale of Two
Cities*, although it might be argued that Dickens, like Blake, is
driven to construct some kind of extra-social space in which the
terrorists can perform, a space which will serve as an evasion of the
human drives and actions which might, to our danger, be considered to form the substance of terrorism; but which to describe as
such would place us decisively outside the law. In Blake, this extra-
social space is one which lasts him through his poetry; it is the
common countryside and city turned into a negative image
through the pervasive nature of the Fall.

In Dickens it locates itself differently. For the supreme image of
the Terror in *A Tale of Two Cities* occurs in a single chapter, 'The
Grindstone', and the nature of the vision that is recounted there is
well described by the paragraph which directly succeeds this
vision and attempts to locate it within a psychogeography. 'All
this was seen in a moment, as the vision of a drowning man',
says Dickens, 'or of any human creature at any very great pass,
could see a world if it were there'.[8] So: Dickens says that the world
of terrorism, that world which it is impossible to 'see' at all in the
normative terms of the historians, is some kind of incarnation of an
uncertain, shifting perception which might have to do with one's
own death; or is, at any rate, in some comparable way unreliable.
The important thing is that this vision is not one that can be located
within social space, it is too violent, its colours too awesomely
transposed, for that, it is a foreign body.[9] Part of the vision itself
is described thus:

> The grindstone had a double handle, and, turning at it madly
> were two men, whose faces, as their long hair flapped back when
> the whirlings of the grindstone brought their faces up, were more
> horrible and cruel than the visages of the wildest savages in their
> most barbarous disguise. False eyebrows and false moustaches
> were stuck upon them, and their hideous countenances were all
> bloody and sweaty, and all awry with howling...
>
> (pp. 248–9)

The question here is of how to represent an excess; we might
therefore hypothesise that one way of charting the representations

of terrorism would be by charting the specific excess depicted. It is clear, and remains so throughout the rest of the 'vision', that what really engages Dickens's attention is not, for example, the connection, perhaps more obvious now than then, between this portrayal and other portrayals of alienated industrial labour in Dickens's canon, but the suggestions of transvestitism, of distortions of the gender-specificity of the body – and, perhaps, faciality – contained in the scene (and Dickens was by no means unique in this). This issue of transvestitism, or perhaps of imputed perversion in general,[10] has wide implications for the representation of terror, and, as it will transpire, for the Gothic in general. For it is evidently the case that any revolution has to do with a transfer of power, a remaking of legalities and social orders, and this involves a threat of the re-assignment of the 'mark' of impotence; and, in a patriarchally gender-coded society, impotence and feminisation are inextricably interwoven – and frequently recoded in the all too common tropes of sadism and masochism.

But here there is more to be said; yet the question is, given this terrain of excess, a terrain which, as in Loomis's account, we might fairly delineate as a terrain of multiply displaced hysteria, more of what? In this representation, are we looking at something emanating from something we might, perhaps too conveniently, regard as Dickens's pathology, or at something which speaks more broadly to a set of nineteenth-century social anxieties? The argument for the latter interpretation would rest upon the way in which the space we are here talking about is not within the power of one 'writer' to control, but also upon the way in which, as we read on through the vision, we realise that the real fear that lies behind the picture, the latent content of the vision, is again a fear of undifferentiation, a fear that all distinction, hierarchy, mark of honour might be obliterated in a terrorism which is, of course, a symbolically distorted image of democracy – democracy's nightmare, as one might put it, a nightmare in which the only way to reduce difference is through bloodletting, because, presumably, it is blood which carries distinction and rank. The marks, the signs which are to be obliterated are here to be replaced by false marks of power, the eyebrows, the moustache, although even there the wires of gender are significantly crossed.

Yet through all this runs the mysterious, boundary-breaking mingling of the blood of women, which might be said to carry altogether different connotations:

The eye could not detect one creature in the group free from the smear of blood. Shouldering one another to get next at the sharpening-stone, were men stripped to the waist, with the stain all over their limbs and bodies; men in all sorts of rags, with the stain upon those rags; men devilishly set off with spoils of women's lace and silk and ribbon, with the stain dyeing those trifles through and through. Hatchets, knives, bayonets, swords, all brought to be sharpened, were all red with it. Some of the hacked swords were tied to the wrists of those who carried them, with strips of linen and fragments of dress: ligatures various in kind, but all deep of the one colour.

(p. 291)

One wonders, first, who it is that is 'stripped to the waist' here, and what the unacknowledged connections might be between the phallic violence and the distorted nurture by the wounded breast which are both represented in this section of the vision. More important, however, is the notion that all sense of 'various in kind' has gone; the notion is that to the terrorist all is one, and human distinctions have ceased to matter. And we can go one stage further than that, for this vision depicts, undoubtedly, an ocean of blood, a dipping, a sanguinary baptism from which nobody can escape, and in this sense recapitulates, among other 'primal' scenes, the ocean of blood on which the Ancient Mariner finds himself adrift as a punishment for his transgression of the law. What we have here, then, as a representation of terrorism, and more particularly as an all too literal 'incarnation' of the bodies of the terrorists, is precisely an inverted replication of the ocean which we might otherwise associate with the repose of the mother, or, to put it another way, we are confronted with a night-mare image, a 'Life-in-Death', of the bad mother. In this particular context we might be impelled to call her Kali, although she goes by many other names, and the Furies are among those names; her task, which is not restricted to female vengeance, is to unman, to threaten with the clothing of impotence, and thus the terrorist, here at any rate, becomes the repository of these feelings of impotence, political feelings, perhaps, which could otherwise not be carried and even here threaten the boundaries of legal representation; the terrorist as scapegoat, the projection of a deep inner fear of not being recognised unless by the embracing hand of death; the apotheosis of our own fears, no matter what the legality of our lives, that when it comes to it our case will not be heard.

Leavis referred to Conrad's *The Secret Agent* as a supreme masterpiece, an unquestionable classic;[11] given the recherché nature of the subject matter, which is terrorism, as compared with, for example, the subject matter of Henry James, equally valued in the 'great tradition', we might reasonably rehearse briefly what it was that Leavis found in this novel of the social margins, this representation of a world beyond the law yet within which we can from to time detect the emergent shape of a different law, which could so enliven a judgment which was, so habitually, dedicated to the approval of that which adumbrated and defended the centre ground, the stability of the legal and social space. And the obvious, and surely the correct, answer is the enormous fecundity with which Conrad here explores and describes immediacies of feeling and event; in *The Secret Agent* there is a sense of inexorability which can only flow from an absolute fit between plot and character.

Or so one might say, using basically Leavisite terminology; yet even within this terminology one might still ask, what here is Conrad's stance? How is he approaching these characters, and what is the ideological subplot (as Leavis would not have explicitly asked) according to which they behave? And here we come upon many features, but to begin with one: *The Secret Agent* is a brilliant, developing description of an unsuccessful group. Verloc, Ossipon, Michaelis, Karl Yundt are members of an inverted body politic, and the failures of communication and trust which beset them and bring them down to ruin, the ruins, if you like, of an alternative if mediocre and already banished empire, the apparent distinctions between their motivations, all these constitute a critique which is uncannily inverted: inverted because Conrad puts it across as a critique of an isolated group, whereas it might fairly be said that what we as readers are here observing is a collection of individuals each one of whom represents – admittedly, and pointedly, at an extreme of the legally permissible space – an attribute of their society; or rather, to be more precise, of the society which is *not* theirs, in which they occupy a succession of positions which are always liminal.

Thinking back again to the work of Loomis, we might expect to find in this representation of terrorism a penumbral field, perhaps in the form of a character or characters beside whom even these pained grotesques can be treated according to the rules of some recognisable *Psychopathia Politicalis*;[12] and there indeed he is, on the sidelines, in the figure of the Professor, supplier of arms and potential suicide extraordinary. We might rephrase this thus: beyond those people who are driven by *purposes* (or, perhaps better, have sublimated their drives into purposes), whether those purposes are conceived as genuinely political or as the outcroppings of inner perversions and distortions, lies the questionably human symbol of that realm in which even purpose as such has no hold, the monster which cannot be brought within the confines of the law: the Professor, who has ceased to defend, protect or secretise himself, and exists now only as naked, temporary threat, a troubling and destabilising of the boundaries. His approach, we might recall from the text, is simply that it does not matter to him whether or, rather, when he dies; he is concerned simply to ensure that at all times he carries sufficient explosive about his body so that any arresting officer – and, indeed, anybody else within a certain radius – will share his moment of blind physical apotheosis. We might fairly embark upon the question – although it is perhaps a question of too great an enormity to permit of embarcation – of what it is that this 'professor' professes; any attempt to answer such a question would have to deal in terms we have already deployed, for here we have again a figure, akin to ones we have come across before, of a curious undifferentiation, one who brings final release, repose of the soul, one by whom all petty matters social or moral have already been resolved, one who has given up the ghost, one who resides – and presides – in the ruins; this is surely one part also of the problematic 'wisdom' of Gothic, and one which is visibly inherited from its progenitor graveyard poets,[13] albeit their meditations upon tombs were more circumspect and less brusque than those we hear from the lips of this 'wise man' *manqué*.

From another point of view, however, the Professor is only an extreme example of something which most of Conrad's revolutionaries have in common; which is a resistant, nay combustible, approach to being touched, to having their bodies appropriated by devices and feelings which might tie them too closely into the legal space. For these are literally the untouchables: they are people who have placed themselves – for the most part with considerable care – on the far side of the boundary which delimits the socially acceptable. But human they are for all that, and here perhaps lies the great strength of Conrad's portrayal of terrorism. For in the battle between anarchy and the law, between chaos and order, which is characteristic of representational strategies in this field, Conrad manages through his remarkable attention to detail to avoid caricaturing his caricatures. Planning there may be and accident there may be, order and chaos, the law and its enemies: those twin poles between which the representation of terrorism is always strung. But the two intersect, always and everywhere, so that neither conspiracy theory nor the liberal theory of total muddle will match up to the 'facts' which Conrad gives us.

There is, of course, a 'factual' basis to Conrad's story in the 1894 attempt to blow up the Greenwich Observatory, perhaps one of the clearest and most apparently neutral sources of all physical law, and it is clear that Conrad's method of writing *The Secret Agent* (which is also, of course, the agency of the secret, the prime mover across the space between concealment and revelation) derived from his attempts to construct a retroactive history, a sequence of events which 'could have' led up to the 'event', if thus we may describe it, as reported. But in representation there none the less always remains the question of the symptomatic; if it is true that the symptom in Dickens – and the analysis of these symptoms, according to a critical pathology, will have a specific function in these representations which are close to illegality[14] – was his dealing with transvestitism, so in *The Secret Agent* we might find the symptom in Conrad's dealing with squalor.

Nobody in the text is permitted a moment of cleanliness of body, soul or moral fibre; all is stained, dyed. The book is built on a substratum so fouled as to call to mind the dreaded and dreadful marriage bed of *Hamlet*. Thus it is that these representations of terrorism automatically turn back on themselves; for if an extra-social space is to be depicted, it can only be in the company of a social space, however vestigially drawn, and thus the attributes of the terrorist gang become the inverse of the community threatened, although there will continue to be differences as to whether that community is presented in actual or ideal mode.

In Conrad, we could say that the unstated presentation is in the ideal mode, a social space in which there are no longer such ambiguous corners as Verloc's shop, with its trickling trade in pornography, its dusty hopeless shelves. And, of course, in which there are no longer such ambiguous names as those which Conrad gives to each member of the terrorist gang, names which send the reader searching for origins, anagrams, reversals (although the name of Inspector Heat is similarly challenging). For the kind of dusting out, the kind of purity, the kind of cleanliness which this hovering idealised society offers is one in which no more secrecies will be permitted, but one in which there will no longer be any hint of the foreign, of a contaminating foreign body which might taint the brave new world with its own unaccommodated antithesis, its 'residence' outside the law.

H.G. Wells wrote *The Holy Terror* in 1939. It is a bad novel. Indeed, it is a paradigm of the several bad novels Wells wrote (although he also wrote some very good ones) in that after an auspicious beginning it trails off into the worst of dreary didacticism. Indeed, something still worse happens here, as it also happens in *The Shape of Things to Come* (1933), which is that Wells runs into a problem of scale. The protagonist of *The Holy Terror* begins very small, indeed very small indeed as a baby, a ghastly toddler, an even more ghastly child, and then in early maturity as an infiltrator of various fringe political groups, hardly to be taken seriously as a figure of power even by the novel's other characters. In these infiltrations, in the background to the alarming gift of amoral eloquence which, in an interesting development of the attorney's craft, is the Holy Terror's purchase on the world, there is the sketching of a social space, but it is a small one, and is marked by a lack of understanding on the part of the chief character himself as to how the world actually flows. In due course, however, he discovers this, and we are expected to believe that this discovery, fortuitously accompanied by the outbreak of war, facilitates his translation to a higher stage entirely, whereby in the space of a few short pages he becomes – no doubt to the envy of many another Gothic hero – world dictator.

Although the book is called *The Holy Terror*, it might be suggested that thus far it may seem to have only a rather faulty connection with terrorism; but there is more to it than that. For the protagonist, largely known only by the name of Rud (a confusion here, which Wells points out, with Rudyard Kipling, but also, which Wells does not point out, with the rudder of an otherwise rudderless State),[15] represents a legal limit, but in a particularly worrying form; for Rud does not need to go forth and commit terrorist acts, instead he is permitted to position himself on the margin and others will flock to him. Naturally, he gathers around him a ruling group which personifies the terrorist gang, imbued with that peculiar mix of perfect functioning and presumed total lack of mutual trust which, as we are now seeing, has become the principal representational strategy with which the political and legal consensus needs to invest this 'excessive field' of delineation. One of this ruling group, the oddly named Thirp, who becomes head of the secret police – and in this context the continually repeating notion of the *secret* is so obviously resonant as perhaps to need no further spelling out – possesses all the necessary qualities to figure himself as a kind of matured outcome of Rud's still intriguingly infantilised pathology:

> Thirp did not do this work himself, but he made all the arrangements for its being done. His essential quality was a feline curiosity in the less obvious motives of his fellow-creatures. It was this that had first attracted him to criminology and prison reform. He was interested in human errors and misconceptions, his life as a watcher and shepherd of rebellious spirits, was primarily one of vicarious anti-social activities. He had Rud's fear and hatred of stark power, but in a subtler, more penetrating form. He had worked with energy, he had become a party man, because he realised the trend of the old order towards a mosaic of military and spasmodically moral tyrannies, but he had no desire whatever to establish a new order with possibly even austerer disciplines of its own.
>
> (p. 342)

Again the unresolved conflict between order and desire; again the fatal imbrication of the criminologist and the criminal, the contamination of order by that which might come to use the tools of order against itself. What lies at the root of this secret policeman, this watcher of secrets, this connoisseur of the hidden and the illicit, is his knowledge of the hidden, anarchic roots of an order which is merely apparent, but his power, which lies in a certain kind of ethical freedom, is in his ability to fluctuate between unresolved poles of imposed discipline and libertine privilege, an ability which allows him empathic access to minds in similar states of disturbance.

We could say, at a simple class level, that this oscillation is a representation of a dual bourgeois fear familiar to us in Gothic, on the one hand of the semi-disciplined army created by alienated wage labour, on the other of the libertarianism of the displaced aristocrat. But the point about the depiction of the terrorist is

precisely that the potential analysis along class lines is so frequently displaced by different, more fraught kinds of analysis,
more reminiscent of Loomis's dealings with his grotesque portraits.
Here, for example, is part of the lengthy textual commentary on
Rud's psyche:

> At the bottom of Rud's nature, covered over and suppressed
> there had always been an acute sense of his physical inferiority.
> He had even an exaggerated sense of his own ugliness and
> bodily feebleness. He had a passionate impulse to exercise
> power, but his primary method of exercising power was to
> destroy, and he consented only to the vast constructiveness his
> movement was developing, because that alone guaranteed the
> complete disappearance of the institutions, restraints and com-
> pulsions he hated.
>
> (p. 339)

There are many things one might say about this passage; here
perhaps it is most important to dwell for a moment on the interesting word 'compulsions', which seems a key term for the representation of terrorism. For of course Wells means here literally a
term in tune with institutions and restraints; that which compels,
that which forces individuals into a shaping process, the body of,
for example, the law, a process which Rud, for one, finds repulsive:
repulsion and compulsion, repulsion as compulsion. But compulsion carries another meaning, as the irresistible force that drives the
psyche on a course not of its own choosing;[16] and thus we find
ourselves standing starkly against a backdrop of the dilemmas of
determinism and free will which, we may now see, underlie these
portrayals of terrorism. Is it possible that a person might choose to
become a terrorist, might choose to lead an illegal, untextualised
life? Where might we have to look, into what dark, dusty or distant
corners, or into what all too familiar corners of family life, in order
to find the possible origin or source of this apparent misplacement,
this placing beyond the boundaries of the law for which we can
only account by stripping such individuals, such groups, of their
human clothing? Better, surely, to claim that such a person is a
reptile or an insect, and thus (we anthropocentrically presume)
devoid of that power of choice which he or she has so certainly
abused. For if choice at this limit of the human can be so extreme,
then how shall we accommodate ourselves to the extremely limited

nature of the choices we take in everyday life, how accustom ourselves to a revelation of the way in which it might be we rather than the terrorist who are, and always have been, in chains, in fetters, in prison, criminalised by our own collusion?

In saying this I am aware that I may now be verging onto territory which veers away from terrorism and into, for example, the material of the existentialist novel, and I can hear the shades of Camus's deadly choices whispering behind me; and so perhaps it would be good to return centrally to the issue of terror with a final text, Doris Lessing's *The Good Terrorist*. Perhaps also it needs to be said at the outset that the title is subject to a certain doubling: the heroine, Alice, is a 'good' terrorist in that Lessing brilliantly depicts her involvement with a terrorist group as stemming from indeed a mixture of motives, but some of them of the best quality; but also there is a question in the text about what makes a 'good' terrorist in the other sense of the word, that is, an effective terrorist in whom a comprehensible and felt motive harmonises with efficiency of execution, in both senses of that word.

It is a superb novel, and displays the knotted strength of prose of which only the later Lessing has been capable. It is a novel in which there is nothing to spare, indeed almost no description at all; everything is conversation and motivation, an exemplar of the novel of ideas in a form far more stripped down and apt for usage than, for example, the over-popular mode of an Iris Murdoch.[17] It is also very much a text for our times, or perhaps one should say, as the years go by, for its own time, however recent that may still seem: centrally it depicts a group of young people – for so long Lessing has seemed interested only in young people, albeit in varying lights – who are, or at least initially seem to be, amateur terrorists, and how their flirtation with the world of real violence leads them into an ascending spiral which culminates in bloody death. What is also left at the end is Alice: 'smiling gently, a mug of very strong sweet tea in her hand, looking this morning like a nine-year-old girl who has had, perhaps, a bad dream, the poor baby sat waiting for it to be time to go out and meet the professionals.'[18]

Lessing does not ignore the possibility of psychopathological explanation; as one might expect, far from it. But what distinguishes her from so many other writers who have attempted to represent terrorism is that she leaves such explanations hovering, as a possible part of a constellation of cause and effect but one which can never be sufficient; and in fact the very dialectic of cause and effect, with its legal ramifications, may seem somewhat suspect by the time we meet Alice at the end with her mug of tea. True it is that Alice cannot stand sex, and true it also is that much of her hatred of her mother stems from a particular re-introjection of the primal scene; yet we are also made to believe that this in itself deserves to be ranged against other realms of explanation, different kinds of determination which have far more to do with desperation about the kinds of trap which are set in contemporary societies for the poor and the underprivileged.

A conventional characterological explanation of what Lessing is doing would reside in the evident 'goodness' of Alice's personality, and leave it at that; a reading, on the other hand, opposed to the politics which Lessing allows, if she does not explicitly espouse, would accuse her of finding excuses for a type of behaviour which threatens the sacred nature of stability and the rule of law. Moving, as the text subtly impels us to, beyond these kinds of 'explanation' – which are in fact merely reproductions of their own terms of argument – what we actually find is an attempted humanisation of a threatening boundary, so that Alice and her fellow terrorists can be comprehended as determined beings (in both senses of the term) and also as people with choices to make – the crucial point being that the way in which those choices are conceived, the grounds on which they are predicated, are not of the characters' own choosing.

What is not shirked in *The Good Terrorist* is that parts of ourselves, as readers, as social beings, as terrorists, may be bound up in these liminal depictions. It is this admission of involvement which saves Lessing's text from the difficulty which invades and colours all the other pieces we have looked at, precisely the difficulty Heaney describes, which is the inevitability of complicity, the feeling of voyeurism, the colouring of the salacious which, to return to our starting point, is present in so many of the Gothic and related works which in the late eighteenth and early nineteenth centuries attempted to find a stance towards the unthinkable events in France, the major examples again being Burke and the numerous displaced further representations of the Terror which we find in so many of the novelists of the period.[19] It is, seemingly paradoxically, the case that while we continue to depict the terrorist as uncompromisingly 'out there', or indeed further out the more (like Frankenstein) we pursue him or her, then we remain at the mercy of our own projections, always running the risk of revelling in a fear which we can justify as representative of a State legal system 'in terror'.

What Lessing does is to bring this fear back along the long, slow bend of maturation: to show us Alice as our daughter, our sister, our former self, our 'baby'; and thus to involve us in a less than – and simultaneously more than – thinking way with that shadow self which we have come across before in the dock, or at the limit of our involvement with the law, and which always ends up going for the easy but dangerous option; that part which from time immemorial has felt in its moments of infantile fury, no less true of States than of individuals, that the only solution is to 'blow it all away', and has also felt that by doing so one might not actually commit real-life bloodshed but merely demonstrate that which our dream self hopes, which is that in this moment of destruction, this incarnation of the destroyer, these oppressive forces might reveal themselves as things of cobweb and gossamer; so that we can have what childhood always wants, the destruction without the following guilt.

In ranging, then, across these various representations of terrorism, we have in various ways intersected with the cardinal points of the text, the body and the law. We might list four particular themes which cross on this field. First, there is the question of the connection between anarchy and the 'rage' for order, those linked imperatives which threaten the balanced, always compromised and legally sanctioned State from both directions. Second, there is the question of individual responsibility and group determination, which will always have a bearing, inevitably somewhat distorted, on the actual limits of legal action within a conventional social space. Third, there is the vexed issue of the State within a State, always a way of phrasing the threat of the terrorist cell but germane also throughout the complex dealings of fiction with the law, expressing as it does, pressed into the shape of secrecy, the nature of the existence of small social units within a larger unit which seems unresponsive to local demands. And finally, and I think especially revealed in Lessing, there is the question of the stance of representation, the extent to which this representation is delivered from inside or outside: inside or outside the terrorist group, inside or outside the legally sanctioned space on the boundary of which it stands.

To return to my initial caveats: I make these points not to suggest an external or suprahistorical essence of terrorism, for there is none,

nor to suggest that there is any way of handling in satisfactory
fashion the real issues of deprivation, transgression and death, a
fashion which would be free from the moral and political problems
which attend on our dealings with representations of the terrorist
moment as an emblem for the moment in which history is distorted
in Gothic fashion by the encounter with that which stands beyond
the law. But I do suggest that in the depiction of terrorism there is a
continuing, and probably perennially unbalanced, dialectic between
the body and the law, figured as anarchy and order, and in turn
between both of these forces, which we may of course alternatively
figure as the unconscious and the superego, and the massive projections of the assumed stability of the licit ego which we normally
take for social organisation, and which form, writ large upon the
world, our realisations of the acceptable and the legal.

By way of conclusion to this chapter, here is a further brief
quotation from Wells's *The Holy Terror*, in which one of Rud's
followers, Chiffan, is musing on the attractions of terrorism in its
manifested form as world dictatorship:

> 'What I – what we have always liked about him,' said Chiffan, 'is
> a sort of diabolical energy. His drive. There is some-
> thing outrageous in his make-up that won us all. And something
> that still intrigues me. There are times when I want to follow that
> man about like a child following a circus show. *Why* does he do
> things? He's an abject coward...and also he is a desperate
> fighter. Do you know I think at times that he is the master of
> the world to-day simply because he has a frantic fear of power –
> in the hands of anyone else'.
>
> (p. 369)

'Diabolical energy', 'drive', 'something outrageous in his make-up',
the 'child' following a 'circus show', the 'frantic fear of power', – in
all these terms, I believe, reminiscent as they are of the description
of the classic Gothic hero, we can also see the struggle to move
beyond the limits of the law, the struggle to find a space outside
the legal where other representations will still be possible; and at
the same time the devastating fear of thus moving into a world
where order will disappear and we will reveal ourselves to have
been merely fascinated by the possibilities of writing, and in particular of a writing which finally declares itself to stand where
perhaps all writing positions itself: beyond the law.[20]

6

Identification and Gender: The Law of Ligeia

A word is neither totally absent, nor present, it lives on *as a kind of life-in-death.*[1]

In tracing these elements in the Gothic, however, we need also to return from the Gothic hero to the crucial question of the female Gothic, and in this chapter I mean to start from a partial reading of Elisabeth Bronfen's *Over her Dead Body: Death, Femininity and the Aesthetic* (1992), which is relevant in many ways. A great deal of the material on which Bronfen bases her argument is Gothic; indeed, almost all the canonical Gothic texts in the British tradition, and a good many of those in the European and American traditions, are referred to and many are treated at some length. The triple linking of death, the female and the aesthetic seems to take its place naturally on the terrain of the Gothic; we might say that the extra-ordinary force of Bronfen's analysis seems gained at times precisely from its recapitulatory status: these images, these connexions, are latent within modernity, but here they are brought together in new and subtle ways, and in the service of an argument which might be characterised as relentless in its accumulation of detail in the service of what, in another context, might be referred to as a master-narrative of Western culture, a narrative of abjection and necrophilia, of the disavowal of the body.

But Bronfen's argument is a massive, a 'monstrous' one, in many senses of that term. Here I have no space to look at it in the fullness of its articulations. I am concerned with only one question, but I think that question is an important one for the Gothic, and for the articulations of the text, the body and the law. It may be put thus: is the psychoanalytic model used by Bronfen among many others – and the psychoanalytic is certainly not the only model she deploys – not itself at the service of a set of binary oppositions which, seen from one point of view, appear to reinforce precisely the *necessity* of the binary collocations she describes? What way forward, what way 'away from', the dire inscriptions she painstakingly unearths and analyses, might, as it were, *next* engage our attention, when the shifting tapestries have been stripped away and we are face to face with the horrors of female abjection demonstrated on the bodies of her chosen texts?

I shall concentrate only on one brief argument in her book. It may be emblematic of the whole, but that is not a point I would want to press here. The argument is the one she advances 'around' the text of Poe's 'Ligeia'.[2] To say that she advances it 'around' the text is already too simple, for the articulations of text and theory here are complex; but certainly 'Ligeia' – and Ligeia – is/are a *topos* which can fairly concern us, for various reasons and not least for the compressed figuring of female death and problematic resurrection, the reoccupation of an 'illegal' space, which the text proffers and for the extraordinary interactions present in the story between these figurings and questions of memory and recollection.

Alongside 'Bronfen' and 'Poe' I want to deploy in this chapter a third term: the writings of Mikkel Borch-Jacobsen. If I flinch before offering a general account of the complexities of Bronfen on the Gothic, that tremor of fear is compounded by the anguish of reading and rewriting Borch-Jacobsen who, in a series of recent texts, has himself undertaken a wholesale rewriting of Freud. That, of course, is not how Borch-Jacobsen would put it; but then, in the rewritings of Freud from Lacan onwards there has been a curious and symptomatic hesitancy in precisely this area of 'rewriting', emblematised for example in the persistence of the fetish of the *chose freudienne*, in the (compulsive) repetitions of claims to 'embody' – to re-embody, to resurrect? – the 'presence' of the master.

This makes for one curious and significant difficulty in trying to work with Borch-Jacobsen's arguments, a difficulty of voice: in attempting, for example, to excerpt quotations from his texts it is often exceedingly difficult to know when one is encountering the 'voice of the author', or Freud's voice coming, as it were, from beyond the grave. All this seems properly Gothic, and it also seems properly psychoanalytic, in one particular sense, namely, in that both Gothic and psychoanalysis share a task of dealing in the dark background, an approach to the *topos* of death, and it is here that the argument doubles back on itself and enters into a hall of mirrors, of refractions which I shall try to set in further motion – to 'subject' to a further 're-animation' – in this chapter.

To turn back for a moment to Bronfen's general argument. As
best I can summarise it, she argues, by detailed reference to works
both literary and pictorial, that a major source of pleasure, and thus
a major 'object of desire', in modern Western culture has been the
dead female body. Sometimes this pleasure and this desire are
cloaked, however thinly: cloaked in early examples, for instance,
in the raiment of the anatomist, of the 'pure' seeker after bodily
information who nevertheless finds it necessary to dissect and display the female body as his (always 'his') major site of evidence.
Behind this – as I imagine all would agree – lies a terrain on which
the apparently pacific certainties of aesthetics code and decode
the grinning mask of power. Power, force, violence; passivity, the
swoon, sickness unto death: these are, at least on my reading, the
kinds of category which Bronfen sets in motion, these are the terms
which, correctly named and arranged, form the tombstone below
which 'Western culture' buries 'its' women and which is now to
fall on the heads of the writer as gravedigger, of patriarchy as the
Covering Cherub, as the signature of the crypt. We could add to
this the whole problematic around these dealings with the female
body as both death and exposure, as the consigning of the female
body into a space of terminal privacy at the same time as exposing
it to the full public gaze of the reader as anatomist's pupil.

The next step also seems to me uncontentious; which is to see
behind these *ambiviolences* the threat of the mother, that fear of
undifferentiation on which I have already touched in several different contexts, conceived everywhere and always under the sign
of negation, the woman as ideal erected to be cast down, 'set up', in
all senses, to demonstrate a weakness, with the aim of confirming
the (masculine) ego in its upward trajectory towards the realms of
light, beneath which lies buried, under the sign – which can perhaps never be fully a signature – of the female, the figure of the
sailor's wife (for example) waiting and waving – or drowning –
while the masculine sails off to brave new worlds. The 'soul of the
plot', to anticipate Poe,[3] is not so much horror as the painful
masculine excuse-making which we find in, for instance, the age-
old resonances of a song like 'Boots of Spanish Leather':

> I got a letter on a lonesome day,
> It was from his ship a-sailin'
> Saying I don't know when I'll be comin' back again,
> It depends on how I'm a-feelin'.[4]

Undifferentiation – feeling 'like it' – or not.

With this quasi-Homeric image of the masculine in mind it is no surprise, then – turning now to Bronfen on 'Ligeia' – that her analysis begins with the comment that 'Ligeia' is a tale told 'in retrospect', although it might indeed be more of a surprise to find a tale which is not. Bronfen naturally proceeds to refer to the tale as a tale of 'mourning', wherein Ligeia is 'psychically resuscitated' and 'textually resurrected in [Poe's] written narrative'. The argument is that there is here an only faintly disguised collusion in mastery: as the unnamed narrator exerts power over Ligeia, and even more over his second wife Rowena, so Poe-the-author reinforces textually the masculist power which 'represents' the work of the ego, Gothically threatened in its mastery by that which might infringe on its sovereignty. Ligeia's absence of a 'given name' is further invoked in the service of this argument about lack of identity, lack of will; she becomes, at least in part, the literary equivalent of the objects of the pictorial gaze which graphically and memorably figure in Bronfen's book.

Bronfen shows us how the narrator, in his inability to 'recollect' circumstances and facts about Ligeia's earlier life and indeed about their life together, and in his concentration on her 'appearance', reduces her to an ideal, a shadow. She speaks also of the narrator's pride in his 'analytic' abilities, his minute cataloguing of the parts of her body,[5] which has obvious relevance to the Kleinian conception of the role of the part-object;[6] and she speaks also of the ways in which the narrator incorporates and appropriates Ligeia for himself – or perhaps *has already done so*, because the time frame of the story is notoriously unstable. There comes a moment, Bronfen says, when 'he now fully possesses the knowledge she had', and she goes on to amplify this by saying that 'Ligeia is the complete possession of her lover'.

This is the first textual crux, the first aporia in Bronfen to which I want to call attention, and I shall return to it below when I look at the tale in more detail, but perhaps it will indicate the next directions of my argument (and feasibly save some unnecessary expenditure of labour on reading) if I say now that this appears to be an undecidable sentence. From this phrasing we are meant to infer that Ligeia becomes completely subjected to her lover; but as soon as we begin to think of unambiguous equivalents which will employ any modulation of the term 'possession', we become textually lost. For perhaps indeed Ligeia is that state of her own being which is 'the complete possession of her lover', in other words, perhaps *he* is completely possessed by *her*. How might we tell? *Can* we tell? Is the language, at least the English language, capable of informing us unambiguously of how these 'lines' of power operate, of the nature of the law of possession, or is there always an ambiguity at the heart of possession, an ambiguity of the 'possessed', precisely an ambiguity, essential to the logic of the phantom, in which Gothic is always locked and which also renders the law's grasp on possession tenuous and phantasmal?

Bronfen continues:

> The resurrection assures the repossession of a lost love object, implicitly a repetition of the maternal body, which promised infinite knowledge and at which the child first experienced a sense of unity and wholeness.

To my mind, 'repossession' here suffers from the same linguistic instability as 'possession' (although perhaps redoubled); but there is also here another question which I would address to Bronfen's text, but as a way of putting it more widely, which concerns the term 'experience'.

I should have liked to keep my three discussions – of Bronfen, of Poe, of Borch-Jacobsen – separate and water-tight; no doubt the desire behind that is explicable, but equally it is obviously flawed. Instead here I must invoke a formulation of Borch-Jacobsen's:

> ... the *same* subject has and does not have access to a given representation, remembers and does not remember a given 'scene', experiences and does not experience a given pleasure. In this sense, the cleavage or division of the subject that psychoanalysis keeps talking about takes place against a background of unity, a *unitary* subject.[7]

To explain this comment at all requires also a little background to Borch-Jacobsen's work, which hinges in part on a rejection of Lacanian versions of the concept of Otherness.[8] It may not be wrong, but it is certainly not *adequate*, according to Borch-Jacobsen, to speak of the unconscious as the site of the other, and in fact to do so is precisely to underestimate the force of our own disturbance. It is to substitute a rhetoric – attractive in itself – based on exile and differentiation for the facts of co-subsistence, within the subject, of ego and unconscious (we might more usefully call it a 'consanguinity'); for how else, Borch-Jacobsen asks, could we speak of differentiation at all except on the basis of a concept of unity?

It is therefore not clear that the child has ever 'experienced' unity and undifferentiation; there is, we might rather reluctantly, and indeed irritably, say, an undecidability encapsulated in the notion of experience. Looked at through a slight shift of frame, this is not hard to appreciate: such a perception – and Borch-Jacobsen's arguments about suggestion and hypnosis as the bases of Freud's practice underline this – is slowly dawning on us in the West as we are presented with the unfolding and agonising epistemological and legal problematic of child abuse.[9] Or, we might say in the present context, of Poe's narrator's treatment of his wife; or hers of him; or the removed narrator's treatment of them both – if indeed there is more than one character position in the text, a point which I should like to leave open for the moment.

Perhaps we can usefully find the thread of Bronfen's argument again in the following passage:

> ...as such a figure of death she becomes completely Other and defies any unity with the survivor. Ultimately eliminated is the disturbing and threatening factor of hesitation, the hovering between anxiety and desire. Poe's narrative articulates the fascination with the revenant materialised as a living representative of the dead and stages an imaginative triumph over the intellectual hesitation it induces.

I have already indicated a dissatisfaction with the notion of the 'completely Other' which I shall develop further below; but here the problem is already textually indicated in the terms of 'she' and 'the survivor'. 'She' here could certainly be either Ligeia or Rowena (but for that very reason is probably most usefully thought of as neither of them); 'the survivor' could again be 'the woman' but could also be the narrator; or indeed the reader, and it is this instability of discursive position that seems to me the heart of the tale, or the tale of the heart. What I also find curious about this passage is the notion that hesitation, or hesitancy, is exiled in the tale, most interestingly within a structure where 'fascination' could be seen to be invoked as an 'opposite' to hesitancy. Although I am now straying here from my three-bodied text, I would, were there space, wish to invoke Kierkegaard's remarks in *The Concept of*

Dread (1844) on sin, psychology and fascination:[10] in all manner of ways, but particularly around the crucial term of 'dread', a key to the text of 'Ligeia' but also a key to relocking the terms of hesitation and fascination into the enduring rebus which they – to my mind self-evidently – constitute. Certainty needs no fascination; where there is fascination there is doubt. Dread, one of the words in English which – as is so clearly evidenced in Blake's 'Tyger' and in the political usages of, for example, 'Judge Dredd' and 'dread-locks' where potency and impotence are so crucially intermixed[11] – automatically – perhaps hypnotically or somnambulistically, according to Borch-Jacobsen – signifies within itself an entire structure of opposites. Who is doing the 'dreading' of what in 'The Tyger'? Where is the (always disguised) judge in relation to dread?

'The frame of the story', Bronfen continues, 'presents the success-ful exchange of uncanny ambivalence or intellectual hesitation, for canny uncertainty'. For the moment, I want simply to call attention to the implications of the notion of 'frame', of the presumption that 'Ligeia' *has* a 'frame'; in other words, that within its text one can discern differences of discourse, which might seem to imply, at the very least, *difference* of voice. Bronfen's own rhetoric here clearly picks up on the notion we have come across before, the notion of 'triumph', that the story represents a triumph of the male over the female, of the surviving masculine over the dead female body, all assumptions, I think, which are difficult to stake out on the lawless body of the text itself, which, like many of Poe's short stories, appears to be pathologically monotextual, unrelieved, short of release, stuck in a quagmire of ... shall we call it undecidability or uncertainty, and is the difference Bronfen assumes between the two psychoanalytically sustainable? Or, to put the question in a differ-ent register, what kind of *evidence* does 'Ligeia' present us with, where the possibility of any 'corroboration' has already been sur-passed, dissolved into an obsessively unitary consciousness which has lost all sense of time?

Bronfen concludes her analysis by saying that 'Poe repeats the scenario enacted in his tale in a description of his own response to his wife's dying', and goes on to query the structure of this 'repeti-tion' (what precedes what?), then quoting a relevant paragraph in which 'Poe' is presumed to be recounting his 'real' reactions to 'real' events. If I were here to be trying to get at fundamental difficulties in Bronfen's overall argument – and thus, of course, in other approaches to the Gothic – it would be on this point that I would hinge a lengthier response, which would consist of several moves.

First, and most obvious, there is an assumption here of a 'difference' of textual status, between, shall we say, biographical veracity and fictional distortion, which is given no textual evidence (for there can be none); indeed, the reverse happens, and significance is extracted from the supposed 'biographical' setting of one piece of text at the expense of the other. But this is an unsustainable argument, based on the presupposition that one can 'produce' or evidence one's mourning direct onto the page, in an unproblematic relation between experience and writing. It would be at least equally credible, were one to want to work in such terms, to say that 'Ligeia' 'represents' Poe's response to his wife's dying in a form more 'true' than his letter, in the sense that the unseating of the ego which accompanies mourning has more in common with the delusive structure of 'Ligeia' than with the heavily defended account we get in this quoted piece of supposed 'autobiography'. But as soon as we say this, as soon as we enter into what is clearly a legal quarrel about the status of evidence, we see that the overall 'frame' will not do. To imply it is immediately to simplify the complexities of repetition – mimesis, imitation, which terms will do, which terms are better? The assumed insistence here is on the primacy of the 'outer world' as corroborative evidence for some kind of accuracy or inaccuracy in the inner world: such a structure is epistemologically primitive, although its significance is that it does portray in miniature the problematic struggles within feminist criticism as to the status of 'real-life' evidence and its complex relations to the (patriarchal) law, struggles which are of the first political importance.[12] Can we ask, 'Did Poe really "feel" this way?' If we can, then all the psychoanalytic sophistication goes out of the window, and we are left without an interpretative 'frame', left with suffering bodies and their direct or indirect representation in text. We are left, indeed, in a field where mystical or hieratic moves – all of them moves between genders and between sexualities – will indeed continue, but merely 'dramatised' without benefit of interpretation – and again in this introduction of the term 'dramatised' I am betraying further arguments about the work of the dream and the text.

Let us now turn to 'Ligeia', the 'tale', and begin from the undecidabilities of the epigraph (is there, for example, or was there an incarnation of 'Joseph Glanvill' who would own to this quotation?):

And the will therein lieth, which dieth not. Who knoweth the mysteries of the will, with its vigour? For God is but a great will pervading all things by nature of its intentness. Man doth not yield himself to the angels, nor unto death utterly, save only through the weakness of his feeble will.

(p. 310)

I have made this point elsewhere,[13] but I will make it again, in I hope a different theoretical context and certainly with a different development in mind: the fifth word of this epigraph, 'lieth', is the soul of untruth. To say that the will does not die, is this to tell a lie? Or are we to suppose that the essence of 'will' resides in its undying quality? Glanvill cannot tell us; Poe will not; the narrator, interestingly, repeats the epigraph a little later – or does Ligeia? Or is the epigraph a pre-repetition of, a pretext for, the moment in the tale when this (pre-)quotation becomes narratologically apposite? All those who could tell us are dead, and their evidence is thus, in a sense, legally inadmissible.

The list of questions about 'lieth' could go on for a very long time (as can/does the will? as does the lying which we call fiction? as does the 'lying' in the grave which is here unmistakably 'foreshadowed' and simultaneously, in the same rhetorical gesture, negated/contradicted?). But in this story, what persists and what is superseded or sublated? To take only one example of what we might also call in under the heading of textual parapraxis, we might place side by side two brief scenes. In the course of his textual remembering of the forgetting (or forgetting of the remembering) which contains his *apologia* for his first meetings with Ligeia, the narrator rather doubtfully hypothesises that he 'met her first and most frequently in some large, old, decaying city near the Rhine' (p. 310) which, we presume, he can hardly 'recall'. When Ligeia dies, however (and we have, admittedly, little idea of how much or how little time has elapsed between the two scenes – the reading time is perhaps some ten minutes, but that may not be entirely relevant), we learn that the narrator 'could no longer endure the lonely desolation of my dwelling in the dim and decaying city by the Rhine' (p. 320) where he, presumably, *still is* (whatever that means). Past and present clearly do not fit under the same law; also, to be 'still there' is clearly the pathological condition of the text, as it is the condition, perhaps, of Ligeia.

Let us, for the moment, ignore the barbaric hypothesis, little to be entertained by students of text, that Poe, for reasons we can well imagine, had forgotten what he was doing/saying. What we might more interestingly ask here is the question I momentarily raised above, which is whether there is more than one 'character' in this text. There are obvious things we can say about this old, decaying city beside the Rhine, for example that it is the dream-house,[14] the house of the decaying body, constantly undermined by the flowing of the river, where no memory 'tells', and where more importantly the crucial problems of recollection and reconstruction, to which we shall necessarily return, are constantly re-enacted. But *whose* house? For the wealth, the dubious 'possession', that the narrator comes to 'possess' was Ligeia's; as with so many Gothic castles, the 'tenancy' of this house is under constant threat of erasure, its inheritance unproveable at law.

However, this is the first point at which I believe that Bronfen's 'reconstruction' of 'Ligeia' falls down: for behind it there lies a notion of recollection, of, as I have said above, an unproblematic 'experience' of undifferentiation – and here I mean to refer back to the various mentions of undifferentiation I have made in previous chapters. Is there any 'recollection' in psychoanalysis – any at all? The voice of Borch-Jacobsen again – although in this particular respect it is by no means a unique voice:

> ... however the analyst may attempt to communicate this 'construction' to the patient, he [sic] will not succeed in bringing about real adherence, or real conviction, on the latter's part – in short, there will be no recollection.[15]

And how, we might ask, in this light might the law, if it cannot succeed in bringing about true recollection, proceed towards what may very justly be called the 'reality of conviction'? In the process of psychoanalysis – let us be radical here – there may be no memory *whatsoever*. The subject remembers nothing, not even, perhaps especially not, the (primal) 'scene' of the crime. S/he does not 'remember' some 'experience' of primal unity (the house on the Rhine cannot be 'assigned' to some set of preceding conditioning factors – or, it was probably not even where the murder took place; or, the wrong house, or grave, has been robbed) any more than s/he remembers the intrusion of the father (or the murderer, or burglar). Did Oedipus remember Jocasta, or Laius? Did he even 're-member' them in the other sense, did he put them together as an enduring and satisfying text beyond loss? Hardly.

This decaying city on the Rhine is thus not a 'scenario', it is not some kind of representation of a daytime residue, any more than 'Ligeia' (the story) is some kind of recapitulation of Poe's 'feelings' on the death of his wife, or vice versa. The radical – perhaps though in the end Heideggerian – hypothesis continues: we are *without memory* (in a paradoxically Gothic world, for in Gothic, memory is constantly evoked to be consigned to the abyss), we are in a realm where we need endlessly to compensate for a lack; or better still, for the lack of a lack, for the inability to own even to amnesia before the law. And this brings me back to the very first point which Bronfen makes about 'Ligeia', which is that it is a tale of mourning, for there is a redoubling in the notion of mourning which needs further attention.[16]

Tending the grave; preserving the 'evidence'. For mourning too is the lack of a lack; it is, if you like to speak mechanistically or hydraulically, a compensation for doubled loss. It is a symbolism in the outer of a loss in the outer, and thus it can only compensate for what is *not* compensated in the inner. But then, the whole effort of the narrator in 'Ligeia' is, endlessly, to 'deaden impressions of the outward world' (p. 310), to blur distinctions of time and frame. 'While I write, a recollection flashes upon me' – we are still on the first page of the story – how are we to unpack this alibi? To 'recollect' would be to gather back together (legal) evidences of a beginning, of, we might say with regard to the gender implications, an entry, a penetration into some presumed primal field. We are told pretty soon that this is *not* the pre-structure of *this* story, at least, which has no concern with discerning the origin of oppositions. The image of the 'flash' is an apt one: it occurs when the narrator tells us that, having already apprehended the all-important 'shadow' (p. 311), he finds that what he never can 'recollect' is a moment at which Ligeia entered his study. He never saw her come in; she was always there. To anticipate a little: there is no intrusion, no otherness here; there is no dealing with a simple binary psychic field (even a *fort/da*);[17] there is instead something quite different, a discourse of hypnosis and somnambulism (Borch-Jacobsen's terms, but also terms, or at least modes, familiar to us all through the Gothic), which takes us back to a level not only before the symbolic but also *before the imaginary*, a level of primary identification. Even if that seems incomprehensible in itself, I suggest that it does take

on a force from precisely the structure into which the symbolic
and the imaginary have been forced, as heuristic terms, as they too
have been moved into the position of opponents in a (gender-
based) power play, and it takes us also, to my mind, back beyond
gender, although in ways which will, in the end, refer us to gender
again; although by a different route and by way of different questions.

Poe knows these ambiguities of recollection:

> There is no point, among the many incomprehensible anomalies
> of the science of mind, more thrillingly exciting than the fact –
> never, I believe, noticed in the schools – that, in our endeavours
> to recall to memory something long forgotten, we often find
> ourselves *upon the very verge* of remembrance, without being
> able, in the end, to remember.
>
> (pp. 313–4)

Why this 'detail' should be thrillingly exciting is perhaps a question which can be best left to the sexual psychopathology so evidently suggested; but what, we might fairly ask, can this narrator
then possibly remember of, for example, the work of the 'schools'?
What is certain is that within the text he moves from one site of
'decay' to another, recalling the instability and undecidability of
atomic half-lives; this process of decay is one which had no beginning, no origin – 'have I *ever* found Ligeia at fault?' (p. 315) – and
no destination – 'the unforgotten Ligeia' (p. 321). There is no shad-
ing of experience here, no ability to wield power in the name of, or
on the body of, the Other; instead there is a radical openness of the
subject to unrecognisable influxes, which might be memories or
might be something quite different – sensations, imprints, substitu-
tions – which have little bearing on the ordering mechanisms of
psychic structure:

> I have said, that I minutely remember the details [*sic*] of the
> chamber – yet I am sadly forgetful on the topics of deep moment;
> and here there was no system, no keeping, in the fantastic dis-
> play, to take hold upon the memory.
>
> (p. 321)

'No system, no keeping': but *where*, precisely, is the narrator
finding this 'absence', this lack or deficiency? Textually, he could

be referring by 'here' to 'the chamber', or he could be referring to his own psyche; again it is the indissoluble link between the two, or rather the impossibility of discrimination between the two, that grounds the story.

The search in the tale takes, it seems to me, little of its form from Ligeia, or Rowena; even the elision of the one into the other seems curiously beside the point. What this search is about is two things. First, it is about the problem of possession, the problem Borch-Jacobsen emblematises in his discourse of somnambulism and hypnosis, of what it might mean to be possessed by another, of the ambiguous presence of the foreign body within, yet not within, the soul, of not being legally responsible for one's own apparent actions (yet of being illegally responsible for them, whatever that may mean). Towards the end of the tale the narrator tells us this, as he searches precisely for a formulation of 'possession' which will step beyond its illegalities and ambiguities, the ambiguities in which, to take another example, analyst and analysand perennially find themselves as they struggle with each other's suggestions, and struggle further with finding something which lies beyond the egoic demands that are all we have to succour us in the floating world of somnambulistic discourse. He (the narrator) finds it – where else? – in a text, in a phrase: 'to restore my self-possession' (p. 327), which we may gloss as 'to establish a boundary', or 'to prevent invasion', or 'to disentangle myself from the scenarios, the dramatisations, of death by which I am surrounded'. Or, indeed, 'to expel the foreign body'; but if the foreign body were expelled, then not only would the structure of the psyche be assailed, the very notion of psychic structure of any kind would disintegrate and we would be returned to the psychotic state that 'Ligeia' barely and painfully holds at bay.

But regrettably such a conclusion can never be reached, as the tale itself does not reach a conclusion – certainly not in terms of gender and power. For the narrator's second search, linked to the first, is for certainty: to be restored to his perception of faultlessness (ascribed to Ligeia) but in some way without the Gothic taint of sleep and dream which has hitherto accompanied it. In a sense, this is achieved: ' "Here then, at least", I shrieked aloud, "can I never – can I never be mistaken..." ' (p. 330). This 'revelation' is, of course, unmistakably linked to death, to terror, to the dawning knowledge that the world beyond mistakes is also the world in which one's worst fears become real; but what is also interesting about this 'final' formulation of the narrator's quest is its repetition within itself ('can I never – can I never'), or, we may say by way of return to the earlier *topos* of fascination, the moment of textual hesitation which necessarily undermines, in the very act of speaking, the attainment of certainty. We might usefully summarise these doubts in terms of a myth of the law, the notion of the 'identity parade'; who is recognising whom, who is dreading whom, as we stroll, lost in the funhouse, before the gallery of lookalikes and enact, no doubt, a repetition, or rather a number of different repetitions, of the primal crime?

I want to turn now away from the story and to Borch-Jacobsen, and to begin (again) with a short series of quotations which seem to me to have a strong bearing on 'Ligeia' and the kinds of fears about psychic structuring it might represent, and also to shed some light on the complexities of Gothic. For Borch-Jacobsen, issues of 'reading' in any sense are inextricably bound up, as was Freud's life's work, with hypnosis. 'The hypnotist awakens in the subject', Borch-Jacobsen quotes from Freud, 'a portion of his archaic heritage which had also made him compliant towards his parents and which had experienced an individual re-animation (*eine individuelle Wiederbelebung*) in his relation to his father.'[18] This 're-animation', it seems to me, describes the dénouement of the tale; as it also goes some way to describing the chronic confusion of affect in the narrator, for the emotions he feels towards Ligeia are not emotions which he has managed to cathect away from himself, they are instead mirrored emotions within the elements of his very subject, and they cannot be extracted from the background of a suffocating, fatal compliance; which we might also connect with the 'longing to confess' which underlies, while, rather like the Rhine flowing beneath the dream-house, it also undermines both legal process and the technique of psychoanalysis.

> ... hypnosis leads us back to the very type of identification – devouring identification – whose relation to the ideal Freud was trying to define.... All things considered, incorporation must instead be viewed as *incarnation*: one subject emerges incarnating the other, body and soul.[19]

This takes us close to the heart of the problem. Bronfen speaks – and in critical dealings with 'Ligeia' and others of Poe's tales she is far from alone in this – a rhetoric of incorporation and appropria-

tion: a language of power and assimilation. Now, that rhetoric is of
the utmost importance; but it has none the less to be predicated on
a clear set of demarcation lines within and around the subject; it
has, in the end, to be based for instance on a notion of sexual
boundaries as stable rather than processual.

What Borch-Jacobsen is suggesting is quite different, appropriately because it is based on a different theory in which primary
identification lies *behind* (but is never absent from) the later complexes and mechanisms. Borch-Jacobsen's theory is indeed the
more truly 'Freudian', we might say if we wish to pursue the
'more-Freudian-than-thou' game, in that in recognising the primacy of identification it also, perhaps paradoxically, takes more
seriously the issue of contradiction. It is not hard to see how bodies
or minds – or texts – incorporate or appropriate each other: we are
dealing here with basically physical models, with everyday processes. But to understand the (Gothic) notions of re-animation and
incarnation requires an approach which is far more genuinely
'uncanny', and which recognises that the perceptions we need as
we try to inspect the subject cannot be predicated merely on models of takeover and devouring.

This is not at all to say that there is not violence, either in the
psyche or in Poe's story; but for Borch-Jacobsen it will have a
'different' origin, and one with a general relevance for Gothic. We
will not be looking at 'a buried sadistic instinct joining forces with
the Oedipal impulse' – a developmentally belated formulation –
but at 'the aggressiveness that the Double inevitably arouses' – as,
Borch-Jacobsen adds, was so well-known by Hoffmann, Dos-
toevsky and Poe himself.[20] Why is this aggressiveness aroused?
Not, Borch-Jacobsen says decisively, because of some formation of
jealousy arising from the intrusion of the third party, however we
might want to frame the Oedipal hypothesis, but before that: 'no
doubt the double is loved, since I love myself in him [*sic*]; but that
is also why he provokes hatred and hostility, precisely inasmuch as
he is close to me, too close.'[21] This is an older, originary formation:
seeing ourselves scares the life out of us.[22] What infant wants to
share?

Thus far, perhaps, we may go with Borch-Jacobsen, but it will be
readily seen that there is a yawning hiatus in my argument, which
is precisely in the central area of gender. If the tone, the mood, the
repetitions, the symbolism of 'Ligeia' all go towards suggesting a
text struggling with problems of primary identification rather than

with later Oedipal structures, this nevertheless explains nothing
about Ligeia; if the figure of the Double, in Borch-Jacobsen's new
reworking of it, gains a new kind of primacy, then what has this to
do with the text, for the narrator has no double, and surely the
doubling of Ligeia and Rowena, important though it is, has all the
textual hallmarks of an evasion, of a series of attempts to deal in a
projective way with buried subject-matter?

We are back again in the realm of the object of desire; or rather in
that problematic world before desire comes to an object; and we are
thus with Borch-Jacobsen's reading of Freud on object orientation,
which 'is homosexual at the outset, and the libido at first cathects
only doubles'.[23] Now, this hypothesis – or, as we might hope to see,
the body of clinical evidence that might confirm this hypothesis –
has, to my mind, an immediate and destabilising effect on many
arguments about the Gothic. For what we have to face here – what
Gothic seems frequently, hesitantly, to have tried to face – is the
sense in which heterosexuality itself, the basis of legalised sexual
relating, is always tainted with 'perversion'.[24] Far from figuring as
an 'emergence', it figures *also and at the same time* as an entry into
the forbidden, into taboo: not because of the 'memory' or 'experience' of the maternal body, whatever that might be, but because it
opens a fissure, or 'fault', in the subject and thus has always to do
with death.

Hence, therefore, the way to deal with this is to deal with the
other sex, but only under the sign of death; and therefore the
massive preoccupation with dead women which Bronfen finds in
her texts is bound up not so much with primary psychic structures
in themselves as with the way in which they are mediated through
text, through a patriarchal institution of writing. At a simple level,
of course, Bronfen connects this instituting with her subject-matter,
but what we might further want to see is the way in which the
dealing with the apparent other 'at the site of death' is precisely in
itself a process of subject-formation, with all the ambiguities which
the problem of individualisation invites.

The problem here can be recast in terms, again, of the relation
between ego and the unconscious, and in his central argument
under the Freudian heading 'Dreams are Completely Egoistic'
Borch-Jacobsen quotes Freud to this effect:

I have spoken above of the egoism of children's minds, and I
may now add, with a hint at a possible connection between the

two facts, that dreams have the same characteristic. All of them are completely egoistic (*absolut egoistich*): the beloved ego appears in all of them, even though it may be disguised. The wishes that are fulfilled in them are invariably the ego's wishes, and if a dream seems to have been provoked by an altruistic interest, we are only being deceived by appearances.[25]

Perhaps the reference to a possible altruism of dreams seems now old-fashioned; but the central point about the egoism of dreams none the less remains all-important. The 'play', the dramatisation present in 'Ligeia' is, as we are reminded in the title – and thus the promise – of the poem within the text, 'the tragedy, Man' (p. 319).

And who, or what, are the characters in this poem, and/or in the play 'within' it?

> Mimes, in the form of God on high,
>   Mutter and mumble low,
> And hither and thither fly;
>   Mere puppets they, who come and go
> At bidding of vast formless things
>   That shift the scenery to and fro,
> Flapping from out their Condor wings
>   Invisible Woe!
>
> (p. 318)

Let us immediately place this alongside a passage in which Borch-Jacobsen speaks of:

> the same ambiguous *lexis* in which the 'I' speaks (and desires, and enjoys) in the name and in the place of another, without our knowing for certain whether that 'I' has ever been located any-where except in resemblance, where it plays all roles and simu-lates all identities.[26]

Has the narrator of 'Ligeia', locked in his dim city on the Rhine or in its later equivalent, ever 'been located anywhere except in resemblance', or indeed in all-important 'appearances' – and if so, how could the law ever find him or, one might aptly say, 'bring him to book'? These 'mimes' are surely precisely the forms of the ego which entertain us nightly with their dramatisations of desiring processes – never, we must add, simply of the desired

object itself, dreams are not like that, but enactments of the ego's
own continuing drama, which does not stop when the lights go
out. *Oedipus Rex*, after all, is not an epic poem; it is a play.

Naturally, in this literal process of *mimesis*, what gets acted is – at
least – the form of God on high, the ego-ideal, and thus the Gothic
revenant who can achieve immortality by defeating death or execution – Ligeia's strength of will is the strength of the narrator's own
will, his own desire towards re-animation, towards incarnation.
But the voices here are unclear, they 'mutter and mumble low';
even here, on this stage, the censorship (the death or murder of the
will) cannot be evaded wholly. Most striking though about the
poem and its situation in the text is surely its obscured readerly
position; who *is* this in the witness box?

> At high noon of the night on which she departed, beckoning me,
> peremptorily, to her side, [Ligeia] bade me repeat [*sic*] certain
> verses composed by herself not many days before. I obeyed her.
> (p. 318)

Leaving aside the curious and suggestive formulation 'high noon
of the night', leaving aside also the apparently conventional but
still unsettling reference to Ligeia's 'departure', what we most
significantly have here is a 'merging' of voices, an incarnation, a
re-animation. The words may be dead; how can they be brought to
life? Not through Ligeia's own voice, for she does not have one; but
neither again through the narrator's voice, for he has no words to
speak, he is spellbound and thus tongue-tied; we might say that he
is under hypnosis, which would render him not responsible for his
actions, unable to give evidence, and would also distort time
through a series of unpredictable repetitions. The poem instead
issues from a doubled process of writing and reading, script and
speech, text and evidence (did Ligeia write these verses down? has
the narrator learned them 'by heart', as perhaps he indeed 'learned
Ligeia by heart'?), it is in itself surely such a 'motley drama' as is
the play it purports to describe, and in relation to which it effects a
further move away from certainty of origin or attribution.

We can also look at this from another (albeit quasi-Oedipal)
angle, and say that we are dealing here, as we are throughout
'Ligeia', with kinds of blindness. Borch-Jacobsen speaks of 'a non-
specular identification (blind mimesis) in which consists (if he/it
consists) the entire "subject" of the fantasy'.[27] Who or what is the

'subject' of the poem; or of the tragedy 'Man'; or of the tale itself? The complexities, the slippings and slidings here cannot be reduced to a notion as simple as the 'gaze'; if there were space enough it would indeed be good to go on to look at the remarkable play of discourse around Ligeia's extraordinary eyes, but what would be shown would only be a renewed, a redoubled blinding which is, in a way, a doubled inversion of the rhetoric of scopophilia: the narrator may indeed 'behold' Ligeia, but in doing so he is dazzled, and the object is removed from his sight, just as it exists in a condition of continuous erasure in his memory. The narrator cannot remember where he met her, cannot plumb the fathomless depths of her eyes, can indeed neither recollect nor reconstruct her at all: of course not, because he *is* Ligeia, but more importantly, while he is being her he obviously cannot see her, he is locked into a 'blind mimesis' in which all his gestures become unintelligible to himself and he is reduced to the condition of sleepwalking, the 'subject' of a somnambulistic passion which, to return to an earlier point, I would name, if name it has to have, as dread, that dread which, we are told in the story, at least Rowena feels as 'the fierce moodiness of my [the narrator's] temper' (p. 323), a dread which, however, appears to give the narrator pleasure since after all, according to his own account – or is it? is it not rather the reintrojected account of Ligeia's feelings towards her live successor? – he 'loathed her [Rowena] with a hatred belonging more to demon than to man'.

'I was possessed', we should by now not be surprised to find the narrator saying elsewhere, and in terms reminiscent of those one might use in a court of law to explain the grip of the passions, 'with a passion [*sic*] to discover' (p. 313); like, very obviously, Frankenstein and so many others, but the redoubling of possession is if anything more stark here. The question which I have not answered, obviously, is about specificity: to what extent might the processes I suggest to be operating in 'Ligeia' be general processes of textuality, to be general to the interchanges between the text, the body and the law; to what extent might they be genre-specific, endemic, for example, to Gothic; to what extent might we see Poe as a writer particularly open to the backward moves, to the regressions and somnambulisms which abut onto these primary (or pre-primary) psychic structures? And finally, and just as important, if what I am uncovering here is a masculine writing position, would it be

possible for women writers (of Gothic, for example) to move
beyond the identificatory processes offered to them in patriarchy?

It may not be possible to be sure of the answers to these questions: but one way of tackling them is by pointing out that the
notion 'female Gothic' suffers from an undecidable doubling of
language reminiscent precisely of the problem of possession
(which, as we know, is on the one hand nine points of the law,
and on the other a criminal offence). Gothic by women, Gothic
about women, Gothic possessed by or possessive of women; female
Gothic because there is some intrinsic link between femininity and
the Gothic imagination, or because the Gothic imagination is
peopled by women – not 'merely' as mothers, but as forbidden
heterosexual objects of desire, or as prior occupants of a desired
domestic space, symbols for the vicissitudes of identification,
within a masculised writing process? What is sure is that in Gothic
we are frequently in a world where the dramatisations of the ego
are nakedly revealed as locked into a series of specular identifications, where legally verifiable 'character stability' is beside the
point: the ferocity of the connexion between women and death in
modern culture seems to me to be a mark of the intensity of the
sense of inescapability, being locked in front of the mirror where
vision only comes in the form of the most unthinkable (sexual)
transformation of all – as Angela Carter, for example, knew so
well.[28]

An inconclusion to this chapter, which is also in part, of course, a
repetition: 'Man doth not yield himself to the angels, nor unto
death utterly, save only through the weakness of his feeble will'
(Poe? Glanvill?); 'it [the ego] never avoids yielding to an identification and always confuses itself in some way with another' (Borch-
Jacobsen? Freud?). Which story, which narrative, would we prefer
to believe, a narrative of precarious transcendence and immortality,
a narrative of the inescapability of hypnosis? Are the satisfactions
offered by either of these 'dread-ful' tales separable from each
other? When we are acting all the parts in the dramatisation, a
dramatisation which ends in the death of the characters before an
absent audience, an audience which has already left the theatre, or
perhaps the court of law, before the dénouement of the tragedy,
how, if at all, can we tell the difference?

7

A Descent into the Body:
Wuthering Heights

In the system of jealousy, it is not unusual for the subject to end up destroying the sequestered object or being, due to a sense of the impossibility of completely averting the misfortunes of the world and of his own sexuality. Here passion reaches its logical and illogical end.[1]

And how, indeed, can we 'tell the difference' in/of *Wuthering Heights*:

> I lingered round them, under that benign sky; watched the moths fluttering among the heath and hare-bells; listened to the soft wind breathing through the grass; and wondered how anyone could ever imagine unquiet slumbers, for the sleepers in that quiet earth.[2]

The well-known final paragraph of the novel, in its action of 'closing', reintroduces us to many of the problems which have been with us from the 'start'. The originating 'I' is unfixed, as we have now seen so often in Gothic, hovering phantasmatically between Lockwood and the potential 'unlocking' of an authorial persona, itself the withheld subject position of the text. The accounts we have already been given by Lockwood, Nelly Dean, the diary, the pieces of evidence which we are implicitly required to fit together to constitute a presentable 'case', slot into each other only like a badly tessellated pavement; between the slabs of description and history the weeds of uncertainty sprout through and hint that we could, at some always deferred future time, infer the authorial position from this strange geometry of the unintended, the return of base, organic, unsorted matter through the over-neat rearrangements of self-serving character/narrators. Were this to happen, then we might find ourselves in the position of the resurrection of the body; but the consequence of this re-eruption through the ground would be the destruction of all textual reliability, a further and possibly disastrous assault on evidential veracity in line with the continual attempts made by Gothic to probe and search for the illegal possibilities of writing, the provision or discovery of papers with no authenticity, the manufacture of false passports to countries of whose very existence the authorities (we are to suppose) remain in ignorance.

Yet to take the image through another twist, we might say that here the position is reversed because what is imminently forcing itself through the quiet/unquiet surface is not an incipient authorial decision, a solution to doubt, but instead the irresistible presence, even after death, of the characters themselves: 'heath' and 'hare-bells', Heathcliff and Hareton, not lost beneath the earth but *imprinted* on it from beneath, so that the continuing existence of the terrain of the natural itself is inseparable from the various twists and turns, at all sorts of interpretative levels, which these characters will unstoppably continue to 're-present'. Here there is no final burial, and in this sense we have a figure for textuality itself; if textuality is predicated upon loss and absence, upon the putative irrecoverability of experience except in the form of the phantom, then burial itself is denied by the very existence of text, and we may see the processes of writing as themselves an affirmation, as Poe clearly saw, of the fact that all burial is premature; we might even say that it is a mere excuse, in a realm where death and somnambulism are indistinguishable, for the inscription of the epitaph.[3]

But the destruction of decidability which keys this last paragraph of the text, this final *sentence* (of death, or a life sentence?), is – not surprisingly – at its most intense in the last clause, which carries to the limit an undecidable freight of two opposing meanings. The construction 'how anyone could ever imagine' may mean at first glance to propose to us what a desecration of these quiet slumbers it would be to fantasise the fate of the sleepers otherwise; but an equally valid alternative reading would be as a summons to imaginative fire, a challenge to portray adequately the unquestionable 'unquietnesses' to which these graves might really be subject. What is crucial is that both readings are, as it were, in the future; both represent *projects*, and jointly they therefore imply the impossibility of using past narrative to achieve a fixity of reference (an epitaph), even while simultaneously suggesting and withholding the way(s) in which the future might come to the relief of a past perceived as intolerably burdensome and vertiginously freeing in the same instant. In this motif of our mixed desire to elude and relive the past (the sleep, we might say, of Verezzi/veracity) we touch again on our ambiguous relation to that truth about the past which the law comes to demand of us: where indeed were we last Tuesday week at 6.30 in the evening, and how many other evenings, nights, days, have to pass before us in a constructed panoply of memory before we alight on the correct 'version'; a version, perhaps, which, when it emerges, will turn out to be one which nobody, even ourselves, has ever 'heard' before, a perversion of experience, an experience of 'perversion' (of the truth, of justice)?

I offer these introductory comments on an 'introductory conclusion' merely to set the scene for an encounter with *Wuthering Heights* in which I want to try to produce a journey. This journey will proceed through five levels of depth; at all points this hierarchical metaphor will, naturally, remain open to (site) inspection, but I should like to go into the ground before the ground seethes upwards to meet me, to inspect the crypt before it spews its contents out and prevents forever the possibility of a (premature) ending; to take such a journey as *Wuthering Heights* [sic] invites. My way of arranging these levels will, therefore, be open to criticism, but I shall try to justify it as I go along. I am fully aware too that the whole depth metaphor is itself open to a further range of objections,[4] but I do not think we can do without it. Our waking lives are spent in realms where space is largely encountered in the two dimensions representing the surface of the planet; in our dreams – and without dream there can be no interpretation, for we can, in my view, have no image of the Other to provide the dark background against which we can pick out our design – it is, perhaps *for this very reason*, not such a world that we encounter, but rather one composed of fallings, risings, elevators and staircases, transformations of depth, upside-down-nesses, trapdoors and spaces beneath the ocean, oppressive mines and vast halls below the earth, all the imagery which we see in the continuing mythical elaboration of Hades.[5]

I am constantly aware that the discourse of the text, the body and the law, secured if anywhere on a Freudian and deconstructive terrain, might seem to offer little space to a term like 'Hades', or to other mythic figurings; yet it is also, and compellingly, true that in the Gothic, in the logic of the phantom, such mythic constructions are inescapable; indeed, they frequently image this in

themselves by taking on the ancient form and feature of the pursuer. Hades, however, was no pursuer; what we might need to
'remember' about him, as I have mentioned before, is that he was
the darkest god, the richest, and also the wisest; so every attempt at
interpretation, at such an activity as literary critics (commonly?)
'pursue', is necessarily an attempt at an encounter with him, an
attempt, always shadowed by fear, to come into the full view of a
figure so attractive that, as the myths tell us, once we have seen his
face free from the shadows we will never wish to leave.[6]

Five levels. I do not include among these five levels the field or
'heath' which we have already encountered in our quotation,
which we might usefully figure as the field of Demeter;[7] but it
must always be from here that the journey begins. This is the
field on which characters wander, gathering flowers, performing
ritual dances, placating gods of the natural world, as do we 'students of nature' when we read text as though these characters of
fiction might be the object of real encounter, when we assume an
unproblematic account of experience. This is the world of corn-
gods and harmless fertility, the world where we can as readers, at
most but sometimes to considerable effect, work at our self-images
and identifications, fall into the ambiguous passions of Catherine,
stride the twisted moorland with Heathcliff, warm the dangerous
fires of romance in Nelly Dean's kitchen.

Yet on this 'fair field', interpretation itself figures as the Other:
interpretation is dark where these opennesses are full of light and
brightness, imbued with the sense that we are all companions here,
parts of the same human order, an order to which even the divine
and the animal are not foreign for all things are 'under that benign
sky' – not of course in the sense that everything that happens is
good but in the wider Panglossian sense, which is basically negative and claims that nothing that happens can terminally disturb
our linked senses of the possibility of truth before the law, of the
fitness of life, of the significance of personality, of the uncomplic-
ated reality of slender reason and the yielding affections.

Wuthering Heights in the world of the fields of Demeter is, we
might unoriginally say, a love story; and it is from this version of
the text that its main progeny have come, in the shape of the entire
subgenre of romantic fiction in which dark brooding villains pursue innocent blonde women across terrific landscapes; Gothic with
a slight but pleasing 'flash' of intellectual sophistication. There is
tragedy in this version, certainly, but the emphasis within the tragic

feeling is upon the sigh of mingled sadness and relief, with underlying it a sense of the beauteous rightness of things, the working
out of a doom or destiny which now leaves *us*, perhaps, freer
through our temporary readerly immersion in, our purgation
through, this curious consummation.

We can now move, then, to the first interpretative level – that is,
we descend the first staircase, or the first tunnel leading down from
the grave, figured as this garden of earthly delights – when we
tackle the sociological and historical implications of all this. We
move down when, for example, we see the text as telling not only
the story of individuals but also the story of a 'house', *oikos*, a
family vacuously yet potently infected by a hollowness at its
heart, that 'heart' which Derrida speaks of *as* the poem;[8] a hollowness of succession which is filled by the expansion of Heathcliff; as
something will always come to fill a shell, for example, or the trunk
of a rotten tree, something dark without real substance, something
which will, in the end, triumphantly kill off the lingering 'semblance' and challenge legal identity at its root.[9]

Here we are in a world where a master can be named a master,
and a servant a servant, with all that implies. We might say,
searching for a mythic correlate, that we are in the brutally effective
world of Zeus (or indeed of the 'divine' Caesar in, for instance,
Antony and Cleopatra),[10] where all is in its rightful place and hierarchy and order prevail. Zeus rules over the other gods: he does so,
paradoxically, by occupying this median position, holding the keys
to all the depths while allowing the fictions of Demeter to hold
sway on the surface, concealing his reign and his determinations,
the disguised judge.[11]

Precisely because of the insistent barriers we encounter in this
world – Zeus is also frequently and in many guises the god of the
nation state, the god of racial and class separation – our attention in
Wuthering Heights rightly focuses on the 'president' of the narrative,
Nelly Dean, and what comes into view is the ambiguity of her class
status, an ambiguity which she shares with a much wider tradition
of governesses, nannies, housekeepers, but which is here allowed a
rare freedom of voice, what we might call the 'medium's tale'
which speaks to us of the passing of an age, of the end of an
order to history: 'Joseph will take care of the house, and, perhaps,
a lad to keep him company. They will live in the kitchen, and the
rest will be shut up.'[12] 'Shut up', closed off, silenced; an end with
no possibility of regeneration, of rebirth, for there is no agency by

means of which this could occur. We may be consigned to an endless life in the kitchen, but the world we are in is nevertheless recognisably the world of revolution, whether achieved or denied, the revolt of the sons against the father, Zeus set in the darker background of Cronos, a world of class oppression and the ineffectively deferred bitterness of social change.

At this first level of depth, then, the rule of law is mooted and sanctioned; we are, of course, allowed our views as to whether this sanctioning is justifiable or tyrannical, but since all revolutions in this realm, all temporary outbursts of terrorist activity, end the same way, this is a merely temporary hiatus in the 'body politic'. Indeed, the *body* politic might be taken as emblematic of this realm, the body, perhaps, of Foucault, subjected to a series of regimes of surveillance which certainly claim an erotic potential through the games of sado-masochism, through the oscillations of discipline and punishment, but which is centrally reduced to a site of lines of power, of thin threads which operate through and through the meagre body and which reduce it to the status of a puppet at the mercy of rule from a disembodied sovereign.[13]

If we travel below this, though, it is further to question these notions of continuity and discontinuity: to ask what features of the psyche are engaged transhistorically, what it is in this text, in any text, which provides us not only with a transformative historical account but also with a transformed image of the psyche. At the next level we find ourselves, where we have (always) been before, in the world of Narcissus. We can also name it the world of psychoanalytical interpretation, which spins out the endless thread from the heart (poem) of ourselves and thus places in question our notions of integrity and disintegration.[14]

A psychoanalytic interpretation of *Wuthering Heights* could begin from many points; let us alight upon names and family trees. The family tree, the graphic account of our legal origins, is textually present in the Introduction to most current editions;[15] but what it does, I would say, is to provide *one* version of interpretation against which the text itself determinedly and repeatedly, in a spirit of delinquency and chaos, poses another, according to which it is emphatically *not* the case that all can be sorted into different categories and what remains crucial is the *re-naming*: the two Catherines, for instance, or the slipping and sliding of patronymics, which is all evidence of *unwillingness* to name as the ego tries to protect itself from danger. The illegality, the resistance to the law, with which *Wuthering Heights* engages is here signified precisely in the *impossibility* of the family tree; all genealogies (even genealogies of morals) encounter the same problem, which is that the facts are irrecoverable in their complexity; and they also come up against the paradox that as they move backwards through time they are subject at once to the pressure of extreme multiplicity and to the pressure of a unitary myth of origins. Genealogies, family trees, thus figure precisely that dilemma of psychoanalysis which we have come across before, the imponderable coexistence within the same subject of differentiation and undifferentiation, even as they enact a rally in relation to 'family secrets', an exposure which will turn out to be an even deeper burial.

These dangers are many, but in *Wuthering Heights* we might see them as focused on incest, and incest as the taboo which the text ceaselessly (and circularly) tries to circumvent, finally even placing, as we have seen, Heathcliff and Hareton in the same (linguistic, symbolic) grave in the hope that something new might be born. Here 'lies' (endlessly, as the soul of untruth, resisting all legal simplifications, beyond the 'will' in both of its most common meanings) the 'end of the line', but dead now not from historical necessity but out of psychic exhaustion, the victim of the pressured intensity of family. These problems of duplication and reduplication are basic to the structuring of the text and also to our reading of it: because the ego squirms, because the 'I' slips and slides through a multitude of voices, we never know where it is: to pick up any random paragraph is to engage immediately with a grappling to locate the unfixed narrator, to convert the undecidable unconscious into the material of judgment and decision.

These worlds of Zeus and Narcissus, we might further say, are themselves twinned images: images of masculinity *as* a dual realm where freedom of choice has not prevailed, and also in terms of the struggle between hetero- and homosexuality, between prolific fathering and self-fathering, between myths of human fertility and older notions of the wind-born child.[16] In these two worlds we are driven by force: a force endlessly modified yet endlessly repeated through the master/slave dialectic, through the incarnation of the Name-of-the-Father, which, as we have seen, is a surrogate for anxiety about the female.[17] These worlds construct themselves through fictions of stability, no less fixed because they are constantly enacted through the revolutions of the under-class, the primal horde, the criminalised body.

In our next, third realm, however, neither god can prevail and even Zeus – who eventually rules this level as he rules all others, as the myths tell us – does not care to visit it. It is ruled instead by a plurality, a collective: known within psychoanalysis mainly by its Jungian name as the multiple force of anima, which lives precisely through fictions of unity and separation.[18] In terms of interpretation, we might say that we are in the realm feminism knows as gynocracy, and we immediately, and appropriately, encounter a difficulty about mythic naming, which is clearly related to the naming difficulties which run through *Wuthering Heights*. Apart from the simplicities of Demeter, the deeper, darker goddesses overlap as they commune, Artemis, Aphrodite, Persephone; these cannot be pinned down to specific attributes because to do is to collude in the worlds of masculine vision and replication, it is to assert the separability and immunity of the body. But this realm is also one of mutual contamination, of 'unspeakable' and non-reproductive couplings, perhaps in Hecate's world of household waste (a commutation of the kitchen as domestic space), which carries with it all the symbolism of the infected body, the body which bears the mark of its involuntary immersion in a world where the control systems have gone down and which is thus subject to a failure of immunisation.[19]

In this realm *Wuthering Heights* becomes, in the terms of James Hillman, further 'darkened'.[20] We see it as a tale of gender oppression; the materials for these readings are not, of course, wholly distinct from those engaged with on the levels above, precisely because it is of the nature of these sorts of interpretative exercise that these materials are always pre-processed, always partly digested by predecessor psychic forms, always gesturing us backwards towards the undifferentiated and the pre-Oedipal, to the dark murmurings of the child 'still' within the womb. Thus, then, we have seen already the fate of Catherine but we have not seen this placed against the dark background of unavoidability, the fearsome repetition of violence towards women of which we have heard Poe and Bronfen speak. Yet this 'unavoidability' feels different from the determinisms of Zeus and Narcissus: for it contains also the seeds of an equally unavoidable fury, the echo of savage goddesses – again often multiple – who hover around the mythic fringes, whose force, at the end of the day, might be to say: Let us bury them *all* under the surface, they have offended against the Great Mother and the time for discriminations is over.[21]

This reading – which I take to be 'feminist', though others may not – says also that the shapes of masculinity fall under the ban on discrimination: no modification of behaviour, no Thrushcross Grange, no quiet and gentleness, no stilling of the will or Wordsworthian attempt to reincorporate the masculine with the forms of nature, will atone for the history of phallic bloodshed which is *Wuthering Heights*. From now on there will be only ambiguous prophecies, following from the withdrawal of unconditional nurture signified by the untrustworthy Nelly, re-perceived now as enacting righteous indignation at masculine betrayal of the species. Heathcliff's orphan status, his accession to the fatal law of the orphan, makes him an *instrument* but not the moving cause of vengeance: he is the shape men produce for themselves in nightmare when there is no mother-training in passion, and passion is consequently transformed down the evolutionary scale into obsession.[22] The fate and intention of obsession is death, of the self and of the Other; but its root, seen at this level, lies in our failure to sacrifice to the goddesses, by whose means alone do we remain stable on the turning world.

It is at this point that we might begin to grasp the alternative form of the law which *Wuthering Heights* proffers, and with which the Gothic has always been concerned. I have called it 'the law of the orphan'. It is worth remembering that all these connexions with the law have a root in those figurations of the law which we discussed in the second chapter, in the paradoxical image of the law as the soul of injustice and untruth; for the writers we discussed there, the counter-position to the law (as to the 'family' with its imponderable secrets and desires for blood vengeance) lies within narrative positions which know no parenting, within characters whose patronymy (and 'will') is uncertain and unstable. Thus, certainly – and here emblematically in Heathcliff – one source for the 'search', the quest: to find one's name, to find a way of inserting oneself into a world in some other way than 'merely' as a 'foreign body' to the other (although this remains Heathcliff's own location). But thus also an emblematic relation between text and world; where the birth of a child adds to the world (in metaphor), the birth of a text detracts from it, multiplies the possibilities of loss, of worlds into which one may not enter, of events through which one cannot live.

On the fourth level, all this has changed. Here there appear to be no gods; there appears also to be an alleviation of the hitherto increasing darkness of our journey. There appears, in fact, to be no discrimination at all: no substantial objects are visible, but only a shadow-play of differences where curious shapes, neither wholly threatening nor wholly pleasing, emerge and recede in the shadows; a world where all passion is spent and colour has ebbed away. Mythically we are in limbo, interpretatively we might say that we are in a realm adumbrated particularly by deconstruction, where anything can take place but nothing can remain. We are, if you like a more positive image, on Prospero's island, where we hear strange echoes and 'twanglings' in the night, but although we can catch them for a moment in the flow of memory the morning is always imminent in which nothing will be remembered and, in any case, nothing will be the same; there will only be traces for us to interpret (though never in freedom) how we 'will'.

A deconstructive reading of *Wuthering Heights* can begin, of course, anywhere: its 'generative gesture' is always 'For example:...'. For example. For example, we could say that the text is a text *about* naming, and thus we would reverse the flow of previous interpretations: there is nothing real behind these forms, but the sign of 'Emily Brontë'/'Ellis Bell' stands as the sign *towards* which our efforts must be directed, and all the problems of namings, genealogies, characterological overlaps, are stages in the impossible 'signature' of this name which is not a name, adventures of discourse of which the goal is the unpeeling of the individual name itself, the inward deconstruction of authorship always already presignified in the pseudonym, that trope which folds endlessly back on itself by its implicit claim that because some names can be identified as *not real*, other names somehow *are* (real).[23]

Or, for example: we may see the text as centred on the issue of written and oral language. When Catherine records in her diary the speech of Joseph, she does not keep up a coherent fiction of the written, for 'she' surely would not have reproduced so variously and so oddly the (presumed) peculiarities of Joseph's *speech*. Thus we may see this as an example of the broader problem of the primacy of written and oral, and we may see it furthermore as the endlessly fertile unpacking of a particular trope: the name of the title, for is 'wuthering' a 'real' word or not? In what might consist the reality of the word? Does it have a 'correct' oral form, a correct pronunciation – like the 'pronunciation' of Catherine's name, and of Heathcliff's, which form the generating gestures of so much of the passion of the text?

What we know of *Wuthering Heights* is not, cannot be, reducible to written text; perhaps more so than any other canonical novel, it is also the incarnation of a sound, of a sound which, uncannily, might or might not be a voice, the long-drawn-out sound of the wind which Coleridge tried so often to replicate.[24] In dealing with this voice, which is the voice of the phantom, we necessarily find ourselves beyond the law; we do not know whether we heard these words, these names, and even if we did we do not know their point of origin (we suspect they have no point of origin). We are perhaps 'called', summoned, even interpellated; but only in the most ambiguous of terms, for here perhaps we are after all, and despite all the denials and disavowals, in the hidden, secretive presence (which might also be referred to as an absence) of a god: Hermes. And one of the significances of Hermes was that, although he took messages between the other gods, there was no check on whether he got them right or not, no quality control. In Hermes' cloak what we find is precisely the misaddressed letter, the postcard which has not gone to its correct destination, the envelope which has no address, or an insufficient one.[25] Who, after all, is the implied reader of *Wuthering Heights*, and what has that reader been doing since s/he died?

Perhaps then at this point – although nothing is certain in this shifting light – such a god does emerge from the shadows, and he wears a hat and carries a peculiar staff. It has always been impossible to tell which way Hermes is facing: is he looking inward at this world, or back and down, where the entrance to another level has opened up behind him? At any rate, we know whom we have to face now, for we know from the myths that Hermes and Hades share a hat; and that Hermes is always to be found around the final threshold.[26] We know also that for Hermes there are, in another sense, no thresholds, the hermetic and the hermeneutic functions merge into each other, secrets and solutions bound indissolubly into one whole, the soulwork potentially completed; and as we look for the last time on the throngs gathered in this limbo-like fourth realm, we see the curious resemblance between their shadowy forms and the figures on the banks of the Styx, condemned by memory and by loss of memory, stuck between two worlds, victims of a supernal radical scepticism which cannot even be alleviated by death.

Wuthering Heights, as we descend to the fifth level, opens into a different shape. There is some sense of vertigo in this final opening, because part of it is to do with an emerging parallelism between the creative and the interpretative activity: as Freud was so fond of saying, the creative artists and writers have 'always known this already', and now we find that *Wuthering Heights* has preceded us on our descent and is, indeed, the account of a descent; that it has predicted, almost cybernetically, our attempt to uncover its secrets and is, in fact, about the problems of uncovering secrets.

For where is the heart of *Wuthering Heights*? It is held in silence and in absence. It is, I believe, situated within the absence of Heathcliff, his three-year sojourn 'on another scene'; from which he returns transformed, reborn, as Donne puts it in the 'Nocturnal upon St Lucie's Day', as a 'quintessence even from nothingness'[27] – that is to say, compounded of an alchemical substance called nothing, a substantive and material negation. And of course, Heathcliff returns darkened from this central 'moment' of the text; for in his three-year absence he is re-enacting an ancient myth, albeit with a peculiar slant. He goes through a process of maturation, but this is coloured, perhaps fatally, by his lack of an accepted male mentor and by his lack of female nurturing, the absence of any means by which this 'maturation' might figure as a real insertion into a society or a culture, into an acceptance of the law, might figure as the, albeit dangerous, purgation of a foreign body.

To this absence of the heart, Heathcliff responds with a further absenting of the heart; he has learnt this from Hades, because this is where he has spent those three years and because this is the teaching which is peculiarly Hades' own. We know this not only because he comes back with a darkened soul; we know it also because he comes back wealthy, and there is only one possible mythic source for this inexplicable wealth, and that is Hades, the giver of gifts, the source of all riches.[28] In sensing this, we are of course also again touching on a mainspring of the novel, the 'will'. The will as last testament, in this sense and in some ways not so differently from the apparently different meaning of the will which I foregrounded in 'Ligeia', is the magical source of wealth; and within the family system that dissemination of riches is figurable only as a response to death, as an accompaniment to mourning, and simultaneously as a denial of pain, as, in effect, the non-talking cure. Of course, Hades represents absence and wealth also because he represents the unconscious, and we conventionally speak of the 'riches of the imagination', which is to say the wealth and fertility of the unconscious; but this wealth, this copiousness, is necessarily double-edged. It should not be brought back. It exists, but under an interdict; it should not be fetched out into the light of day. This is what magicians and alchemists through the ages – and we include here the late twentieth century, and probably also the twenty-first – have tried to do; they have tried not merely to probe the secret of the philosopher's stone, the elixir of life, but also to bring these secrets back to life, whereas these secrets are indeed available, they can be held; but only in death.

Let me be clear here about what I am saying, and how I have been trying to approach *Wuthering Heights*. I am not saying that Emily Brontë was writing a mythic fantasy, I am not even saying that the text enacts such fantasies at the 'unconscious level', whatever that may be. I am saying that there are certain archetypes – although I do not wish to restrict them to their Jungian definition – which shine, albeit darkly or dimly, through narrative; and that at this level, which I understand to be the deepest we can get (this side of the grave?), *Wuthering Heights* is the account of the descent of a soul to Hell. In now substituting Hell for Hades, of course, there are a host of implications: certainly the Greeks' encounters with Hades contained nothing of the passionate torment which infects our dealings with Hell; Hades was a gentle place, 'death's other Kingdom', echoing with the murmurings of sleepers quiet and unquiet, softly rich, full of shadows but not lacking in colour and texture. It had no fires; its worst torments were effusions of cold air.[29]

But Hades was demonised by Christianity; and so, we may fairly wonder, what does this text tell us about the parallel process of demonisation which constitutes a large part of its narrative structure, the demonisation of the orphan, the passage of the 'unhoused' beyond the law, represented in the figure of Heathcliff? Here, I believe, we come to a crux which has mostly to do, again, with the question of passion (which is always one way of phrasing questions about the body). For thus far in my account of the 'fifth level' of interpretation, I have been following and applying suggestions made by the mythic analysts, up to the point of the demonisation of Hades; and hence I have also been following their sources, which lie principally in studies of the Western mythic tradition but which also extend occasionally to other cultures. But on the crucial subject of passion, which is the linchpin of Gothic, they have very little to say.

Let us begin to try to remedy this defect by looking again at *Wuthering Heights* itself. Two things about it seem incontrovertible:

that it is a 'text of passion'; and that it is a text lost in uncertainties and undecidabilities, and therefore in a certain sense irrecoverable – in which respect it is only emblematic of the irrecoverability of a version of the text which will stand before a court of law. It shines forth with a dreadful and ominous single-mindedness; yet it is simultaneously wandering the maze, the labyrinth, names calling other names which turn out to be the same name, the generations redoubling upon each other, plot forever hidden behind conflicts and dramatisations of the ego, castles and houses where the terror- ist might lurk in forgotten rooms (particularly, of course, bed- rooms); we are, for example, in the dreaded presence of the 'secret agent', who is also the foreign body. Psyche is drawn to her utmost pitch, in the screams of Heathcliff and Catherine, of passion and doomed omnipotence; yet Psyche is also under con- straint, is forced to avoid speaking her name, is made to creep through subterranean windings and – and perhaps this is the crucial point about our originary text, the last paragraph of the book – never finds her way out.[30]

In terms of relevant alternative myth, that, for example, of Orpheus and Eurydice, or of the dark queen Persephone, what happens in *Wuthering Heights*? Heathcliff descends to the depths to regain his lost love; and in those depths he is reincarnated – the whole text is a story of reincarnations, for Heathcliff and Catherine both die and are reincarnated *within* the text, and at the end of the book they stand again as symbols for a further kind of reincarna- tion. One question we might ask here, though – and the text asks it constantly – is about the extent to which these deaths and rebirths are experienced *together*, about the difference between the ever- aloneness of Heathcliff and the force of love which drives the 'heroes'; it might seem that the price the law exacts for the rein- carnation of the body here is greater in the end than that which Orpheus pays, or at least different in kind.

If we want to look more closely at reincarnation as a site for that which might occur beyond the law's purview and fatally disturb the simplicities of signification, we find a paradox, and a useful parallel. The paradox, of course, is that reincarnation holds its own contradiction within itself, in an obvious form: if we are reborn but without memory of previous lives, then who is to say whether this is any different from not being reborn at all? To recast the question more relevantly, does Gothic re-enact previous traumas and encounters with darkness, or bring them into being trailing a ready-made illusion of the 'past'? The *différance* is not rebirth but the problem of memory. The useful parallel can be seen in, for example, the Tibetan *Book of the Dead*.[31] Here the soul is detached from the body at death, and enters a curious realm known as the *Bardo* plane. Here it is the soul's fate to attempt to avoid the grasping of many wombs: to avoid, if nirvana is at all close, the possibility of rebirth into the material world at all; but if this remains necessary through unshed attachment, to be reborn to the right womb, to be reborn in such a way as to increase one's standing at the next birth on the long road to real death and absence.[32] The extent to which the soul is equipped to fight delusion on the *Bardo* plane and thus to ensure a correct rebirth is proportionate to the soul's *freedom*, in its previous incarnation, from 'attachment' itself, from the delusions which obscure our sense of ourselves as foreign bodies.

But the inverse of this successful detachment is passion, the lure into *crime passionnel*. And thus, according to this myth, the acme of passion will represent the worst possibility, of rebirth into a non-human form; and this is in a sense what happens to Heathcliff, but with several provisos. He is reborn as a thing of vengeance, true; but it is a curious testimony to the alternative power of passion that he escapes from the deepest depths at all. In his encounter with Hades, we may say that, like Hercules, he wrests a concession from Hades – one that Hades is not entirely unwilling to give for, again like Hercules, in the lower realm of tranquillity and peace Heathcliff represents an impossible and disruptive potential inhabitant. He is returned to the surface like a black bubble ejected by the sheer force of his own outrage, but also, we may surmise, because the very nature of attachment represented in Heathcliff is unnatural: his passion is itself born of an earlier configuration of absence and deprivation, it is the culmination of orphanage, and once one has roamed – perhaps been born roaming – the map-less castle of desire, no further fate, the text seems to suggest to us, can alter the constellation that has built up one's resistance to the law.

Thus we admire Heathcliff because he has defeated death; and we fear him because we know, at some level, that that defeat is temporary and can only be achieved at the cost of his loss of humanity, of human feeling. In the battle represented here, the outcome is truly undecidable. To say that death shall have no dominion is Promethean, Herculean, speaks of grandiosity and even of the faintly ridiculous; but it also speaks of courage and survival, and here the various myths are crossed, as they are, for example, precisely in the succession of Buddhism to Hinduism, where the intensity of the attention to family responsibility, duty, law, even to the wifely funeral pyre, is transformed by the cunning of history into its own opposite, the life of the celibate worshipped as the truer alternative to the life of the legally protected and domestically/legally active 'householder'. That life of the 'householder' is the one led by all those who accept an inevitability of attachment, who live within the human world and seek to add to their *karma* through acts of goodness, through accepting social role, through living, moving and having their being within a cultural structure.[33] To live the life of the celibate – and here we are no longer merely talking about Buddhism, for we can find parallels for this in many other religions including Christianity – is to pursue the path which crosses the human with the non-human, which speaks of the possibility of transcendence,[34] which talks of the negation of passion in terms which frequently suggest that this is really a redirection of passion, a transference or translation which has come to consist in the passionate attachment to the notion of destroying by surpassing one's own sociopsychic configuration; and here the implications for the body and for the body-imago are perhaps obvious.

Am I speaking here too much of Heathcliff, ignoring the other 'characters' and especially the women in the text? Perhaps I am. But I would say that what we might call the 'soulstuff' *is* carried largely by Heathcliff, and that this is enacted in the text itself as Heathcliff drains and absorbs power from the others, indeed from the world of the human. This is vampirism, in one of its oldest senses: the power of the dead to draw off force from the living, to leave them pallid and trembling, on the verge of that death which is pulling them towards the misty threshold. I am not talking here of moral issues, although in any culture these events will take on moral forms: but of the shaping of our encounters with death, that shaping of which we have already spoken in the context of the relation between Gothic and psychoanalysis, where what we, for example, refer to as the 'masculine' strides forth alone; and returns, in this case, alone, having battled with itself and thereby become a creature of battle, re-confirmed in its obstinate and disastrous solitude.

The violence, the violation of 'Catherine' is the attempted destruction of anima; such an activity as may seem necessary for a woman writing under the multiplied sign of patriarchy and therefore necessarily without a textual 'signature' that can be legally validated, for here we are returning up through the levels of interpretation, surfacing from our journey. Up through the level of deconstruction we may carry with us a (sceptical) suspicion that scepticism itself exists only as a superstructure, that below the shadow-play there is a realm of dark stasis which will not be moved or altered by the play of *maya*. Up through the vale of the goddesses we carry a knowledge that they too have their counterparts in the lowest realm, but down there always associated with a sign which goes beyond naming, not in mere psychic 'difference' but in the insistent move to the depths themselves, to the hidden 'inner', which has no name because it is, as Borch-Jacobsen hints in different terms, beyond birth and death alike. Up through the analytic level we carry the knowledge that individual psychic mechanisms *may* be seen as re-enactments of that which has already happened, that the timelessness of the 'unconscious' is itself a replication of the absence of time and timelessness alike (and has thus to do with the distortions of time and history which form part of the grounding of the Gothic). And up through history we carry a sense that the very striving for change takes place against the 'dark background', and that unless we know what is inside, our dealings with the outer will never take place in the full knowledge of what accurately pertains to the human and what to the non-human, to the world of gods, devils and animals;[35] we may not recognise their access to superior and older knowledges.

And so we emerge onto the field again; not to dismiss the cheerful interplay of characters, but to know that each character has her or his own intimate connection to the depths; that each one represents a variant of the essential journeying which makes *karma*, soulstuff; and perhaps here, to continue our metaphor to its conclusion, which is also to carry it back to the creative source, we might find ourselves calling again upon Hephaestus, who knows many different depths including the peculiar ones of craft and creativity, to arm and prepare us for a further journey.[36] This is not the stuff of mysticism, not the stuff of looking away from what is there; it is about the power to *endure what is there*, to endure the presence of the dream-knot, to place undecidability where it truly belongs, in the overlaying of realms, in the ceaseless process of negotiation between levels which constitutes the examined life and which therefore precedes and shapes all narrative and its attempts to incarnate and exorcise the body, to manifest and elude the law.

8

*Psycho*pathology: Contamination and the House of Gothic

'It was purely accidental,' he said. 'I did not put any glass on her head. If she did, it was a joke. I certainly did not intend to shoot at it.'[1]

Of all the Gothic horror scenarios which have sunk into the Western unconscious during the twentieth century, *Psycho* is one of the most powerful, although principally in its manifestation in Alfred Hitchcock's film of that name. Here I want to approach instead Robert Bloch's original story, published in 1959, and to put some specific questions about it in relation to the psychological, and to the text, the body and the law. It needs to be noted at the outset that this is an odd and difficult, perhaps an uncanny, task, because of a peculiarity in the story itself: which is that it contains its own psychological explanation, attached near the end as an authenticated account by a psychiatrist of a series of events which were, so we are led to believe, closely based on 'real' incidents.

The narrative, then, which will of course sound uncannily like a pre-text to the better-known film. In Bloch's *Psycho*, Mary Crane, engaged to marry Sam Loomis but compelled to wait because of Sam's financial problems, steals $40,000 and drives off to join him. On the way she stops at a lonely motel, run by Norman Bates and, apparently, his sick mother. Bates rents her a room which is connected by a peep-hole to his own office. Observing her undress and go into the shower, he starts to drink while meditating on the dirtiness of women, and briefly passes out; or, we might say, reflecting on previous motifs, passes, rather than 'out', 'into' a hypnotic, somnambulistic field in which he is, perhaps, no longer legally responsible for his own actions.

When he wakes up, he sees that she has been brutally murdered, and concludes, it would appear, that only his mother could have

done it. To protect her, he disposes of the (female) body. Meanwhile, Sam is disturbed at his (very masculine) hardware store by
the arrival of Lila, Mary's younger sister, who is searching for
Mary; and they are simultaneously visited by Arbogast, a private
detective hunting for the stolen money, who has tracked Mary this
far but has not found her.

Arbogast discovers the motel, the last on his list, and suspects
Bates. While Arbogast goes up to the house behind the motel where
Bates and his mother live(?), a worried Bates again starts to drink
and, as before and yet totally differently, because the reader by
now has internalised something of the experience of repetition,
passes out; and when he too heads for the house, he finds Arbogast
also killed, and goes through the same procedure as before to
protect his mother from the legal consequences of 'her' deranged
crimes.

When Arbogast does not return to town, Lila persuades Sam to
come to the motel with her, where they book into the room Mary
had occupied and discover enough to make them suspect Bates of
murder. They plan for Sam to keep Bates in conversation while Lila
goes off to phone for help. Bates is again drinking, and as he does
so he tells Sam something of the truth (just as, perhaps, in his
previous states he has also been telling, or rather acting, something
of 'the truth'). However, before Sam can act (can repeat and in
some sense react towards the 'truth' which he is being told), Bates
knocks him out, or rather, perhaps, reproduces on his body the
condition of somnambulism which has been the key to his own
past actions; before doing so he has warned Sam that, in fact, Lila
has not gone for the sheriff but has instead decided to explore the
house on her own in a search for further clues.

We next switch to Lila, who explores the house; we have, of
course, been present at this scene of the 'exploration of the house'
before, in so many previous manifestations of the Gothic. She discovers Bates's bedroom, which is oddly untouched (pristine, virgin)
although the bed itself bears traces of recent occupancy. She eventually goes down to the cellar and, while searching this most remote
yet most intimate fastness of the body of the dream-house, she
discovers instruments of the taxidermist's craft (we already know
of this hobby of Bates's). She then, however, hears footsteps over-
head and, in her panic, accidentally finds herself in an inner room.

Within it, she finds to her horror the decomposed corpse of
Bates's mother, and screams 'Mrs Bates!', surely by any account a

rather odd thing to scream under the circumstances. Yet an answer comes; not from the corpse but from Bates himself, the alternative body, who is descending the cellar steps wearing his mother's clothes and wielding a knife. Before he can get to Lila, however, he is overpowered by Sam, who has conveniently 'come round' in the nick of time.

In the first aftermath, we are told that 'in fact' Bates's mother had died some twenty years before, along with her lover. It was supposed at the time that they had made a suicide pact; Bates had been committed to hospital at the time because of his supposed grief, loss and mourning transformed, Hamlet-like, into madness. However, it emerges that Bates has forged the suicide note and had himself killed the couple, and had subsequently, in a fit of remorse, exhumed his mother's body; it is this body he has been living with ever since, and thus it is he himself, of course, who has killed Mary and the detective; or at least it is thus if one is to believe that the Norman Bates who stand 'convicted' is the unitary signatory of a set of 'deeds' of which he is only spasmodically aware.

The psychiatrist's explanation follows and takes fairly conventional lines, dwelling on Bates's early domination by his mother, who had 'conceived' a morbid hatred of men when Bates's father had walked out on her shortly after the son's birth. Bates, we are told, had developed a triply fragmented personality after murdering his mother: the conventional adult who ran the motel, the child who could not escape from under his mother's jurisdiction, and the mother herself.

In a chilling footnote, we encounter Bates in his psychiatric hospital (which has certain crucial resemblances to a motel). The previous gaps in his fragmented personality are now closing as adult and son vanish into the psyche of the mother; a mother who, having, as 'she' says, been silent for these twenty years, must now remain silent for the rest of her life, and so motionless that everybody will realise that she, rather like Renfield in *Dracula* (1897), 'wouldn't even harm a fly'.[2]

Overall, this narrative of psychic splitting is told tersely and even conventionally: the characters of the Crane sisters and Sam Loomis step straight from the pages of pulp fiction, Arbogast with his cigarettes and trilby is another avatar of Humphrey Bogart. The power lies in Bloch's ability to manipulate our uncertainties; although quite early on we learn that Bates's version of his mother's life/death does not square with other known 'facts', the reasons for this discrepancy remain in doubt until the dénouement.

There are also a number of significant blurrings of boundaries. At the beginning, Bates is in conversation with his mother, and one could say that this hardly squares with 'external' reality as it is apparently revealed later in the text. But Bloch could have a ready answer for this: the personality with which he is dealing (the personality which he is also ambiguously 'constructing') is so far disintegrated that rival accounts proliferate, and the conversation between Bates and his mother may be seen as a spur to his actions as much as anything which happens in a validable outer world.

Psychoanalytically, though, *Psycho* should be seen as not mainly the story of the disintegration of a personality, but rather of a massive attempt by the psyche to *re-seal* itself, to find some way of disguising and recovering the gaping wounds in its (masculine) construction; and of course, it could be said that in this it depicts a successful strategy of the unconscious,[3] albeit a strategy which returns us to the notion of the relation of unconscious to conscious as a version of the master/slave dialectic in which the ego, unknowingly and uncomplainingly, walks direct into the trap (death) which it has all along existed to avoid. Faced by the strain of maintaining a multiplicity of personalities, Bates has to perform actions that will make this situation unsustainable and will make possible its replacement by a forcible reunification on one side or the other of the border of psychosis – which side matters little, because either way there will at least be a recognisable human being reassembled which can then be surveyed, policed and dealt with 'in the usual manner' – or, we might say, thus will the personality take its place in the identity parade, the line-up of 'the usual suspects'.

Again, it is no accident that this re-sealing takes place in a mental hospital, precisely the place where the original splitting occurred as a paradoxical effect of Bates's attempt to heal the gaps in his *outer* world through the double murder – a double murder itself replicated by the slaying of Mary and the detective. It needs to be pointed out here that this is a very direct reference to the connection between mourning and murder; a reference to the taboo point that some of our feelings in states of mourning are 'unbound', that they might well take the form of an unfathomable revenge.[4] It is no accident that mourners and figures of death both wear black, for in the night which succeeds the decease of the loved object there is no way to tell them apart; and perhaps the still silence that surrounds the bullet to the sky at an IRA funeral is a more fitting emblem of this complex and destructive process than sectarianism knows.

Farther than these uncanny doublings, these 'duplicities', one might say, Bates cannot go, because to encounter triplicity, the one step beyond these locked pairings in unimaginable sexual symbiosis, would be to encounter, without insulation, a replication of the pattern on which his own inner life has stabilised and become modelled, a pattern in which all three corners of the Oedipal triangle have to be held together in an act of quivering terror, because to let any of them go would be to permit once again the possibility of 'loose ends', ends (of the narrative) which can never be picked up and which therefore leave all the personality's hopes of order shattered on the floor (of the shower/'show-er'). We could go further and say that this is precisely why the salvation of Loomis figures as structurally non-accidental even within the terms of the *deus ex machina* ending.

It is at this point that we may start to think more deeply about what is told in this 'tale of the unexpected', and this will involve looking not only at the 'story' itself, but also at the triple structure – account, diagnosis and aftermath/'footnote' – into which the text itself, in some ways like Bates's psyche, falls; and I propose to do this by asking some questions which remain unanswered in the text, and by looking at other fictional analogies for the psychic structuring explored in Bloch's *Psycho* and the problems of legal accountability which it represents.

One of these questions concerns what we might call *the spur to action*, and it is simply: why does Bates kill Mary Crane? The diagnosis does not offer an answer. It offers, indeed, an account of Bates's psychic structure and of the originating traumatic events which sparked the present shaping. It also makes suggestions as to why Bates might indeed be spurred to murderous thoughts by the sight of a naked female body. But we are not surely meant to suppose that, given his apparatus of peep-hole and adjoining room, this is the first opportunity for murder Bates has had in twenty years of running a motel, even if it is somewhat off the beaten track.

I believe the text principally offers two possible answers, without fully validating either of them. We have already alluded to one of them, which is the conversation between Bates and his 'mother' (that is, we might reasonably conclude, the conversation within

Bates himself) at the beginning of the novel, the originary dialogue (monologue). It could be said that the tenor of this conversation suggests that Bates has had enough of his mother's dominance, and that this provides him with the impetus for a make-or-break attempt to reintegrate what has been severed within him; although it has to be added that this assessment is itself psychotic in its recognition of the independence of the 'mother' agency within the psyche.

But the texture of the conversation simultaneously undermines this interpretation, for we are told that this kind of interchange has occurred many times before – in this sense the disturbance, the troubling of time here, the sense of further vistas where memory fails us, takes us again back to 'Ligeia'. We are therefore enjoined by the text to see it precisely as part of a continuing process of rememoration, and as such it cannot be considered within the simplistic terms of a model which would offer us concepts of rupture within a traumatic – and traumatised – structure. Certainly it illumines the tension betwen Bates-as-child and Bates-as-mother, but it does nothing to account for the specific slaying of Mary Crane.

The other possibility occurs, significantly, on the final page of the story, when Bates-as-mother is recalling the 'evil' of Bates-the-adult, whom she now holds responsible for the murders, 'the deaths of two innocent people – a young girl with beautiful breasts and a man who wore a grey Stetson hat'.[5] One obviously interesting point here is that it is precisely a 'doubled' death that is referred to, the deaths of a man and a woman; although the deaths do not occur simultaneously, we are inevitably reminded of the way in which Bates continually supposes, once he has murdered Mary, that somebody will turn up looking for her (although this is to impute a kind of psychotic prescience for which there is little other evidence); yet Arbogast is really too shadowy and conventionalised a presence to stand in for Joe Considine, the mother's murdered lover, who has already been 'consigned' to the mortuary, or to the pretext from which all else follows. Also, the link between Arbogast and Mary is non-existent; they have never met, or rather, if they are now 'meeting' it is on the other side of the river, aside from their in any case very different relations to the law.

The allusion to Mary's breasts, her specific physicality, is, I believe, more interesting. It is the only such allusion in the book, although Hitchcock, with his 'masterly' use of voyeurism, emphasised Janet Leigh's physique in the film version, to the point where this notion of the body (the attenuated body, the body in pieces, the body in parts) might be considered to be the entire hinge between written and filmic treatments, and what could be more apt than the image of the breasts as the point at which the inscribed and the visual signal their coincidence and at the same time their breaking point on the terrain of the rupture between the imaginary and the symbolic?

Again, we would be hard-pushed to believe that Bates has not observed a naked woman through his peep-hole before; but the issue does take us back again to the beginning, where Bates-as-mother accuses his childhood self of being a 'Mamma's Boy', with all that implies of failed nurturing.[6] The battle continues: is the breast or the bottle best? While Bates entertains murderous thoughts about the breast, he indulges in the bottle, and in doing so falls into precisely the trance of unknowing which is the pre-rogative of the most primitive of all forms of human union, he falls into that somnambulism which we have now come across several times before; and while he does so, exempted from the law and riven also by a series of hiatuses in the text, he seeks out whom he may kill, because this sense of sleep-filled wellbeing is also one in which nightmares come, and one in which we are all, in one sense or another of that deeply ambiguous word – if it even is a word – 'psycho'.

So these images too can be clearly connected onto Bates's drinking, his decision to suckle himself in compensation for the mothering he has not had, or rather which was diverted, at least in his fantasy, onto Considine. It is precisely the drinking which acts as the sign for a kind of freeing – here we come again across Cholly Breedlove's [*sic*] curious 'freedom'[7] – of a part of himself from constraint and, through the medium of blackout, allows the murderer to take over in the attempt to find psychic unity as sublimation for the failed unity of mother and child (son). Within the complexities of Bates's attitudes to women, we can trace a double attitude to being nurtured (in turn, a doubled relic of the experience of being nurtured, fraught with all the ambiguities we have pointed out in an earlier chapter, to do with the notions of experience and memory[8]) : the image of peace fatally conjoined to a re-childing and removal of parental, legal control.

Under these circumstances, Bates's culminating attitude towards the feminine can only be one compounded of absorption and re-animation. He murders Mary, and in fact decapitates her, paving the way for the moment when his own head/mind can finally and fully become that of a woman, a female brain to match the female attire and resolve the sexual split. That this sexual 'split' has also to do with a notion of castration, the split between the possessor and the possessed, the gap betwen fullness and lack, goes perhaps without 'saying', just as Bates's excesses do not find their representation in an impossible textual 's[l]aying'. In his gaze through the peep-hole, Bates (or would it be better in these ever more intimate surroundings to call him Norman?) begins the process of taking Mary inside himself; but he can only complete this cycle in an insulated way, by permitting his 'mother' to have the (murderous) contact which he, as child or as adult, regards as forbidden.

We need thus to see *Psycho* as a drama of the vicissitudes of the psyche entrapped in a wish to be loved; and more particularly, of a male psyche caught between images of the woman-as-mother and the woman-as-lover. Under the circumstances described, what is experienced is a mismatch between the inner and the outer, between the presumed full splendour of the 'adult' inner self, as a (Gothicised) adolescent may often experience it, and the accidentally acne-pitted outer countenance which will render this splendid person invisible.[9]

The terrain on which we now find ourselves is one on which we have found ourselves before: we are back with the 'case that cannot be heard'. We are back with all the distortions of narrative that arise when trying to recall either the route back to the past, which seems to be blocked by the rubble of an unreliable memory, or the route to the future, to the summit, which seems unbelievably risky and in any case already grossly over-occupied by those others who are trying to make their way to the top. Between these poles, it is unclear how we (particularly as adolescent selves) may be able to make out a case for ourselves that does not convict itself even as we utter it; is there any way of assuring anybody that, if they were to look into the cellar of our house, they would not find down there the abandoned and rotting body of our dead mother?

In Bates's case, the split is floridly displayed in transvestitism, a transvestitism which not only hides the shamed male contour from the outside world but also hides Bates's own actions from himself – in, perhaps, a guise of 'female' passivity which the spirit of his mother constantly denies, even within her own re-remergence within his own psychic frame.[10] The parallel which I should like

to bring in here is with another text which we can fairly characterise as a psychopathological novel, and again as a text which moves
among the difficulties of the encounters of the body and the law,
Patrick Süskind's *Perfume: The Story of a Murderer* (1985).

Here the protagonist Grenouille is again, and particularly,
starved of mother-love, being born and abandoned on a garbage-
heap (thereby enacting literally the conviction of so many of our
dreams and simultaneously re-calling Hecate before our astonished
eyes), and his mother executed shortly afterwards. But Grenouille's
story is mainly oriented by Süskind's chief device, which is to make
him a unique master of scent and perfume, and the central trope of
the story is to do with Grenouille's superior, indeed remarkable,
olfactory abilities. It is therefore these he uses, for two separate but
linked purposes: first, to reproduce the perfume which, of all
others, has most attracted him – which is, perhaps unsurprisingly
in terms of Gothic conventions, that of a pure and innocent maiden
– and second, to provide a perfume which will make him, Grenouille, loved by everybody, a perfume that will convince the
entire world that he is a man of the sincerest and noblest intentions.

Like Bates, then, he is in the business of taking on the outer
contours of the bodily feminine in order to provide him with an
'internalised' source for the love of which he has been starved.
What we might say about both Bates and Grenouille is that they
have discovered within their own psyche images of themselves
which are such frighteningly 'bad objects' that they cannot be
contemplated at all but must be covered in the feminine clothing
or perfume which will simultaneously conceal this horrifying, ugly
inner man from bystanders while recreating that person in a form
that will contain within itself the ambiguously comforting yet
destructive form of mother-love as it has been experienced by
them, perhaps at a pre-Oedipal stage, in all their fantasies and
yearnings.[11]

What is obviously confused here is the line between person and
object. If the personality is split into fragments, then there may
follow a tendency to perceive others as also in fragments, which on
the one hand absolves us of the responsibility for treating them as
persons, while on the other making them appropriable by us as
substitute parts for our own missing organs; this seems to be one of
the suppressed meanings behind the ambivalent yearning for
the 'body without organs' of which Deleuze and Guattari so
lasciviously speak.[12] Some of these parts, in this case the breasts

perhaps in particular, will in turn remind us precisely of the deficiencies which are motivating our own forgettings and evasions. They must thus be dealt with in some way, for there are only two possible outcomes to this psychotic splitting: psychotic reunification, as with Bates, or physical obliteration, for Grenouille is finally torn apart by people precisely because he has made them love him so much, in a late Dionysian resort to distraction/destruction/ deconstruction.[13]

We need, in *Psycho*, also to speak of (in) the *third person normal*. In the above, I have talked mostly about two of Bates's personality fragments, Bates-as-mother and Bates-as-child. But Bates has, as I have said, a triple personality, and alongside, or within, this continuing conflict there is also Bates-as-adult, the 'normal' Norman who continues to feed himself, to run the motel, to gather firewood; all three of those named activities have their own symbolic equivalents in the processes of cannibalism and incorporation which characterise the underworld of the text, but nevertheless they also proceed within a more surface structure. And this prompts us to recall a third *différance* in the encounter between Bates and Mary which may serve at some level to set it apart from its previous incarnations, for we are told that she is the first, and thus the only, person whom he has ever invited to the house behind the motel.

We may thus hypothesise that this penetration of the inner sanctum is the source both of intense desire and of intense fear: Bates wishes his inner illegal secrets to be probed in at least a single flirtation with the reality-principle, but at the unconscious level he also uses this invited penetration as symbolic evidence of the threat which is posed to his fragile personality by the outer world – will this be the 'evidence' which is finally used to condemn him and to 'consign' him to the death-chair (his mother's chair) of which we have such abundant 'evidence' within the text? Mary's presence in the house itself constitutes the only evidence of a 'normal' interest on Bates's part in the opposite sex; but it is precisely this moment of 'normalcy' which contributes to placing the long-delayed question about stability at the forefront of his warring psyche.

What is important, I think, about this 'normal' adult within the traumatic structure is that it represents routine; and routine is the sign for a reversible mastery, the adult's mastery of outer events through prediction and reliability, and at the same time the dominance of the person by events which will continue to flow in predestined ways despite the individual's attempts at control, reminiscent of more general issues of habit and addiction.[14] It is of course also routine which renders the individual retrospectively available to the processes of the law: again, 'Where were you on Thursday, 14th April at . . . ?'. We may thus see the 'normal' Bates as representing a midpoint of power: where Bates-as-mother and Bates-as-child stand for unresolved problems about omnipotence and domination, about retrospection and prediction, Bates the harmless motel-keeper stands on a conventional edge where power is actually limited and clear.

We are thus returned to the underlying symbolism of Bates's drinking, which again takes on the form of a triple sign. First, as we have seen, it forms a substitute gratification for Bates the thwarted child. Second, it forms a moment of escape from the control of the mother, both in its revolt against social convention and also in its loosening of constraint. Third, it represents, to Bates, a 'normal' male adult activity, and in this sense it again returns us to the problems of control and legal responsibility, because it stands as the sign for a habit which, so Bates thinks, is under the control of the rational mind whereas in fact it is vividly demonstrated to us that the mind loses its control precisely under this influence (although no court of law would accept that view, whereby the punishment meted out to the drunk would be seen as always landing on the wrong person).

Bates the adult needs objects to validate his adult status; but in this respect his status is that of a collector. He gathers firewood; he collects stuffed animals; he collects books of various kinds, including pornography, which can be seen as the motif of the collector *par excellence*; feasibly the 'collection' is always and everywhere a pornographic object,[15] an excrescence of latency, a suggestion which would certainly be supported by the curious dialectic, within the notion of collection, of secrecy and exhibition, reminiscent as it is precisely of Bronfen's dialectic of the exposed and withheld body. In these attempts at collection (recollection, collecting oneself together), we may see Bates as trying to establish a psychic and physical terrain of his own (through an impossible memory), away from the omniscience of his mother (or indeed the narrator, or the judge); we may also think metaphorically about his attempts, as I have hinted, to 'collect' a self, to get himself, as it were, all in one place at the same time (despite the disseminative, dispersory activities which characterise motels).

In this respect, it is important to note, Bloch's portrayal of Bates is startlingly different from the Anthony Perkins portrait in the Hitchcock film. Where Perkins is dark, moody, halting, Bloch's protagonist is fat, balding, gingery, perhaps even benign in appearance. He has, in effect, protective colouring; and it is this ability of the psychotic to sink into the texture of everyday life which repeatedly fascinated Bloch as writer and film-maker in his own right.

And this reminds us of another question, which is about Mary herself. Why, after all, does it matter to the text that she has committed a criminal act, an act which has already placed her (body) beyond the law? Bates never discovers the money, which is in fact hidden in the car which he buries in the swamp; the secret is, in one sense, never revealed. I would suggest that at least part of the point here is indeed to underline the structure of 'hiddenness' in the story; for Mary herself is in significant senses a 'hidden' person. First, we know that she hides her own motives from herself; she believes herself to be in love with Loomis, but we are also given strong hints that this is really a mask for her increasing fears about isolation and emotional waning. Second, she makes a self-defeating and ultimately unsuccessful attempt to 'hide' her own tracks: seen from, as it were, a low angle, the journey in which she several times exchanges cars seems momentarily likely to succeed, but in fact Arbogast follows her easily.

Third, and most important, we are told that she has, in fact, always been largely 'hidden' from her lover Loomis and even from her own sister; they do not know what to make of the accusations that she is a thief, and as they draw closer to solving the mystery (shades here, perhaps, of Shelley and Jane Williams[16]) of her disappearance they simultaneously draw closer to realising the enigma, the inexplicability of her personality. In fact, then, she is dispensed with in a double way in the novel: physically by Bates, but also emotionally by Loomis and Lila, who, it is hinted, may 'get over' her absence by getting together themselves, thus eradicating the trace of her presence and simultaneously renouncing any hope or intention of uncovering the secret; another version of re-collection.

In fact, when Lila first appears in Loomis's store, he initially mistakes her for Mary, and this underlines a general point in the story about the problem of the identity parade, and more specifically the replaceability of women. For Bates, clearly women are no longer 'real people'; his vision of them, akin to the spyings on women that feature so heavily in the 'anatomical' tradition, is wholly a matter of bits and pieces, and is at the same time a mapping onto the template of his mother, which is deeply inscribed on his mind. But we may then hypothesise that the very *structure* of the story underlines this replaceability, and we are thus urged to read Bates's plight, and the ease with which it is passed off as normalcy – the ease, in fact, with which mother and child in Bates have cohabited with Bates-as-adult for twenty years – as symbolic of a general structure in the community, whereby women are objectified and can thus be dealt with as replaceable commodities (to be purchased, perhaps, in a hardware store) rather than as people; because their real power is too awesome for men to deal with, because they have come, in a substitutive way, to represent the mystery of personality which is taken as having caused psychic and social damage.

These motifs of collection, objectification and 'normal' ritual, with their implications for the limits of legal process, find a natural analogy in John Fowles's *The Collector* (1963). Here again we find the representation of a psychotic subject who is perfectly able to hold down an ordinary job, who also evinces a strong need to collect living things – in this emblematic case, first butterflies then girls – and who also kills in an atttempt to reincorporate within himself his own absences, to compensate for a overwhelming and irremediable sense of loss. Fowles's novel, which might thus otherwise be referred to as a text in mourning, is also a parable about the damming up of creativity; his protagonist's habit of collecting is counterposed to the 'genuine', if questionable, engagement with art symbolised by his art-student captive, Miranda.[17]

What lies behind this is the damming up of any creative possibilities for the self, their encasement within a (legal) framework of rules and regulations, the impossibility of escape from patterning, habit, addiction; and here we may call to mind Walter Benjamin's resonant account of the habits of the collector in modern society, and the role of collectable objects as substitutes for real relationships.[18] The collector believes himself to be in control of his collection; but at the unconscious level what has happened is that the person has consigned control to a set of routinised paths which serve to deflect and reduce the feared area of freedom. The theory of collection is thus not unlike the notion of demonic possession, whereby the feared and desired other takes over the hollow spaces inside 'the shell' and one experiences a moment of release which is simultaneously the pleasurable settling down to a greater and potentially irreversible bondage.

We therefore find ourselves questioning the 'third person normal' in Bates's psychic construction. After all, it is this personality-fragment which in fact stands guard over the others, a 'cemetery guard' in the full sense of Derrida's term since the landscape over which he presides is one inhabited only by ruins, and indeed by the ruins of ruins.[19] At the same time this 'adult' figure is protecting these remains, as it were, from the harsh winds or truths of the outer world in a savage parody of the conventional 'male' role as protector of mothers and children. Bates has constructed his semblance of adult masculinity along lines suggested, even enforced, by the law, and it works; the sheriff, the representative of the law and thus of an ordered universe in which identity stands on parade and all is exposed to the might of the law, is able to see Bates as slightly eccentric, but no more than that, for within this community of role models Bates stands out as the symbolic representative of 'family life' reduced to a stark conflation of psychic agony, wherein the entire 'family', the holy family, we might say, has been bound up, concretised, fetishised within the single body.[20]

Bates's 'mastery' consists also in *the control of detail*. One of the characteristics of his condition is a reversal of priority whereby large-scale features of life – love, murder, the rights of other people – slide into the background, whereas the small details of practical arrangements, whether these are to do with the opening hours of the motel or with the disposal of corpses and vehicles, assume greater importance. Bates is obviously proud of his command of detail in, for example, the way in which he meticulously covers up for his 'mother's' crimes; plunged backward onto a primal scene he has never really left, his task seems to be to arrange everything in a parodically seemly order, with the motel itself, that thing compounded of the transitory and the contingent, as the final emblem of a space which is always available for occupation but which is never actually occupied, and which is paradoxically available for inspection by the representatives of the law.

It is as though, in Bates, we are watching somebody in whom the narrator's art has been taken to an extraordinary extreme. What he has done is to set up a 'suspension of disbelief' among the various parts of his own psyche, in the midst of these elaborate dramatisations, 'mimes' in the terms of 'Ligeia', of the ego. In place of the tales told us by our mothers we have tales told *to* his mother to comfort her in her sleep. Once that fiction – that his mother's corpse is alive – has been established and watched over, guarded, then he is free to concentrate on the embellishments, on the precise evidence of verisimilitude, to etch in the clear details against a massive and looming fictional backdrop, the 'sublime' over the shoulder; or behind one's back.

Again, we may sense here some curious version of gender relations. The overarching fiction is, as we have seen, a protective one: that the mother must be protected, guarded against the consequences of her crimes; she must at all costs not emerge into the light of the law. It is as though it is the male role to set up the framework in which play can take place:[21] simultaneously mother and child are thus protected from systems of knowledge which only the adult male should possess (or by which only he may be 'possessed'), and at the same time the more feminine aspects of Bates are allowed to work on detail in the other sense of (transvestite) adornment.[22]

I would like here to mention another of Bloch's novels, *American Gothic* (1974). The central character is again a murderer of women, G. Gordon Gregg; and again here Bloch reminds/persuades us that he is taking the frame of an actual criminal history, a legal case, and searching in it for clues of a different kind, clues about the kind of psychic structure which might lie behind these crimes.

Gregg's story is replete with Gothic trappings: it is set in a modern castle full of secret passageways, hidden doors, even slaughterhouses to complete the nightmare topography of the mind, and comes to an appropriately melodramatic conclusion. Among other things, Gregg is a pharmacist and a master hypnotist, a clear descendant of villainous alchemists in the tradition of Frankenstein but also connected deeply into the 'history of hypnosis', if there can be such a thing, as the very recounting of the 'real-life' tale might be seen to represent precisely the hypnotic effect of 'history' itself. But in the end, it appears that Bloch is as puzzled about Gregg's motivations as we are, and offers two interlocking but disparate accounts.

Below the surface, we are allowed to surmise that this is another pathological account, and that Gregg enjoys his grisly work. But this, of course, is not the way he sees it. He again regards his victims as simply objects; what he wants from them, or so he believes, is simply their money. But he wants this not in any empty spirit of acquisition: 'it wasn't swindling', he explains to

Crystal, who is intended to be another of his (fragile and breakable) victims, 'it was a business matter. Building a place like this, carrying out my plans. You've got to find working capital, that's the primary rule of economics.'[23]

As he goes on to explain, he is only doing what everybody else is doing. The whole story is set against the background of the Chicago World's Fair of 1893. 'Look at the Fair', Gregg continues, 'and you'll see. The big exhibits – the steel industry, the railroads, textiles, armaments: don't you think the men behind them had to do their share of what you call swindling? Banking, insurance, real estate, I don't care what it is, you've got to look sharp, cut corners, take whatever steps are necessary'. The 'big exhibit', then, the exhibited and (re)collected body is connected direct to activity with knives, to cutting and looking sharp, back to the anatomist's craft, or the dissection of the corpse in the service of the law.

'He believes it', Crystal realises, 'he really believes it! A businessman, dealing in death. A salesman, dedicated to making a killing.' But then amid this plethora of images she remembers the other aspect of Gregg's 'work' that she has seen, the hearts of all his victims carefully removed and kept in jars, and goes through a vertiginous process of trying to match the two stories, the businessman's detailed accounts with the psychopath's mania for collecting.

We may go in several directions from this point. On the one hand, we may trace the psychic effects of capitalism, in ways similar to the route that Will Self is later to take in *My Idea of Fun* with his figure of the Money Critic; the implanted need for success and profit, the apparent need to treat other people as objects in the process of engaging successfully in 'business'.[24] On the other hand, we may think about the psychic need for domination and possession which the castle – as so often before in the Gothic tradition, and as is underlined in the book's title, which is, like all titles, a kind of generic promise – represents. The concentration on detail connects again with a need for secrecy; it is only through an intense absorption in detail that one can emerge from the all-seeing eye of mother and simultaneously prove one's command of the outer world, even if, seen from one vantage point, this attention to detail is merely the 'exhibited' outcropping of an extended involvement in infant ritualism, the trace of psychotic subservience.[25]

But this need to command is itself also merely the psychic residue of unaccommodated problems with omnipotence; if anybody were allowed to penetrate the bedroom, all of the child's (or perhaps more particularly the adolescent's) secrets would be revealed, all that lies behind the accurate and neat accounts, the ledgers of profit and loss, the apparently veracious diaries, even the hearts neatly arranged in their jars. And the term 'loss' perhaps reminds us of what is most important for Bates and Gregg: that there should be no loss to the self, no further erosion or leakage of that which is to be so preciously guarded because it is so fragile (as Miranda for Fowles's collector represents exactly the fragility within, to be feared, dominated, brought under control and then wiped away), the sense of a maturity precariously achieved and maintained only through an increasingly detailed elaboration of an overarching fiction, a symptom only barely still visible beneath the layers of psychic and symbolic accretion.

What we have here are examples – Bloch's protagonists, Süskind's Grenouille, Fowles's collector – of men who are engaged in massive efforts to bring back together sundered psyches. The principal means for doing this, however, is not through an exploration back into the dark: the house behind the motel, Grenouille's parentage (his orphan status), these are places too frightening to be contemplated – because they contain the real secrets of birth and death, they represent the live female body which is not to be admitted to the light of day but must instead be pushed ever deeper into the swamp even if that means burying what is most precious along with it; here again we have part of the submerged 'law of the orphan'.

Instead, the psychic effort is directed to the 'front office', the motel itself, Gregg's pharmacy, the exterior of the collector's specially purchased cottage, to ensure that these environments are sealed against leakage – which is also, of course, to ensure that they are insulated against the disclosure of truth, which in turn might be taken up as a kind of evidence that could move beyond the monologue of the all-controlling and inventive narrator, the narrator of detail. Here in these offices and places of 'business', there is a mass of neatly arranged detail, under steady surveillance because in this way the penetrating gaze can be averted from the brutal facts which are meanwhile seen as mysteriously amassing themselves behind one's back.

In this respect, we may also return to *Psycho* and to the originating 'details' of Mary's theft and what lies behind it, which is Loomis's financial insolvency. This is not, Bloch takes pains to

point out, Loomis's fault; on the contrary, what we are shown is a
structure within which Loomis has *inherited a debt*, and it is taken to
be a mark of his rare probity that he is determined to pay it off
before marrying his fiancée. The psychic analogue is plain to see:
that Loomis must repay the psychic debt (to the mother, to history,
to the primal scene) before he will be allowed to move beyond the
systems of adolescence, before he will be allowed to participate in
the world of adult sexuality, a threat so great, not merely to Loomis
the character but rather to and within the text itself, that the brutal
murder of Mary, precisely at a moment of her greatest physical
exposure, necessarily intercedes before the process of maturation
can be finalised. By a significant twist, then, were it not for this
debt there would have been no robbery; and Mary too, perhaps, is
trying to seal her psyche against leakage, against the awesome drift
into middle-aged spinsterhood, by a last desperate effort to gain a
substitute gratification in the outer world instead of looking in to
the forbidden dark recesses (looking back, perhaps, through Bates's
peep-hole), where one's own real death may be a fact which has to
be encountered.

The themes behind these structures, I suggest, are those of *contamination and death*. In 'A Girl Like Me' (1986), a story by a Hong
Kong Chinese writer who uses the pen name Xi Xi, we hear the
first-person story of a girl – like Mary Crane approaching with fear
a time of life when she may be considered, or consider herself,
unmarriageable – who is waiting to meet her present lover, her last
hope, as we are led to believe, of a decent marriage.[26] She is waiting
with a kind of trepidation which also verges on a blank despond-
ency. He has asked to see her place of work. She has told him – as,
she tells us, she had told his predecessors – that she is a beautician,
and in a sense this is true, but as the story goes on we realise that
her actual work is to beautify the dead; she works in a funeral
parlour.

She has no friends; they are, she says, too scared of her pallor,
of the strange, unplaceable odour which clings to her – which
her present boyfriend, in an error of which Grenouille would
not be guilty, has so far mistaken for cologne, but which is in
fact the residue of pickling alcohol. She sees herself as a paradoxical image of contamination; she works too close to death for the
living to want to have anything to do with her, even though she is
also aware that the dead have a pure and sterile beauty of their
own.

The ending of the story is entirely ambiguous; we are not told whether her boyfriend will go the way of the others. But what we are told of is her own prefiguration of failure, her doom-laden awareness that she carries with her the smell of too much reality. I cite 'A Girl Like Me' because I believe it reminds us of something of the fear behind the psychopathologies we have been discussing: which is a fear of death which is made over into a wish to place death entirely in others, to kill them psychically by reducing them to objects and fragments and then 'freely' and guiltlessly – because they are *already* no longer persons – to kill them physically, in order, at least in part, to take on their protective colouring, in order to confuse the possibilities of surveillance, of being arraigned before the inflexibility of the law, of being picked out at the identity parade.[27]

The fate of Xi Xi's heroine is not to enact this series of substitutive acts but, instead, to represent in her own person with its indecipherable but resonant inscription precisely the final caring of which the male protagonists are so afraid. It is as though she takes to a deathly extreme the fate of Bronfen's objectified woman, the object of the collector's pornography. She it is who can admit, has to admit every day, that the dead are dead; but for this clear perception of reality, which is also a recognition of the indomitable power of secrets and yet at the same time a symbol for feminine nurturance, she may never be forgiven.

One thing which is quite remarkable about the four male protagonists we have discussed is their extraordinary *busy-ness*. The elision with the other meaning of 'business', which has already cropped up several times, is here intentional; but the implications extend beyond this. The perversions (if they are perversions and not 'normal') of gender relations from which these psychic structures stem come partly from masculine responses to the role model of masculinity; these are 'heroes' who have to take care of every eventuality, and who, in the particular case of Norman Bates, claim to be doing so in order to protect their nearest and dearest (even if these nearest and dearest are in fact stacked on the shelves of their inner world). It is as though they are each parodies of the man out and about in the world; Grenouille and Gregg are unabashed careerists, Bates and Fowles's collector are driven to further and further controlled paroxysms of activity as they seek endlessly to spin out the web of practical implications of acts which are themselves deflections from the truths of the outer world, in, perhaps, an extended parody of the relation of text itself to loss and fear, fear of the truth and of being reabsorbed within the law.

Against these images Xi Xi places an image of feminine stillness, but this is a stillness of mature acceptance which also knows that, at every turn, it will be objectified and misinterpreted, as the beneficial wealth of significances in death is rejected by societies of achievement which have no use for stillness and which have resigned (consigned) their hopes for psychological integration. In this context, *Psycho* can be seen to pose an ordinary but none the less important question, and one of peculiar relevance to Gothic: what is actually going on behind the facade of busy normality which characterises legally acceptable social life?

But what this attempt to disclose the reality (to betray the secret) behind the cover-story in fact comes up against is a set of intractable splits. A diagnosis can always be offered – in a sense, a diagnosis *is* always offered, and in one sense always preceded the condition of which it purports to be an explanation – but we have also to contend with that further aftermath in which the mother in Bates takes over the controls of the psyche. Clearly there is no world in which these two discourses can be made to interlock properly with or inform each other, because there is no available single subject-position from which both could feasibly 'originate'. The complexity of the disordered psyche, which may be again reverting to a pre-Oedipal undifferentiation, evades scrutiny in a parallel yet opposite way to the evasion that occurs when Loomis and Lila try to remember, to re-collect, Mary and end up by admitting, at least partly for their own convenience, that they never 'understood' her.

And what lies behind this is not only a fear but, as always, a wish: a wish to multiply those aspects of being-in-the-world which deliberately avoid comprehension, a wish to preserve the secret, because comprehension modelled on inadequate mothering figures on the psychic landscape as a deadly surveillance, a surveillance which in effect threatens the assumed sovereignty of the omnipotent subject, whether this be at the individual level, or as hypostasised and projected outwards in the massive systems of the law. In this world there is only absolute power or absolute powerlessness, which could also, of course, be a description of the whole of the paranoid/schizoid position; Bates's peep-hole observation of Mary, or Bates finally wilting, disappearing, melting, locked before the grim looks of his fantasised mother.

9

Laws of Recollection and Reconstruction: Stephen King

. . . the growth of the mind is somehow inextricably tied up with the evolution of the relationship between the self and its internal objects. Consequently, death of the mind is entailed by these objects being expelled, dethroned, invaded, corrupted, or fragmented.[1]

We can further investigate issues to do with Gothic and its dealings with the text, the body and the law by looking at some of the work of a writer who can fairly claim to represent Gothic most fully in the late twentieth century. In his immensely long fiction *The Tommy-Knockers* (1988), to take one of many examples, Stephen King offers his readers a highly conventional scenario for horror. An alien spacecraft is discovered buried in the ground; from it there come forces which turn the inhabitants of a small town variably odd or murderous. This creeping evil spreads, seeming to sweep all before it, until the town is cut off from the outside world, and its inhabitants have become the servants or hosts of those who control – or used to control – the spacecraft. The lone survivors of an untransformed humanity are picked off one by one, until it seems there is no hope of survival.

But then the scenario changes. What has been happening in the small town comes to the attention of the outside world. Greater forces, forces of the State, are mustered; and then the whole illusion crumbles. The power which the aliens appeared to have is revealed as not so very great after all, certainly incapable of withstanding the mass of human weaponry. The 'tommy-knockers', who have appeared impregnable, are revealed for what they are: not the rulers of the universe but a long-dead gang of space gypsies whose weapons are ineffective and fall apart in their hands. Victory goes conclusively to the home side; to the forces of law and order.

This, I believe, is an Ur-plot of King's, a hidden master-narrative, although it is rarely so fully or so lengthily articulated. It hinges psychologically on a swing between two different world-views, which we can conveniently assign as the views of the child and the adult. Those apparently alien forces which swamp the child in terror are revealed to the adult as things of mystery no longer: the power that keeps the child transfixed is at best a concocted affair, and only seems omnipotent because of the shortage of vision – the psychic analogy of King's archetypal US small town – typical of representations of early experience.

What psychic and ideological end is served by this plot? Reassurance, certainly: an assertion that powerlessness will in the end be overcome and we shall all – or almost all – come into our very own and golden city. Or, to put it another way, King puts forward a particular version of communal values, whereby the childish squabbling which makes us weak will be transcended by a stronger power of organisation vested in the law and designed to relegate the power of the Other to its proper place. The analogy with gypsies is no accident: cut off from lines of communication back to wherever their original home might have been, and cut off further by the fact that we are seeing only an *aftermath* of their activities rather than the activities themselves, these interplanetary dealers in space junk are swept aside, sent back to the death on which they have battened.

Or, to put it another way, the text enacts the construction of a 'we', produces a readership which is at all points coterminous with the norms of the law. And this is obviously a major root of King's enormous popularity: feelings of loss in childhood, and also feelings of adolescent separation, are eventually overcome in a perfected version of adulthood; all is legalised. We might see King's project as another overcoming of mourning: the loss of faith in the good parent which is the psychic equivalent of the intrusion of the alien is revealed as available for compensation. A price, of course, is exacted: plenty of other people die so that 'we' may survive, leaner, fitter and apparently more experienced, to take our just place in society.

Of course, to say that this is King's master-narrative is to oversimplify: there are examples where the narrative stops short at a point where resolution does not fully occur.[2] But where this happens, there is often a further device which reassures us that all will come well in the end, namely the articulated presence of the writer.

The 'presence' of the writer in King's texts is doubled in a complicated rebus. In *Misery* (1987), for example, the protagonist is a
writer, captured by a crazed fan and forced, under pain of mutilation, to produce for her the narrative she wishes to read. The
protagonist of *The Shining* (1977) is again a writer, and here his
weakness comes about as a susceptibility to the writings of others,
the texts, perhaps of the hotel itself, which fill up the empty space
afforded by writer's block.[3]

These writers, then, the writers-in-the-text, offer a range of
subject positions; but only in company with the 'presence'
of King-the-writer himself, the King who announces himself on
every title-page, the writer in Maine who is in constant touch
with his legions of fans and who is dedicated to supplying them
with the product they want. Does anybody ever re-read King? Are
his texts susceptible to re-reading? We might reasonably suspect
not: what we have instead is a manic proliferation of texts, texts
about texts, further texts spun from side-hints and ideas, texts
designed to fill an endless vacuum.[4] And if there is such a vacuum,
then on the psychological model of maturation it is clear where it
must be: in the latency period, in that phase of development where
nature runs counter to nature, where development is in abeyance
and we are at the mercy of uncomprehended forces which pre-date
and attempt to resist our submission to the law.[5] King's works
form a vast triumphal arch over latency: below we can see the
devils and monsters reaching up for us, but we are not confused,
for there is a writer at our elbow, a narrative to fill the void where
there are no narratives, a figure invisibly saying that in the beginning was the word, and that the word is still with us and will not
let us down.

In the beginning. But to speak yet again of the beginning, to
speak of the time 'before', to extend and promulgate a series of
narrative acts on the supposition that we can reach back through
time and memory, is immediately to feel the psychological polemic
within King's texts, and at the same time to glimpse the
deeper nature of the problem which King's work encounters and
attacks, and it is the same problem as the one we have seen
already besetting, for example, psychoanalysis, just as it is now
proving the lodestar of literary theory; for these are texts which
grapple directly with the question of origin. They constitute a series
of encounters with our recollection of the primal scene, the 'originary' law-breaking.[6]

We might say, for example, that King offers his reader a series of opportunities to re-experience scenarios of childhood anxiety under conditions of relative safety; the super-fiction *behind* King's fictions is that potential childhood traumas are laid out before us, and we avidly revisit the forbidden places of past periods of our maturation. But of course there are, as we have seen, no guarantees of the accuracy of these recollections. Although psychoanalysis, at least in its earlier forms, claimed to hinge on the possibility of rememorating a primal scene, emblematically in Freud's case history of Little Hans, it can offer us no epistemological guarantee of the validity of these supposed 'memories' – a point, of course, which the Wolf-Man took up during the course of his own analysis.[7]

Ned Lukacher, in *Primal Scenes*, provides another development of this point of undecidability: 'What Freud recognises', he writes, 'in *From the History of an Infantile Neurosis* [the case history of the Wolf-Man] is that the finitude of temporality demands that the origin be sought not in the past, buried by forgetfulness, but in the future, in the projective repetition of the origin as it is elaborated through the transference.'[8] Or again, comparing Freud with Heidegger:

> Freud and Heidegger demand that we understand the relation between forgetting and remembering in a new way. The patient has forgotten the primal scene, and the history of metaphysics has forgotten the history of Being. The remembrance of that forgotten history and of that forgotten scene does not occur within the mode of subjective or personal recollection; it occurs as an act of interpretation, as a construction, as reading.[9]

In other words, are we to treat these primal scenes as memories – memories beyond screen memory, as it were – or as constructions which we build, textually or analytically, to cover over the vertiginous abyss of the forgotten? In what sense is the relation we as reader or patient establish with text or analyst a recapitulation of previous relations or the immediate projection of a desire, a component of the future, a pre-statement of a wish as to how we would like the world to be? We might on the one hand ask what other loves we can ever form than those which are built upon the hidden foundations of the past; or on the other what feasible imaginings we can have of the quality of our past loves except in terms of the present, *but* a present which is dominated by projection towards an imaginal future.

Either way what we would see is that the present itself is that which now figures as the vacuum, as latency: however closely King's narratives may affect us, there is always another sense in which they *pass us by*: we need the guide at our elbow, the *psychopompos*, because we are ourselves blind (in the ways Borch-Jacobsen suggests) and deaf, lost in a world where forces (like those in 'the tragedy, Man') move in ways which we do not understand. The trouble which King persistently traces is powerful because, looked at from the underside, as it were, it is *real* trouble: it is the anguish of establishing a foothold of presence when we are haunted by absences, when we sense that the arch on which we stand, as in one of Martin's paintings, is held there only by the power of the Other. King's 'power', according to the repetitive aphorism which has come to dominate his book jackets, is indeed in his 'words'; but they are also *his* words, and we have no guarantee that the conventional, legal morality into which he draws us has anything in common with the imaginal lines which we draw between past and future and on which we hang suspended.

If we look at matters in this way, then many of King's devices fall into place; for I would say that there is a sense in which his fictions strike at the heart of all loneliness. We can now say, however, that this loneliness, the fearful isolation of his struggling protagonists, always on the brink of being swamped in unidentifiable and unnameable material, is not in itself a recollection of childhood loneliness; rather, it is precisely a re-statement of the Ur-loneliness, which arises from our ontologically peculiar knowledge of having forgotten the past the moment after it has happened.

One of the texts in which King approaches this most closely is *The Langoliers* (1990). The name of these creatures, who roll up the myth of being as night comes and replace it with nothingness, conjoins the languor of somnambulism and unconsciousness with the doubled notion, yet again, of lying: 'lying', in the first place, as our prone position, in sleep, the expression of our powerlessness and of our ignorance; 'lying' also as the untruth of our apparent recollection and of our dealings with the law. The langoliers neatly sum up the lapse, the gap, the hiatus which structures all 'memory': they figure as all our doubts as to what goes on in the outer world while we are absorbed in the inner; they suggest the crucial question of what *else* there is other than dream-time, of what it is which might guarantee continuity despite the manifest discontinuities suggested by dreaming, waking, and the archetypal difference which is encapsulated in the 'recapture' of dream material.

The popularity of King is evidence that the textual psyche he constructs is one which in some sense 'matches' the cultural psyche of the late twentieth century in the West; and here again we have to deal with the paradoxical problematic of latency, for, as we have seen earlier, child abuse stands as a key motif, not only in King's texts, nor even in the West's contemporary preoccupations, but also in precisely the problem of epistemological validation which, after all, haunts not only psychoanalysis but all psychology, law and history, and which is further emblematised in the deconstructions of postmodernism. Nobody knows what happened; we may know, as in the symptomatic title of Joseph Heller's novel, that *something* happened, but our only way of negotiating the detail of past event is precisely through the telling of story, the provision of (suspect) evidence;[10] and thus, of course, King's narrators emerge as storytellers supreme, hovering on the enticing, langorous, infantile borderline between the voice which lulls us to sleep and the voice which whispers of terrors in the dark.

In this realm, for example, we find the novella *The Sun Dog* (1990), which I would like to deal with at some length. The principal structures of the text are easily stated. There is a camera, and it is a gift to a boy. It is dropped, and this event opens in its viewfinder a hairline crack. Or, to put it more mythically, we might say that it 'falls'; and it is important at this point to underline that we have to deal, as we did with *Wuthering Heights*, in mythic discourses, for as we have hinted it is only through these suspensions of temporality that the structure of the primal scene can be approached.[11] But *both before and after* the 'fall', no matter in which direction the camera is pointed, it shows one 'scene' only (and this sense of the obsessive scene, the obsessed dark-adapted eye, should not fail to remind us of the transfixed stare of the child, the inability in latency to escape from prefiguration and repetition, all the ingredients of the 'primal scene' and of its relations to 'possession', no matter how we figure their temporal status): a stretch of white fencing, and in front of it, a dog. But although the 'frame' of the scene is always the same, the stance of the dog and its 'aspect' changes. To begin with it seems a harmless enough animal. Gradually, as the boy, becoming mesmerised, transfixed by the process, takes more and more pictures, first in the hope of

shaking the camera's own transferred trans-fixation and then in the
service of the burgeoning wish to know what will happen with the
dog next, it turns more and more towards the camera and as it does
so it grows ever larger, ever closer, ever more menacing until it
becomes evident that it 'wasn't any dog God had ever made'.[12]

The camera falls into somebody else's hands, the hands of a
bricoleur, a 'tommy-knocker' whom we need only know as 'Pop',
a 'father' such as God never intended, who takes more pictures,
which the boy, the original owner, experiences in the shape of a
sense of growing certainty that the terror is about to break into his
life, into this world and destroy it for ever; for the dog is becoming
a figure of pure hate. The new owner, however, eventually realises
something of what is happening and sensibly decides to desist
from further photography. But it is in this moment that the present
is passed over in, as it were, an unseen flash; or, to put it in the
cognate terms of Poe when he deals with the suspension of life and
death, that the will yields utterly.[13] It is, as we are told in a savage
parody of the flash of the photograph, as if a white light explodes
inside Pop's head; and 'as in a dream' he takes the camera, not
seeing it but mistaking it for something else, and continues to take
more photographs, thereby bringing the dog closer and closer to
the barrier represented by the hairline crack in the real.

This hairline crack can be seen also in other contexts. It is mentioned, for example, by Elisabeth Bronfen; she speaks of 'the breaks
that puncture the imaginary and the symbolic register, the crack
that disrupts both orders so that, momentarily, the real emerges',
and goes on to outline the 'central question' of 'whether the crack
of sexuality/death can be closed, with representation solving the
enigma by virtue of disclosure'.[14] It may seem at first glance as
though this is to put the argument about registers the other way
round, but this is to underestimate the trickiness of textuality,
whereby the crack itself opens us to a world where the registers
fuse, where competing claims for the status of the real, all such
claims bracketed by the role of the semiotic, are the very substance
of which text is woven. It is interesting too how this notion of the
crack is connected by Bronfen with the complex issues of repetition
and mourning and with the status of 'Ligeia' as an essential component of a guide to the underworld.[15]

The dénouement of *The Sun Dog* need not concern us here; what
is interesting in terms of the problems of recollection and construction is the moment when the will yields. Pop has decided that the

trouble coming must be averted at all costs; he is on his way to get a sledge-hammer to destroy the camera.

> And as he neared the door to the back shed, a shutterflash, huge and white and soundless, went off not in front of his eyes but behind them, in his brain.
>
> He turned back, and now his eyes were as empty as the eyes of a man who has been temporarily blinded by some bright light. He walked past the worktable with the camera now held in his hands at chest level, as one might carry a votive urn or some other sort of religious offering or relic.[16]

Yielding, emptying, what we have here is the consummation devoutly to be desired, the takeover, the 'per-vasion' by some force perceived as outside the self, the abdication of legal self-responsibility in the single bright white light at the back of the mind to guide us, the illusion of an origin, and in the process of recognising this external force we are introduced also to the bearing of the votive chalice, the very emblem of the pure symbol. Pop is no longer in need of the myriad stratagems which have been his hallmark: he has moved beyond them into a purer and more unified realm, whose own alternative hallmark is an unwitting, an unconscious destruction. Its agency is, of course, animal; but not animal in any sense of a real perception of the beast, or of the human as an 'ancient animal full of grace', rather he has been taken over, overtaken by the dog.

Or not. Perhaps we should rather say that what has 'taken over', what has 'possessed' him at this point is precisely the force of the threshold, the undecidable gift and withholding of presence, the god who lives, facing both ways, in the hairline crack, whose function is to obliterate the divisions of class, status, gender which comprise the frame through which the law sees (view-finds) the world, and from which we manage to structure the simulacrum of recollection; this god has found himself fortui-tously located in a 'visible' crack (as the forces of malevolence which crowd onto the child, emanations of the will to damage within the child's own self, make themselves visible through the curious interlocking of that which cannot be remembered with that which can never be forgotten, which is the stamp of dream) and able to peer out, in an inversion of Norman Bates's 'peep-hole'. A single glance from 'earth's wide eye' is enough to overwhelm consciousness;[17] it figures as the long-awaited bright light of knowledge (of the imaginal past) before which the will must yield utterly. We should not underestimate the pleasure in this 'experience'.

We should also not underestimate the complexity of levels which we enter, along the path controlled and revealed by this hair-line crack. Some of these are relatively obvious. For example the world of the camera inevitably reintroduces us to the gaze, to scopophilia, thus from a specifically reticulated angle to the whole realm of 'penetration', to a set of mechanical complexes rooted in the evolution of a 'tool', a handle sufficiently strong to rebut or disguise the feared and denied penetrative capacity of the mother, that which has been psychologically (and pornographically) imaged in the equation of nipple and penis,[18] which in turn represents the early silencing of the (male-)child by a force of fascination and nurturance which at the same time stoppers the mouth, violates precisely the *will*, the will to select alternative pleasures which cannot even be 'seen' around the mountainous, necessary presence of the breast. In this realm, what might the crack in the viewfinder signify, apart from but also through maternal genitalia? Presumably the possibility of a new entrance, the mooted presence of a world which is not under the control of mother, which is not at all within the confines and boundaries of 'creation' even when this maternal creativity is displaced and fed back, as it constantly is in the 'real present' of 'monotheistic' conflict, as an allegiance to the one (male) god.[19] The pleasure in yielding to this absolute Other is simultaneously the pleasure of supplanting, replacing the 'natural', removing the hieratic power of the summation of the matriarchal law which the dog does not recognise, which the dog comes with an atrocious permission to savage. To achieve this proffered liberation no price is too high to pay; or rather, our knowledge of the price will be willingly yielded in the moment of the one bright light which comes to wipe out the whole web of ties, of conditionings which we resent from birth, even while we falsely recast them as the chains of our mortality.

That this liberation can only be into death goes without saying, as does death itself; for here what we need to sense in the terms of the master-myth is that Eros is present, but *entwined*; although – and because – Eros represents the possibility of *not* being enwrapped by birth trauma, he is the force which holds the end of, or limit on, answerable questions.

Some argue that Eros, hatched from the world-egg, was the first of the gods since, without him, none of the rest could have been born; they make him coeval with Mother Earth and Tartarus, and deny that he had any father or mother, unless it were Eileithyia, Goddess of Childbirth.

Others hold that he was Aphrodite's son by Hermes, or by Ares, or by her own father, Zeus; or the son of Iris by the West Wind. He was a wild boy, who showed no respect for age or station but flew about on golden wings, shooting barbed arrows at random or wantonly setting hearts on fire with his dreadful torches.[20]

Eros, I suggest, is a crucial figure for our dealings with the problem of recollection and reconstruction; and incest and child abuse, the fatal undecidability – and indecision – of the father (which we might see as the root of all undecidability) are all present here in the myth suggested by the Sun Dog, who is in himself the ironic inversion of the hounds of Hell. The Eros of horror is held in stasis, yet at the same time he approaches, *encroaches* with an irresistible force, not yet to be tamed by the false realisations of adulthood which in themselves amount only to the nervous suppression of the dream. If the primal scene is a refraction of a fear of future powerlessness (in itself the image of the encroachment of death) then the way in which King recounts it has a certain accuracy; for this is not a fear which announces itself along the trajectories and dimensions of the real, rather it is a refraction through the ever-present hairline crack which will always prevent the real from assuming the robes of its own omnipotence, will always assure the dog its own space while building the most complex and sophisticated of defences to prevent its (recurring, imagined) intrusion.

We can see here none the less the liberatory potential of the 'dog beyond the world'; we can also sense that 'entwined' in this set of Eros myths there is a major doubt, a root of much myth-making; we sense that we are here on the cusp of an historic realisation (which will also always be the root of misrecognition) of the masculine participation in conception, and thus we remain locked (in terror) on the site of the primal scene. If it was not incest, then perhaps it was Ares or Zeus; or perhaps it was really the West Wind, a non-human force which might blow through the hairline crack. In the world of fascination evidenced in and by the camera, and for which Eros is a psychic name, anything is believable because all the barriers are down, or potentially so, no force can withstand or fail to yield; the enjoyment of powerlessness is laid bare for all to see and thus becomes the site of the endless recapitulations and reconstructions which become necessary after latency in the name of disembarrassment, or disentwining from the (un)natural proximity of the dangerous mother.

It seems necessary to read the psychological 'level', as we did with *Wuthering Heights*, down the gentle slope towards myth; and there we might find ourselves also encountering a previously suggested etymological level, in terms of the notion of 'per-vasion', the incipient takeover of the vulnerable flesh by a force which is without control or explanation. This per-vasion is again re-contained within, reconstructed in the glare of, the single bright white light which is beyond the world, beyond at least the human-shaped world and thus beyond will or *nous*: what happens here happens under the guise of an irresistible mastery, and is also thereby signed, as Lukacher suggests, as a type of transference. For the image makes itself clear: it is an image of a kind of event which has been 'known before', the photoflash, and thus it fits neatly into the chain of such events which is unfolding (before or behind our eyes); but it is also in itself precisely the unassimilable, the irremediable break, the momentary vacuum – and here it needs to be said that the clinical evidence for latency is not what is textually at stake, for the very image of latency becomes transformed, before our eyes as it were, into the problem of the langoliers, the question of how, in the absence of a history of Being, we might connect one moment to another or surpass the alternative, lake-bed arch constructed by dream not over but under the very site of presence which, in our imaginations only, could effect, succour and cement such a connection.[21]

We see here the point at which there is always an absolute qualitative break in the signifying chain, and perhaps this is indeed the inner heart of the primal scene (and thus the heart of the law is always broken, as is the possibility of its poem): it is that which we hold most closely to ourselves, unremembered, unforgotten – indeed, unforgiven – as a counterbalance to the ineffectualities and incapacities of the tommy-knocker world: while in the apparent present we may fumble about in an absence of convincing narratives, at least we can hold to a notion that there was a cause, an explanation for why all this went wrong, a hairline crack in the past through which seeped an impossibly contaminating matter, such that all our experience is now of the impossible.[22]

We are speaking here of thresholds, and this seems to me apt both in terms of King's work as a whole and also in terms of the problem of the primal scene; for what may be held in the 'liminal' area before remembering and forgetting is evidently a threshold, and perhaps this is the best image our recollection has to offer us. Beyond this threshold, *The Sun Dog* tells us, there is only pervasion: there is only the lack of individuation, the absence of separable event, we are instead now in a different 'presence', sacred, perhaps, holy, such that its agent needs to be carried like a chalice, like an unintelligible precious object, like an artefact which has been made by neither god nor man.

To bring on again, as Baudrillard and others suggest we have to, the 'question of soul':[23] the camera, of course, is well known as the agent of soul-stealing, as the surrogate organ which will drain power, or soul, from any living body which it confronts. If we think again in some of the terms offered by Deleuze and Guattari, we might say that the camera is the organ without a body, the result of an appalling separation, a deflection of and within the gaze such that we no longer know what is our 'own' and we can no longer find anything of our (point of) view; or rather, perhaps, that it is that 'inorganic organ' which attaches itself to and pervades any body with which it has to do.[24] The text here grasps, it seems to me, that *this* process of pervasion is dialectical: it is not a matter of power flowing *through* the camera from object to subject but rather a representation of a process of dehumanisation which is perhaps also a fabricated memory of non-humanisation, in which precisely the link of relationship, the emotional tie, which would alone guarantee humanity to either or both sides of the equation is placed in brackets, and those brackets are again summarised in the frame of the viewfinder. Again, then, and now at the level of soul or spirit, we have to ask ourselves: what of the hairline crack? And here, perhaps, we find ourselves on firmer ground: for it takes only a brief discursive sidestep for us to see, and indeed announce, that the crack *is* soul. It has to be: if the process of photography is an apt image for de-souling, for stealing soulstuff and funnelling it from both sides into a 'black hole' where it disappears (inside the camera, never to emerge despite the even more disquieting implications of the process of Polaroid), then a crack in the fake completeness of this process, a spot of tarnish on the armour of the larcenous ego (Mary Crane's crime), has to be seen in terms of a gesture of letting soul out again, of letting it live in the only way it can, which is in a world of its own devising, engaged in gradual and slow activities which move to the beat of a different drum, the reverberations of which enjoin us to construct the primal scene as a means of rendering intelligible that which cannot be brought under legal control. The shape this world might take, which is here composed of the attributes of abjection in Kristeva's sense,[25] cannot of course be estimated in advance because the only way to approach them any more closely would be by transiting over an impossible threshold; nevertheless, this crack is here the only promise of soul, and the plotline, the master-narrative which repudiates it and colours it with the deeper shade of black which we associate not with the 'darkened' world of Hades but with the absence of coloration of the void or vacuum can be read only in terms of the depths to which the historically real – here a thoroughly etched picture of a regime of contemporary US society – will go to avoid the possibility of that which is – to put it at its very least – beyond the confines of the conventional, that which smacks of the excesses, transgressions and 'transfixations' of the primal scene.

This, at least, is something of what the text appears to tell us; but perhaps we should rather say that it is *there* that the text appears to lead us. We might further say that 'it' – and in putting it that way we are now speaking of what we might term the Ananke component of the text[26] – leads us into the heart of a blocked and static impasse which we might cast in terms of the primal scene; or we might – and the connection is crucial – cast it in terms of that easy and almost uncontested spread of the realm of the law which we know as colonisation. Where, as we have to ask in every textual context and very particularly not only in relation to those scenarios which abut onto an overt historical 'presence', is the colonial agency here? Is it to be apprehended in some relationship, always burgeoning, always disappearing, between the forms of invasion and pervasion? How can we discriminate between them when their basic terms cannot be mutually translatable? Or, to put it another way again, how shall we start to quantify or qualify the exact relationship between the violence of the dog and the violence of the social formation within which it is locked in the common premonition of a mutual doom? Or – and perhaps the rhetoric of 'levels' becomes exhausted at this point – what does dream replicate, at what point are its static images revealed as, although freestanding in *shape*, nevertheless composed of *materials* which are, after all, always and everywhere day-residues, the compacted and sedimented forms of the dayworld, its shaping politics and its own particular violences and imperialisms?[27]

The Sun Dog. If we want to turn this trope of bodily exhaustion further, then we can do it by playing about with these words ... endlessly? For instance: by whom is the son dogged? Why, by Pop, of course: the bad father, the wicked uncle, also Coca-Cola and the invasion by ghastly plastic juices of the innocent bloodstream. Sun God, Sun King, sunspot: the blindness which cannot see for brightness, the dazzled obliteration of difference in the face of the blinding presence of the One God, the Sun God, which is also Oedipal blindness but yet again the blindness we feel in our ecstasies before the throne of, indeed, who else but the sun god, who is the god of the masculine, the primary force, presiding (and usurping) deity in the primal scene, the force endlessly claiming primacy, seeking to replace the West Wind and thus demonstrating the inseparability of ego-based monarchy and usurpation, the force in whose face we find ourselves bending as we experience revelation, seeking the obliteration of multiplicity in the form of woman; the great replacer of lunar matriarchy, the force which will in fact not permit lunacy because the multifariousness of the shapes of madness will destabilise and upset the Sun King's throne.[28]

With this particular god, to continue to spin out the tropes, the *son* feels profound sympathy: he wishes to yield because the alternative is continued humiliation. To yield at the altar of macho, to internalise the images of masculine hunting-and-shooting normality (small-town ethos) which (sun/son) King's texts proffer might now seem precisely the solution to being haunted; and naturally the promise of release from such birth-directed haunting comes through an extreme exacerbation of the hauntings which have first driven us to the brink, to the threshold.

At this threshold we find the figure whom we might call the 'god-son', the blessed youth who will have a firm white light to guide him through the perils of a dog-infested or even dog-embodied universe, a world where Sirius reigns and the dog comes to end our days; the faithful friend is precisely he who, in the world envisaged as small-town USA, is the only one who can really betray us, the one dog who will in the end round on us and proffer a new life if we will accompany him through the gates of

Hell, through the hairline crack (which is also Alice's looking-glass) beyond which all the registers will be rearranged through a process akin to the constant mistaking of the concrete for the symbolic which is the hallmark of psychosis.[29] He is there in the inverted form of the sundog, the only sure guide through the morass, the tearer out of throats; we can see here the further traces of an inversion of the 'great goddess' in her subjugated, abject role of assuming the vestments we wish her to, those with which we want to clothe her – although here again we are on a terrain of ambivalence, for we want always to see her both hieratically arrayed and stripped bare, concealed and exposed, secreted and exhibited, 'scene' and 'ob-scene',[30] the holder and betrayer of her own and our secrets. In this array of imagery we also see the ambiguous form of desire itself, the distortion of the soul with which we have to work if we are to get further in the effort to comprehend the *aporias* which underline and undermine our lives, and we thus glimpse some of the ways in which we seek to transform these incompatibilities into a legally acceptable textuality.

I would contend, then, that in *The Sun Dog* we see a clutch of projects struggling within the text, centred on a wish to develop a primal scene. We look back at the protagonist in the textual past; but what we find is a project for maturation, ideologically coloured, and the construction of an explanation for the fatal flaw, the hairline, the crack of mortality which is *at the same time* the only evidence of our continuing connection with death, and thus with mortality and life itself. What the white light comes to do is to 'remind' us of the rebus-like intertwining of memory and forgetting: within that white light there is no past at all, only the naked terror of an unimaginable future which we need to populate with figures resurrected from the dead, from the void which provides memory with all the structure it has.

If we turn more briefly to another of King's texts, *Misery*, we can see a similar set of projections. On the surface we have here a text which concerns the primal horror of the all-encompassing mother; the writer's deranged female fan has all the power, the protagonist is sick and motionless, imprisoned, oppressed unto death by the overwhelming presence of her large, rigid, unyielding body, in which is also transparently coded the withholding of the breast. He is all too literally transfixed, all the more so as 'mother' starts to cut off parts of his body. But this apparent primal scene serves only as, precisely, a 'pre-text': the narrative is centred, in a Gothic trope, not on the 'facts' of imprisonment but on the possibilities of escape, and one of the principal pieces of evidence for this occurs in a scene near the end where the protagonist, free at last, walks into his own living room to discover 'mother' there, bloody and axe-wielding, only then immediately to realise that this is a trick of the imagination, an after-effect or afterimage, an aftermath which can be disposed of in the same way as the tommy-knockers.[31]

Misery itself, then, becomes an afterimage, in this case perhaps a means of explaining and justifying male violence. For in *Misery* what the protagonist has experienced is a prolonged and extreme form of child abuse; or rather, that is the (obviously uncorroborated) claim advanced by the text. The psychic uses to which this fictive primal scene might be put are manifold: it might be developed as an excuse for stasis, for an inability to progress beyond the rememoration of trauma; or it might be used as a justification for a process of maturation consisting of emerging into the world unscathed and unscatheable, as an imaginal perfect male body which grows back over the literal and emotional scars which the text would have us believe have been inflicted – among other things, as a punishment for the precocity of the masculine writer.

We face here a discursive crux of extreme danger, which has an obvious bearing on current debates about the therapeutic effectivity as well as the epistemological and legal validity of the psychoanalytic process. For the construction of a primal scene becomes itself, seen in these terms, the perfection of the alibi: the ever-present status of discourse as other than what it is, as that which stands in for and, as Lacan says, 'murders' the real through excess of the symbolic,[32] becomes foregrounded and highlighted through the subjection of the past and, naturally, through the equally difficult subjection of the analyst to the (unnaturally) strengthened will of the patient. The primal scene becomes the triumphal site at which the body of truth lies prone, whereupon we find that we have converted the revelatory potential of analysis into the most abject complicity.

But, of course, we do not 'find' this: who, indeed, could the 'we' or 'I' even be on a scene where all has been converted into an apparently present alibi for projection? What we have to deal with here is a vanishing, a disappearance of the self which is simultaneously the vaunting of the perfecting of the psyche which we faultily and hesitantly describe as the 'cure'.

In *The Library Policeman* (1990) the matter becomes even more clear in a variant of the master-narrative which is rare in King, for here the apparently supernatural events of the text are in the end pinned directly and closely to early experience of child abuse and of betrayal of the child by an adult. There are many other aspects of the text: what is interesting is that only an incomplete attempt is made to fit them into the structure, with one of the figures of terror ending up, in a gesture of structural despair, rather resembling a very small piece of chewing-gum. Shades of *The Tommy-Knockers*; but more significantly the occurrence of this scene of abuse is, precisely, a library, the site where the writer learns his trade, the storehouse, the physical body of textuality and at the same time the home of rules and prohibitions, or the point where the hairline crack through which knowledge of sexuality comes to the child is opened but within the order of the symbolic, through books, through the text. Again we might say that as in psychosis the symbolic is rendered directly into the concrete, with the abuser, the man who calls himself a 'library policeman' in order to assault the child protagonist, figuring as a direct and unmediated representation of a knowledge and a quasi-legal power too unsettling to bear.

The summoning up of powerful countervailing forces of defence within the psyche and their projection onto concrete objects in the outer world receives a further incarnation in *Christine*, with the adolescent section headings to which we have referred before: 'Teenage Car-Songs', 'Teenage Love-Songs', 'Teenage Death-Songs'. Here the plot hinges on a car which in some way funnels the evil and resentment of its previous owner and transforms this into a power of malevolent self-regeneration which appears impregnable until one of the protagonists – the one who survives – thinks of the obvious solution, which is to find a motor vehicle, not possessed of supernatural powers, but vast, violent and explicitly female, which has the power to crush all 'memory' of Christine. Whether this attempt is entirely successful is left open: by the end of the narrative it appears that Christine's powers of regeneration have increased, and that it is possible that she can re-create the whole of herself if even one small fragment of her material body is left. It does not take much insight to see here a crushing out of existence of early memories of humiliation, alongside the realisation that this act of crushing, of 'forgetting', can only be complete *if we succeed in remembering the past as it never was*, a past in which there was no Christine at all; neither is it a very long step from this to see the text itself as self-immolating and therefore forever unuseable as evidence. Thus the preservation of a fragment of Christine becomes both a source of terror and the only means of salvation of a sense of self: without the possibility of her return there remains no stock of images, no repository of the forms of love which might in time be transmuted into a mature psyche.

Another way of putting what is going on in these narratives is by thinking in terms of animation, disanimation, re-animation. If the primal scene is constructed rather than recollected, then we have to face also the possibility that all vestiges of the animate, the organic, the spirited face transformation into their mechanical equivalents, that the freedom, the exorbitancy, the unspeakable *excess* of love which is the maternal heritage and which is too inexplicable to be borne, rather than being cathected onto further love objects, is instead reduced, remade as a thing of bits and pieces, reassembled as a lifeless *bricolage* which we might then submit to the law. True it is that many of King's protagonists conclude their stories by leaving us with a sense that there is nowhere very much to go from here: the sheer strength required in the struggle to suppress the problem of the past means that nothing is left over, and thus we can take the notion of desire through a further twist. For the desire enshrined here is not merely for a kind of maturity which has dealt with, to the point of expunging, any possibility of memory of the real; it is also a desire to have done everything forever, a desire to equate maturity with death. This incarnation of the death drive is very strong in *'Salem's Lot* (1975), where the effort of ridding the small town of its vampires drains the energies of the protagonists (or we might say the split protagonist, man and boy, 'father' and 'son') while at the same time suggesting that the rest of life is going to be a vast disappointment.[33] But the desire for disappointment is a very strong one: once we have anticipated the future under this sign, then there is no further damage that can be inflicted upon us. We have prefigured all potential loss, we have extinguished hope, we have engaged in, and continue to engage in, a prolonged work of surrogate mourning which occurs *before the fact*.

And this takes us back again to what Lukacher has to say about the reversal of remembering and forgetting. 'The projective repetition of the origin as it is elaborated through the transference': *The Sun Dog* is obviously predicated on repetition, the repetitions of photography, the repetition of an inescapable scene, but a scene which, although always the same, is nevertheless one in which, uncannily, something is also always happening, an uncanny work of transmutation from familiarity to terror is always going on. Does it go on only when we take a photograph, or lie on the couch, or attend to the promptings of love? Or does the other world, the world behind the crack, have a mode of continuity, perhaps of a non-temporal nature, of its own? To put the question in a different but related way: what is it that we do to dream when we claim to figure it merely as an alternative, discontinuous mode of discourse, and relegate it to the world of sleep? What is it that we forget in waking life, not about the events of the night before, but about the dark background which remains with us – 'behind our eyes' – all the time, even in the court-room?

As Bronfen and Borch-Jacobsen say in their different ways, we have indeed to attend all the time to the *aporias*, the incompatibilities: the real and the symbolic refuse separation, the semiotic and the somatic will not stay in their appointed places, and the name of this set of refusals is death. To take Lukacher's argument one stage further, we can also say that the series of attempts we make to 'stage' the primal scene is also a series of attempts to stage our own death, in that it serves us as explanation of our own mortality. But at the same time it provides us with an alibi; because the construction of the primal scene simultaneously abolishes truth (as do the langoliers), then we remain consummately free to regard death itself as a lie; and this is what enables us to continue to live.

What, then, do we find in King's texts when we try to read them against this background, to see them as a series of elaborations of desire? What we find, not surprisingly, is a circle, and it is a circle heavily inscribed with writing, a circle in which text proliferates and is consumed – as an emblem of the body, which proliferates and is consumed. We can turn, for example, to *Secret Window, Secret Garden* (1990); here again the protagonist is a writer, and he is persecuted by a mysterious figure who seems to know much more about him than he should and clearly has murderous impulses, impulses which he vents not only on the writer himself but also on those around him. The text builds up an elaborate structure of suspense in which we are constantly hovering on the brink of the realisation that this 'second figure' is a double, that he is perhaps a figure from one of the writer's fictions made incarnate, that he is the writer himself during those increasingly frequent times when he finds himself, like Norman Bates, overcome with lassitude and forgets where he has been.

But this forgetting is indeed a remembering, an unconscious and uncontrollable recollection of the death drive: one of the minor characters hypothesises that the murderous and murderously named John Shooter may have been in some sense a character from one of Morton Rainey's fictions,[34] but the hovering alternative version would have things the other way round: that Rainey is in the service of Shooter, that the desire for obliteration, only slightly postponed by the entanglements of textuality, works its way through the use of Rainey's increasingly recumbent body. But other explanations are also possible. For there is no desire for fusion here, no will towards the reintrojection of separate psychic functions: instead there is a peculiar refraction of the impulse I have mentioned before, to be, in Kurt Vonnegut's phrase, 'lonesome no more'.[35] The conjuring of the dark Other thus becomes the ambiguous counterpoint to the problems of community and proximity which are encoded in small-town USA: in a world where everybody knows everybody else, then the only way of protecting a 'secret', of holding onto whatever is in the crypt, of shielding oneself from the pryings of the law, is through a structured proliferation of the self.

But this reminds us too of the extent to which King's very settings have to do with defences, the way in which small-town USA marks itself off as a remembered, imagined past, in stark contrast to the intrusion of the real at the end of *The Tommy-Knockers*. King deals in the vicissitudes of community, but in a way which reminds us constantly of the interchangeability of openness and closure: openness to the behaviour of others, knowledge of their whereabouts and of their daily habits, is a simultaneous closure to the possibility of change. Psychologically, we are speaking here of an intertwining of transparency and opacity, such that certain kinds of 'knowledge' serve only to reinforce the stereotypical. Or we might say that two kinds of knowledge are opposed in the texts: knowledge of 'what is', what Hegel referred to as the quintessence of positivity, which has its own certainty but is immune to difference, and knowledge of what surrounds this island of certainty, a knowledge which opens up the richness of the imagination but simultaneously produces the hairline crack through which uncorroborated versions of past and future flow. One kind of knowledge leads us towards submission to the law; the other leads us inexorably away from such submission.

If we return to reflecting on the Gothic in general by way of conclusion to this chapter, then one key we have to the essence of the Gothic can now be seen to lie in the dual nature of the imagination. We may speak – as did the Romantics – of the bright imagination and the dark imagination, but we can also ally these to highly specific childhood formations.[36] The bright imagination, we might say, is born of security, of a sense of apt containment, of a sense of freedom within boundaries which allows the safe space in which one can withdraw always knowing at a deeper level that one can return and find the essential coordinates of security still in place. The dark imagination, on the other hand, is born of the absence of boundaries, of insecurity which produces fear, of a sense of danger which, unconsciously, requires the elaboration of fantasies of further damage, projected onto the outer in the form of an arbitrary and punitive system of 'justice', in order to survive.

Thus, probably, utopias and dystopias: because the imagination always remains rooted in childhood and because these two formations of the imagination bifurcate sharply, the more difficult imagining of the future would strike between these two poles. But thus also two different approaches to the construction of the primal scene and, although this has yet to be theorised, two different versions of the transference. Explained and unexplained supernatural, survival and obliteration, these tangles are worked and reworked in Gothic: the dispelling of the supernatural achieves nothing because the rational view of the past is as riven with hiatus, as unavailable for corroboration, as its alternative.

The 'memory' of loneliness is the fear of future loneliness: the strategies, textual and psychic, with which we seek to evade or populate this loneliness constitute also an attempt to provide an array of figures beside the deathbed – which is also the bed of the writer in *Misery*, or the bed of misery in the writer. The scenario in which 'mother', in the uniform of a nurse, hangs over our bed bearing a cleaver or a chainsaw is a reticulation of the cultural conflation of the image of the maternal body, the matrix, with the image of undifferentiation. What the writer in *Misery* loses to this composite Fate is a foot and a thumb: he suffers attacks on his mobility in the real world and on his mobility, his authorship, in the world of text.

But around this 'primal scene' in King there are also other figures moving, figures which remind us of something we have forgotten, sometimes of things we continue to forget. In *The Shining*, for example, there are the mysterious forms of the 'topiary animals', which on occasions appear to move, to menace, on others to remain firmly, innocently in place.[37] They are animated avatars of the sundog, they occupy a dimension beyond the human, they are the limit of what the Overlook Hotel can 'overlook'; or, to use a different meaning of the word, they are symbols for what has always been overlooked, that which has been omitted from the equations of the law, that which reminds us that no equation is possible because when we are 'subjected' to love we are subjected to excess, to embarrassments and humiliations, and conversion into terror, to touch again on a central theme of Gothic, is the only way that we can escape from this sense of unworthiness. There is a sense in which the protagonists in King achieve their 'worth' through grappling with these terrors, these dangers; but there is also a sense in which this can only be done through massive reincorporation, through forming a perfected body, whether of the State or of the individual, which is built on lies, which lies through its teeth, which seeks to reject the sense of *aporia* and replace it with a web of narrative strained to breaking point, the evolution of a clenched and resistant body which will suffer – and be lonesome – no more.

10

The Body Sublime:
Liu Suola's *King of Singers*

In Western literature, the supernatural and the fantastic, as their association with the term <u>fantasy</u> suggests, are conceived mainly from the angle of creative perception (the author's projection of his vision) rather than from that of the reality represented. Within the Chinese context, the opposite orientation is assumed ...[1]

In this chapter I want to discuss a short story, 'The Quest for the King of Singers' (1985), by the Chinese woman writer Liu Suola.[2] Liu has a growing reputation as a writer; she also for a time had the distinction of being one of the very few nationally known pop stars in the People's Republic of China. The writer herself and the story are remarkable products of the 'New China', by which I mean the cultural explosion which was detonated by the liberalisations around 1985.

The story itself is also, I believe, remarkable both in the Chinese context and in the more general one appropriate to this book. I shall begin by giving a brief account of it, and shall then try to identify and describe some features of it which bear relation to Western Gothic and its discourse of modernity, in terms of the text, the body and the law.

'The Quest for the King of Singers' is a story in which past and present mingle in confusing and intricate ways, which invite formal comparison with certain Western postmodernists – perhaps Barth, Calvino, Coover, and particularly Borges – and which make retelling, re-collection, difficult. The unnamed heroine is herself a 'singer star', struggling for identity amidst conflicts between art and commercialisation, and between 'native Chinese' and foreign cultures. She is popular and famous, and lives in a world which, in terms of the PRC, is unusually cosmopolitan and sophisticated; a world of private cars and foreign restaurants, grasping agents and Paris fashions. She believes herself to be in some ways talented; but there is no demand for the kinds of folk song she wishes to sing, and instead she finds herself earning vast amounts of money by turning out ordinary, banal pop lyrics.

Her memory, however, is dominated by her ex-boyfriend, known only, in a Kafkaesque stroke, as B. B is, or perhaps was, a composer: a man of obvious musical genius whose work, however, has now become eclipsed, precisely because he found himself unable to capitulate in the requirements of the new cultural market. The heroine, who also narrates the story, is called upon to make herself into a kind of musical executrix of B's legacy, but feels deeply ambivalent about what this would entail.

Her principal obsession (and this again is a tale of obsession) is with reliving a journey which she and B undertook together. B had heard rumours about a mysterious being called the King of Singers, who is supposed to dwell in the wild places of the earth; on lonely mountains deep in the south, surrounded, perhaps, by hosts of disciples called 'singing spirits', disciples who might be real peasants or might themselves be supernatural beings; or even the voices of the barbaric, of the wind and the wilderness, of the world beyond law.

He decides to seek out the King of Singers, and the narrator agrees to go with him. As she tells us, she is highly uncertain about her own motives; she seems to have little faith in the existence of this living myth, and says she regards the journey merely as part of her 'duty' as B's girlfriend. But below this, we receive hints that she too, out of her dissatisfaction with her own life, is searching for something transcendental, something totally beyond the world of civilisation.

The journey itself is recounted in Gothic hints and flashbacks, lit by an uncertain gleam and illustrated by snatches of half-heard music. The physical environments, though, are at times all too concretely painted, as the two of them go through swamps, picking the gorged leeches from their living flesh, staying at ghastly village inns where the ground is crawling with bugs, maggots, rats.

From time to time they receive hints that they are on the right track; strange peasant women encountered in the murk tell them that the King is just a little further on, up the mountain; but then other adjuvants send them back the way they have come. Fortune-tellers profess to help them, but the narrator grows more and more disillusioned. She speculates on the hidden purposes of the journey; on the relationships between herself and B, between B and the King, wondering all the time whether this whole event might be some kind of awesome monodrama within her own divided personality.

In the end a kind of vision does occur, and B apparently joins the singing spirits. The narrator does not have the strength to follow his example, and instead returns to the city (or, perhaps, she has returned some time before, and the concluding moments are only her fantasy of B's fate); where she finds herself frozen into immobility before the spotlights and microphones of her next concert, stuck in her memories of B and, therefore, of the King of Singers.

That the story is, like the original Gothic of Radcliffe and others, about the search for and the fear of the sublime is made obvious very early on, although the aesthetic correlative for the sublime is ostensibly music rather than painting. The narrator tries to scoff at sublimity: 'Composing music was no religion. All that talk about character and spirit, the heart and the soul, enlightenment and inspiration; about true music being pure, lofty and sublime...' (p. 2). But this dismissiveness proves unavailing when she finds herself actually in the world of the mountains which, again as in Western Gothic, is a world where all the petty detail of the picturesque is 'sublimated' into a kind of terrible purity which also bears the unmistakable contours of dream: 'I kept feeling that the two of us were like somnambulists [*sic*] who had climbed up a high mountain. The wind at the top of the mountain blew away all noise, leaving one wondering whether this was not really a soundless world' (p. 3). But this 'soundless' world, this world where all sounds which might 'awaken' have been swept away, is also one which is profoundly animate, although instead of the cries of banditti, 'the sound that came from the pine forest was like the sound of children sobbing'.[3] Just as in Burke's formulae for the recognition of the true sublime, the human individual is here dwarfed by mighty forces, reduced to an insignificant speck, with the wind 'turning us into its playthings'.[4]

Besides reminding us of our insignificance, these manifestations of wild nature also appear to refer to a kind of natural vengeance for, as again in so much of the Gothic, the unknown sins of our ancestors. These ancestors had left us a legacy:

> Light wind on the lake,
> Moonlight on the mountain,
> These, and these only, are for your use,
> Take them freely, they are always there.

But we had handed back to our ancestors this treasure endowed upon us by the creator...

(p. 8)

What Liu seems to be implying is that the fear we experience in the face of nature's grandeur is at least partly the result of our own misbehaviour towards the environment; this inability to regard the body of nature with innocence is the source of our (infantilised and infantilising) fears, and thus the origin of the mysterious and terrifying ways in which the mountains manifest themselves – at least to the narrator, although B seems to live a charmed life in these regions, no doubt as a result of his uncompromising attitude towards his artistic gifts, which seems to give him a kind of exemption from the cycle of damage, guilt and reparation which we can see as a mainspring of art and, at the same time, as the hidden source of the types of reparation and vengeance writ large in the forms of the law.[5]

For the narrator, therefore, the mountains can never be apprehended clearly:

> The mountains in the south were enveloped in heavy, eerie fog, people who lived there seldom saw the sun. Like the rising tide, clouds and clouds of fog rose from the valley, covering the fields and villages that could be seen from the mountain. All the mountains were alive, were exhaling steam, the steam carried with it monotonous, long drawn-out calls that echoed everywhere. People said that these were the voices of the 'singing spirits' – the followers of the King of Singers – calling to one another. Trees in the burnt-out wasteland, deeply scorched, were stretching out their long fingernails to clutch at the soil. Crash, crash. Everywhere huge boulders collapsed and came rolling down from on high, swallowing all living things in their path.

(p. 21)

I shall return to this burnt-out wasteland below; for the moment, my point is to emphasise the immensity and casual malevolence of this sublime landscape, a landscape obviously but distortedly modelled on centuries-old traditions of Chinese painting.[6] The sublime here figures as that quality of perception which continually eludes classification, which refuses to conform to human laws of proportion and perspective; just as the journey itself refuses to sort itself out into a regular sequence of events, but figures only as a set of chaotic remembrances and alternative scenarios, contorted like Gothic narratives themselves, the soul of unreliable evidence.[7]

At the end of the story, the two travellers find themselves at the central point of this landscape, and our perception sways, as it does in the face of, for example, Martin's biblical paintings, before the scene:[8]

A cliff appeared before us. At the top of the cliff there was a huge piece of rock which jutted out, forming a platform. A group of singing spirits were sitting there, others were still climbing up the cliff from the bottom of the mountain. Those on the platform were swinging their bodies and calling sonorously, with their eyes fixed on the moon. The slow crescendo of their calling was like the rising tide swallowing the dark night. There was no leader here, and no audience; everyone was enveloped in a solemn atmosphere, the naked bodies reflected a silver light.

(p. 33)

An incarnation of a sublime, post-legal politics, perhaps:[9] although it has seemed as though the King of Singers is the goal of the quest, here in the heart of the mountains there is no longer a searched-for and a searcher; all is merged in a panorama of heights and depths, and the apparently human figures reveal their alternative guise as manifestations of the spirit of the wilderness.

The intertwining of the sublime and Gothic in the Western tradition needs no further elaboration; but obviously what is at least as clearly distinctive of the Western Gothic is its troubled, ambivalent textual dealings with the supernatural, and Liu's story provides us with several instances of these, beginning with the 'singing spirits' themselves:

On our way in quest of the King of Singers, I nearly fell into the trap of a 'singing spirit'. It was a woman, she told us that she

could find the King of Singers. She led us up a high desolate
mountain, then sat down at the edge of a cliff. From the heart of
the dark valley came gusts of cold wind, a huge lime crag in
the distance shone with white light in the dark of the night.
The 'singing spirit' was shivering all over, a loud moaning
came slurring out of her mouth and rose and fell like the ebbing
and flowing of the tide. The wolves in the mountain started to
howl at the sky, the moon-lit night became desolate, all too
desolate.

(p. 16)

Ghosts in Chinese culture are in many ways different from Western
ones, in ways too complex to be gone into here,[10] but it is at least
clear that we are here confronted by all the 'symptoms' of possession, and also by a strange linking of apparently human and
apparently natural forces. It is interesting too that this is the third
time we have come across the image of the 'tide'; I believe it
functions precisely to erase distinctness of shape, both the shapes
of the landscape and also the shapes of the human forms who
perhaps guard or perhaps even constitute the ambiguous and
insubstantial body of the King of Singers.

A second telling instance of the supernatural we may summarise
as the episode of the clawed tree. B has a knife, and is eager to
show off its powers; to do so, he unnecessarily fells a tree.

I was about to applaud him. Why did he stand stock still all of a
sudden? I ran over, and found that he was caught by an old tree.
It was black and ugly, its body was gnarled and covered in thick,
spiky thorns. Its long claw, which had B in its clutch, was also
black and thorny.

(p. 25)

There is an elaboration here of the ancestor motif, the motif
referred to in much Gothic fiction in terms of the 'sins of the
fathers'; it is not only humans who have ancestors, the trees have
them too, and they are unsatiated in their desire for vengeance.
Indeed, this tree is only thinly disguised as a tree; it also bears
many of the hallmarks of the traditional witch, as the 'singing
spirit' in the example above bears the trademark of the fox fairy.

The narrator manages to disentangle B, but 'all of a sudden, the
sharp claw of a tree was right before my eyes, I had no time to

dodge, it scratched my face and blood began to stream down immediately' (p. 25). This wound, or rather the scar which succeeds it, becomes important in the story: rather like the various 'visible signs' we come across in Gothic, from the mark of Cain[11] to the Ancient Mariner's albatross, it forms an open code for the narrator's fear, a mark which on the one hand reveals her experience, exposes the frailty of her body, but on the other sets her apart from other mortals while suggesting that she is the possessor (or the possessed) of a secret which cannot be told, the victim of the ever deferred outcome of a case which cannot be heard. It also presages her death; although it is never clear at what level of consciousness the text carries this inscribed premonition.

B himself evolves throughout the journey, but his evolution is a curious one. Certainly he carries within himself an awareness of ideal life which serves as his guiding light, a white light to guide him; but this in turn means that he leaves human existence behind and develops into a strange manifestation of the 'afterlife'. 'By now, B would certainly be able to go without meals. Bury him in the soil for a whole week and he would, when he crawled out, still be alive' (p. 26). What kind of life, though, would he possess, or would possess him? Here again we are on the terrain, or in the crypt, of the premature burial, and in the presence of a Gothic structure of imagination. It is possible for human beings to strain beyond the confines of the law, towards the transcendental, the absolute; but as so many Faustian and Promethean figures within the tradition discover, Maturin's wanderer to take but one example, there is a terrible price to be paid, the price of mounting to a state of being whence there can be no return and indeed no communication, unless in the form of a message, a misaddressed letter, from the apparently dead.[12]

The most problematic figure the narrator encounters is the painter she refers to as Sharp-snout. He carries wisdom, but neither it nor he can ever be pinned down. He 'took out a few masks, all human faces, and wore them on his head. He screamed and shouted, and he shook and swung his body. His shadow flickered on the low ceiling, like the spasmodic contortions of some demon' (p. 27). It is, indeed, this same demon who stands for the true art of painting within the story; but his painting, although done with vividness and high colour, is executed not with a brush but with a spatula, producing huge thick masses of hue beneath which, as beneath the rising tide, all form and shape is purged away.

We are also returned by the story to the theme of the *Doppelganger*, and to strange, or rather estranged, re-collections of the theme which remind us of the *Confessions of a Justified Sinner* as well as of *Dr Jekyll and Mr Hyde* (1886).[13] In the Western tradition, of course, this series of accounts of the split personality – perhaps it would not be too much of a pun to suggest that it might often be better referred to as the *spilt* personality, in recognition of the lack of containment and boundary-breaking which it evidences – take on many articulations: reason and passion, good and evil, body and soul. In this third form it feeds on the images of the wraith, the bodiless soul, and the zombie, the soulless body. 'The Quest for the King of Singers' can be similarly read, especially when, as the two travellers wander through the dark spaces of the valleys,

 ... we met a carpenter who told us that ghosts often appeared in the low-lying areas, walking beside living men, whilst souls of the living would go to the burial ground and cry there. There were certain circumstances in which the soul of the living would leave the body ... At this moment, I couldn't tell whether it was my body or my soul that was walking in the dark; perhaps my body was still in the little wooden house, or perhaps it was in fact in the city, or at a show, or making a recording?

(p. 29)

What makes Liu's account of these phenomena distinctive is not so much the encounters with ambiguous figures who might indeed be mere souls or mere bodies; it is more the sophistication with which she not only depicts these splits within her chief character but also evolves a form of narration in which the very splits are replicated as the narrator answers her own questions about the strange mode of existence into which she appears to be passing, and also the detail with which she underlines that these differences of mode of being are also differences of environment, the marks of a gap between different cultures which have grown apart so that the increasing cosmopolitanism and commercialisation of the city are literally unrecognisable to the older, more traditional China represented in the untapped vastnesses of the countryside.

These meditations erupt into a lengthy speculation on the triple relationship between the narrator, B, and the King of Singers (or: A, B, and ... ?):

What about B? Was he at one with his soul? Was the B I have followed for so long merely a soul? What about the King of Singers? Was he human or was he a soul? If B was a soul, what was he, the man, like? Where was he? If he was a man, why did he not give up chasing a singing soul? What was the natural connection between the King of Singers and B? Was the King of Singers B? Was he B's soul?

(p. 29)

Interestingly, although the terms of the split are offered as double, body and soul, the actual personalia who inhabit this structure are triple: this reflects, I think, a puzzle about idealisation, whereby the King of Singers represents a form of ideal which is *always* in the beyond and thus undifferentiated, whereas B represents, to the narrator, a kind of oscillation between immanence and transcendence, and therefore a phenomenon which cannot be described in terms of the visible or the invisible, the accountable or the unaccountable, the bodily constituted or the immaterially chaotic. It is thus that B both 'goes away', in the sense that his physical being 'crosses the line' (as, of course, in a different context does that of the Ancient Mariner) and becomes, presumably, absorbed into the mysterious 'corpus' of the 'singing spirits'; while paradoxically the shadowy presence of his memory remains to plague the narrator, ineradicable precisely in its absence, which also involves the impossibility of transferring this shadow-burden to other shoulders, whether the shoulders of a further individual or those of the law or State. Yet here too we might consider matters on two levels: the narrator is afflicted by a personal traumatic fixation, and also by a body of purportedly creative work which will, it appears, also always remain to cast its 'shadow' within the spotlight of her transient successes, successes which themselves depend precisely on her 'appearance', in the doubled sense of the aesthetic of her bodily presence and also of her arrival, in fully materialised form, for her next 'show', her dubiously or melodramatically lit manifestation – or 'apparition'.

This puzzle, and the associated imagery of light and shadow, the recrudescence of the visions of a silver tide in which distinct forms melt, recur painfully at the end of the story. At the literal level, the narrator is transfixed on stage, waiting to move into the bright lights (the stage, the city streets); while inside she is reliving the moment when she failed to accompany B on his final, naked journey:

I really wanted to walk naked into the white light, as B had done, but I hesitated, I didn't move. Standing in the dark, outside the white light, I felt surrounded again by the cold, the damp, and the insects. I saw innumerable singing spirits calling to the moon. I could never walk into that beam of silver light; I would always have to stand on the outside, in the dark; I would never become a singing spirit, never see the King of Singers; I could only stand here, waiting, waiting, B, could you appear again with the light of the dawn?

(p. 35)

Read more as a parable of the state of the psyche, Liu here is caught in an unbridgeable Gothic gulf, a gulf which is a kind of de-allegorisation of the 'sublime' gulfs and crags of the landscape in order to manifest the mutual alienation of country-based and city-based life. We see here a reflection of a world where there seems to be no more space for the reintegration of a traditional (in this case Chinese, in other parallel cases it will be different) culture on the precipice of obliteration, as new forms of foreign-based life take over the (shells of the) cities and render the outside rural darkness frightening and ghost-ridden. This, I would like to suggest, is an archetypal structure, which is to say a structure of haunting: the barbarians are always at the gates, we stand always on the precipice of obliteration, and the forms of life which are riding to take us over will always come from elsewhere, from 'outside', will always be in some sense foreign, yet at the same time will always relate in ways difficult to imagine to the death-wish which has its collaborator in the 'foreign body' which is within, yet never within, ourselves.

What needs to be emphasised is that the world of touchable reality, the world of the body, in Liu's story is in effect reduced to two seemingly unconnected realms. On the one hand there is the highly physical environment of the city, which is pictured in terms of hairdressers, beauty salons, reataurants, a world of purely material comfort which is nevertheless in itself in a sense unreachable, in that we receive a suspicion that this Chinese version of Western sophistication bears a duplicitous relation to the 'real thing', is a kind of floating imitation, a 'floating world' to use a resonant Japanese equivalent, an appearance of security which may in fact be not merely transient but even a mirage, something curiously akin, perhaps, to a pleasure dome. And here, of course, we see a reflection of the uncertainties consequent on the PRC's own massive shifts of culture and political freedom over the last decades: it could perfectly well be that all those beauty salons, so the story suggests to us, could be closed down tomorrow, worse, that they will entirely disappear and be erased as China perpetually erases its own history, all the glossy magazines swept beneath the carpet, under another red tide. And even as we say this we recall to mind the figure of Ozymandias and, confronting his ruins, and the other ruins of a life based on factories and trades which have been all but erased as other kinds of tide pursue us across even where we think we are most tending towards progress, most arresting of our own decline.

The other physical reality is the countryside, 'the cold, the damp, and the insects', where absolutely no comfort is available for the body, and where we realise that the citified flesh has become too soft, too specialised, to withstand much of this alternative and older reality, to do so not requiring, of course, the growth of new organs but perhaps requiring the suppression of certain forms of dominance in the internal psychic order. Yet each of these two realities figures as a delusion, a mirage, in terms of the other. Certainly the narrator tries to persuade herself that the life of the journey was a virtual hallucination: 'slowly, I began to plod my way from that unreal delusion in the far away south back to reality' (p. 10). But the city itself also does not remain stable:

> This city was changing gradually. If you went away for several months, you would find it so new and exciting on your return. But if you stayed here all the time, you would be bored stiff. The mountains were just outside the city and could vaguely be seen, grey and hazy. That was where we should be heading for, not here. It was much less crowded there, the mountain ridges were wide, open, empty, and spacious. In the pine forest, the branches from last year were still everywhere, in layers, making a kind of cushion for people to sit on and talk about love.
>
> (p. 12)

What we have here are several conflicting perspectives on novelty, on the brave new world, on the relegation of the ancient and of 'established' (but ruined) history. On the one hand, it is only in the city, as Wordsworth also saw, that things change: only in the city that it is possible to receive news and influences from the outer world and thus to feel 'in touch' (but perhaps more than ever not in *bodily* touch) with wider forces of innovation and development. From this perspective, the countryside figures as a repository of ancient custom and superstition, where nothing has altered for millennia: the episode in which the narrator attends a 'village party', although in effect it shows us a group of urban artists indulging in a little wealth-cushioned pastoralism, is none the less redolent of an older Chinese attitude to the country: the house is full of shadows, ghosts and demonic dancing. And, of course, the city is able to repeat this trick of appearing novel after any prolonged absence.

But on the other hand, life amid this process of forced change rapidly reassumes the contours of tedium: there may be a new fashion in vogue every month, but that cycle of production and consumption upon which the West has barely the strength left to comment reveals itself in China, as perhaps it did in some ways in late eighteenth-century Britain, in all its innate conventionality, the process itself remaining deeply the same despite the minute differences of style which the fashion cycle exists to promulgate and from which it exacts profit.[14] From this perspective, the city is indeed 'crowded'; not only with people, but also with redundant information and exhortation, crowded with a wealth of goods which serve no obvious interpretative needs and with a wealth of lawful regulation which serves only to distance the human from that realm in which it supposedly moves as producer and orderer.

From this point of view, the mountains do become 'where we should be heading for', and it is there that the city fades into oblivion. The narrator is thus caught in a double process of forgetting, which we can relate back to earlier primitive processes we have seen at work in Gothic. It is indeed this which causes her final traumatised immobilisation. The journey was not less real than the show business world of the urban present, but worse still, it is out there in the dark, amid the ghosts and shadows, that she has left B, which means that she has abandoned there a major facet of her own soul which will now not return on demand. Thus in the process of the story, we confront the possibility of the making of a monster; of a soulless and immobilised being whose eyes gaze continually inwards at an irrecoverable (primal) scene. This is very akin to a general definition of trauma,[15] and thus we see, in suitably melodramatic form, an account emerging of what it is like to live in a 'modern' or 'modernising' world, in a world where

modernity is produced by divisions between city and country –
perhaps we should rather say, by their dividing *again*. It is indeed
important in this context to add that 'again', because although in
one sense Liu is describing new phenomena, one of the most
important aspects of her story is the extent to which she is also
describing something that has been a recurrent feature of Chinese
history, the violently hierarchical dissociation of metropolis from
hinterland, a historical disruption which also has clear Western
analogues and has produced its own forms of textuality, Gothic
among them.[16]

I have already mentioned the image of the wasteland; and this
also is important because it is one of the central images of contemporary Chinese literature.[17] It bridges several reference points.
First, it is an obvious image of the Cultural Revolution, and of the
way in which during the years of turmoil much of China's history
and tradition were laid waste; paradoxically, by zealots who
claimed precisely that they were defending those features of
Chinese culture most appropriate to the twentieth century from
'foreign' incursions and ideas. This wasteland is one of burnt-out
temples, Buddhas shot through with bullet-holes, villagers cow-
ering in the dark.

But there is another sense in which the wasteland is also the
countryside itself, that vast land of eight hundred million souls,
souls for the most part without articulate voice; without political
voice, but also without voices that could be understood in the
cultural capitals; for 'at a distance of one hundred *li*, there are
perceptible dialectic differences... at a distance of one thousand
li, only a half of the things said are understood; and ... at a distance
of two thousand *li*, nothing is understood'.[18] The wasteland is thus
damaged, and voiceless; to transfer back into Western myth, we
might say that it requires a healing akin to that of the Fisher King,
but the Fisher King cannot be found. B's quest for an alternative
and also healing King is indeed a knightly quest, in the course of
which he encounters monsters, and along with him he takes –
whether by or against his own will it is hard to say – a modern
version of the propitiatory maiden. And although that wilderness
may have no words, it has music: the narrator's mistake is to think
she can record that music and that it will, thus re-membered,
survive the transition to the city, where, in fact, her upmarket
friends merely giggle over the primitive croakings with which she
has returned.

But B 'left the city and went to the wasteland with his mind filled with scores and methods of composition, for the purpose of becoming the disciple of the King of Singers' (p. 23); he goes in search of the charismatic teacher or wanderer who carries meanings which have become submerged beneath that alternative wasteland of urbanisation, to find something which withstands the endless flow of trivial 'compositions' against which Wordsworth inveighed.[19] In doing so, he embarks on a process of questioning familiar to us from Gothic encounters with forces which both transcend civilisation and underlie it; as the narrator puts it, 'the barbarous – the civilised – the philistine, who defeated whom?'.[20]

Whatever the upshot of this question, if it has one, she does become aware that the apparent order of conventional life is a thin veneer. As she asks herself on her flight back to the city, 'this smartly dressed lump of chaos in a plane – was it flying back to its original form, or was it on its way to completing its rebirth?' (p. 31). Reincarnation, resurrection, re-animation, the birth of a body with a different relation, a relation in difference, to the law; what, in other words, can one bring back from an encounter with the forces abroad in the world; new knowledge, or only a kind of dream-awakening, a repetition, a deepening of somnambulism, which leaves one forever haunted by images of a fantasy realm where both the more destructive instincts and the higher creative aspirations exist in a clearer form than amid the quotidian clutter?

The narrator comes, in fact, to what I would see as a pure and clear knowledge of what chaos is, which is precisely that 'chaos does not know what it is, and it never knows whether it should or should not, whether it is right or is wrong; it always admires clarity but is always dispersed by the airstream' (p. 31). We could meditate upon this image as one of the reader; but perhaps, in its complex and contradictory form, it touches more closely on the most basic themes and questions of Western Gothic; for it is in Gothic, as I have been trying to show, that we in the West most recently confronted again, and continue to confront, the borders of our own uncertainty, of the troubling of our own attempts at text; took up the endless play with the possibility that, below the neatnesses and arrangements of the conscious mind, there lies precisely that vast hinterland where crags loom in the fog and where one's own longings for law and order are revealed for what they are, attempts to cover and conceal the depths of chaotic impulses inside us.

Thus we may again take the route towards secrets, towards those particular secrets which comprise the crypt of the Gothic. But thus, more locally, the difference between the narrator and B. For her, the quest is more or less a literal one; she expects to encounter the King of Singers in the flesh, expects the object of her desire to manifest himself in a clear and recognisable form. It is B who is able to float on unresolved possibilities. What he sees is only, after all, a crowd of singing spirits who may simply be old peasant women engaged in ritual worship, but for him this outward and visible manifestation is enough to take a chance; it is the *feeling* of the presence of the King of Singers which satisfies his imagination whereas the search for a definitive 'incarnation' is always bound to drag itself back to the everyday round disappointed by its failure to meet with an identifiable being from another world, a being who, paradoxically, would only be perceived as satisfactory to the extent to which it would partake of clear, 'this-worldly' status.

One of the most distinctive aspects of Liu's achievement in this story has to do with her emphasis on the consciousness of her heroine, who is more aware than most Gothic heroines of her narrative investment in the tale; which is also to say that we are made to feel that Liu herself is self-aware about the part which narrative processes play in fiction and in the world. 'I exaggerated my experience, dramatised it, fictionalised it. I became a heroine and a woman of achievement in people's eyes' (p. 3). One of the most interesting aspects of this formulation is the way in which it encapsulates the connections between the processes of the heroine (or hero) and the related processes of the self-dramatisation of the ego and thus confronts us with an abyssal potential in the text's dream-like-ness, its somnambulism, its exemption from all consciousness of the law. To put it in another but related way, what Radcliffe does in *The Mysteries of Udolpho* for Emily 'unconsciously', which is to transform her from a sobbing victim into an unraveller of arcane mysteries, Liu does for her narrator with open eyes, contrasting her experiences of fear and cowardice in the swamps and mountains with her version of these events once they have been transformed into the language of the city – which, we are meant to infer, is again a language of exaggeration and melodrama, as perhaps are all languages when seen in the 'light' of their own foreignness.

The narrator certainly wishes to fly above the world, to come to its high places: 'I had never been in a spaceship, I didn't know whether its speed and my music would harmonise. Space could add loftiness to music, even the sound of wood-sawing could be sublimated in the universe. If the atmosphere could be turned into an amplifier, there would be even more singer stars' (p. 11). The ambition is great, but so is the fear; that it would be precisely the inadequacies of her own talent which would be exposed and dwarfed by an encounter with the truly 'lofty' – after all, she has already been told by her agent that part of the reason for her success is the smallness of her singing voice, because more available volume would simply cause distortion and feedback in the microphone, a distortion and feedback that we might want to connect directly to the unsustainable and unevidenced historical loops of Gothic.

The narrator thus has an intensely quizzical attitude to the stories that B tells her. Although she is persuaded, for ambiguous reasons, to join the quest, she is also aware that the stories B tells her are probably not 'literally' true, whatever that might mean; indeed, they may not be true at all, yet even so they may represent a fiction worthy of belief, a voice to which it is worthwhile listening, and thus a belief and a voice unlike the unworthy fictions and street-cries of commerce.[21]

In this passage, we hear the narrator listening to B's words and interspersing them with her own reactions:

'Every year the King of Singers holds a gathering with his disciples'. I knew, it was the same old story again, a gathering with his disciples in the wildest and most primitive region. 'All the people go there to hear the King of Singers sing; the singing spirits dance as they sing, the singing spirits of the entire world would be there'. It must have been an enormous stretch of wilderness, wider even than the sea, or the singing spirits would all fall into the sea. 'The entire wilderness is packed full of singing spirits, they sing and dance, sing and dance...'.

(p. 21)

I believe that we can here sense the doubled attitude within the narrator, a primal split, something always *spilt*: on the one hand, the urban cynicism at hearing the same old traveller's tale all over again, on the other, the wish to fall into this fiction, to make a semi-conscious gesture of belief. The tone, the language of Liu's prose has itself at times a childlike quality, and here we see the double reaction of the child listening to stories of ghosts and witches: the worldly knowledge that Santa Claus could not possibly come down the chimney, coupled with the small, bright hope that, just this once, he might...

The story thus enacts a kind of Gothic suspension of disbelief, and the narrator and B become figures for those two parts of our minds which take up different attitudes to tales of the supernatural. Yet it is unclear throughout which is the more 'enlightened' of these attitudes; the boundary between belief and unbelief is perpetually troubled. The singing spirits, after all, oppose the crass materialism that creates the other kind of 'singer star':

> All of a sudden, a strange sound came with the wind, came moving through the waves of air. It seemed to have come from the earth, it also seemed to have come from the sky; it seemed as if hundreds and thousands of spirits were there match-making for all the things on earth and for the universe, were bringing enlightenment to all living creatures, awakening them from oblivious ignorance.
>
> (p. 33)

The sense here of a 'higher world' is familiar enough; the mention of 'match-making' is perhaps more strange, reminding us of the literal level of the story. For the narrator is indeed uncertain of her relationship with B, and spends some time speculating that the whole fate of her participation in the search might have been conditioned from the outset by her jealousy of the absent King. We could extrapolate from this that Liu is saying that the social world inhabited by the narrator is one where there is no longer any 'appropriateness' to be found, and also that it is one where the individual is thrown back, in a way unfamiliar to 'traditional' (Chinese) society, on his or her own resources or judgments; better, perhaps, to become again part of an older world where, precisely, the impossibility of travel precluded these dilemmas of choice and where, furthermore, the wisdom of the old as embodied in the arranged marriage system and its many avatars was still trusted as a guide for those lost, Verezzi-like, in the mazes of maturation.

I hope I have outlined some ways in which I think that 'The Quest for the King of Singers' is related to Gothic themes and structures: the concern with the sublime, the dealings in the supernatural, the account given of splitting in the personality, and so forth. I would also want to add that the whole *mise-en-scène* of the story, its questioning of the boundaries of reality, delusion and dream for me relate directly back to the principal concerns of the Gothic.

But my main concern here has been to suggest that this set of intertextual relationships is not adventitious. The social configuration within which the Western Gothic was born can now again be conveniently recalled. The late eighteenth century in Europe was a time of massive and frightening change. In part this change was political and, as such, revolutionary: in part it had to do with highly local changes in patterns of work, and hence of family life. I have already alluded to the concern in Liu's story with dissonant visions of country and city life, and this is an aspect of Gothic fiction itself which has been extensively described.[22]

We can offer again an old summary of the early Gothic impulse at the sociological level, and say that it is a specific reaction to a specific variety of alienation.[23] Its excessive dramatisation of the powers of the isolated individual, whether that be represented in the diabolic monk or the tremulous victim, is the inverted marker of an age in which real control was felt to be slipping from the hands of individuals into those of a larger, partly unintelligible and possibly malevolent entity. A different order was being supervened; under such circumstances, it became imperative but also terrifying to question the limits of order and also to ask what older models for the self and its relation to society were disappearing as an industrialised and thus differently organised 'modern' society came into being on the haunted site of the past.

In these ways, then, I believe that we can see Liu handling similar materials: China, between the late 1960s and the late 1970s, underwent a process of change which, of course, cannot be justly compared with changes in the West in that that change cost many, many lives and still more in terms of humiliation and isolation. Nevertheless, one of the upshots of that terrible experience, an experience, as the Chinese still frequently describe it, of being wounded or scarred, was to call a bitter attention to the limits of order and indeed of a legal framework within which that order might be enshrined and guaranteed. It also, of course, exposed urban intellectuals to a long and painful experience of rural life which was quite alien to their hopes and practices.

I understand Liu to be providing a myth within which to contemplate those dislocations, which include and illuminate legal shortcomings, and like all good myths, and certainly like all Gothic ones, it is striated with contradiction. Many of her colleagues of the recent generation have found themselves bound up in feelings of fear, anger and hatred which were generously spawned during those years; Liu, I think, perhaps because she is after all rather younger than other writers prominent since 1985, appears able to consolidate a different distance between herself and the events, a distance which also implies a necessary degree of distortion parallel to the distorted versions of history which the Gothic has offered since its inception. But we need to question the nature of that distance in a number of ways. Is this a distance born of comprehension, or of a trauma so deep that it fixates upon a constant presumed rememoration of distant times and places, as the Western Gothic was fixated on the depths of history and geography because the present was too full of 'difference' to provide any solid grounding?

Chinese writers of Liu's generation often refer to the 'literature of the wound',[24] thus providing us with a vividly bodily image for a type of textual structure, however problematic the relation might be between this scarred textuality and any notion of 'experience'. Following Klein, Milner and other psychoanalytic commentators – and at the same time following Keats and rehearsing a familiar romantic trope – we can say that there are senses in which all art has to do with the wound, with that model of the psyche and of society which has to do with scarring, crippling and reparation, to which we have also referred under the Western mythic sign of Hephaestus.[25] Nevertheless, it behoves us at the same time to keep in mind, as all knowledges are local, that wounds are specific and cannot be wished away through the accretive processes of mythologisation, within text or within the psyche. The ghosts and supernatural forces that Liu's narrator encounters are, in the end, not fully distinct from the entirely natural forces – cold, damp, insectile – which plague her; just as the exaggerated representations of religion and feudal hierarchy encountered by Gothic heroes and heroines from the eighteenth century to the present day cannot be properly separated from the manifestations of incipient power – incorporated in the State, in capitalism, in the structures of the law – of which they are the inverted and sublimated emblems.

The search for the mountains and the valleys is not, therefore, accidental; it is on the one hand a reflection of the new kinds of alienation which are being born, or fostered, in the city, and on the other the sign for a feared engagement with the forbidden social and personal past, the 'immortal city' which may itself be precisely the inversion of its manifest equivalent. But we can always go too far with these parallels; what Liu brings to this general problematic is also a variety of post-modernist techniques which were not available to the original forms of Western Gothic, although in certain distinct ways the early writers may be seen to have fore-shadowed them in their dealings with haunting, the phantom and the boundless text, as with the whole notion of the sublime. Indeed, one should say that it was precisely with that early Gothic that the conception of the *Doppelganger*, with all its complex narrative implications, found its fullest expression, and here, as the expression of the person who can find no match between bodily and social yearnings, it finds a parallel.

What is important is the questions which remain. Principal among these, I believe, is the question of the psychic function of these kinds of melodramatic form, as purgation and/or intensification of experience. It is perfectly clear within Western culture that the images manifested in Gothic have not been purged; that they continue, as it were, to claim prime air-time. What will happen to these images of China, where, as in most things, a paradoxical position obtains; where an official classical realism continues to compete in varying cycles with an underlying stratum of folklore, which we may refer to as 'Gothic' in the sense in which, for example, Hugh Blair intended the term,[26] and indeed with an underlying set of life beliefs according to which the ancestors are no less real than their fellow living inhabitants of the village, and also where the living ghosts of the societal past have always fig-ured as 'real' participants in the political and social struggles of the present?

11

Gothic After/Words:
Abuse and the Body
beyond the Law

*Incorporation then is the situation of a secret lodged in the uncon-
scious (a false unconscious) as a monument to the dead, which at the
same time keeps the dead alive. This secret – which is always illegal,
and always circulates deep within the body of the living (even if it is
the surreptitious (written) body of the dead) – is perpetually dis-
closed, albeit secretly.*[1]

Where, then, have I reached in this series of interrogations of the
Gothic? How can we begin to approach a summary of a phenomenon which is crossed at all points by improbabilities: improbabilities of subject, improbabilities of interpretation, improbabilities of
longevity and survival. It is, perhaps, as if the Gothic admits subjection to no law; as if it flourishes in the undergrowth, to an extent
immune from the fellers of trees, always able to shift its terrain,
always able to find other more apparently sturdy forms on which
to batten. Yet the life that moves within it cannot be written off so
easily in images of ill health, disease, parasitism; there is clearly a
form of nurturance here too, but how we may specify it, historically, psychologically?

I would begin – as I began this book – by saying that the Gothic
is indeed extra-legal; it is illicit, contraband, always at the mercy of
comings and goings, mysterious translations which pass through
no controlled frontiers. It is always on the point of dissolving into
something else, as are phantoms and spirits. Yet the position which
Gothic thus assumes is in no sense a comfortable one, as the life of
the outlaw is not comfortable. And the outlaw is a common theme,
through from the *banditti* of the late eighteenth century to the
cyber-'cowboys' of William Gibson and the mercenaries and
space rovers of Iain M. Banks.[2]

But to be outside the law is not enough (as it is also, of course, not possible); in the Gothic text, we must experience this exteriority, this sense of being in an abyss where the writ of the law does not run, from the standpoint of anxiety. It is in no sense as though the extra-legal space were some kind of simple inversion of the civilised space from which it is exiled; on the contrary, to move from the space within to the space without is to encounter the chasm, the abyss: to discover a world which has not been measured and where creatures appear in the night which no 'God had ever made', yet which appear to have a type of chthonic existence of their own. This, certainly, is the substance of anxiety, but it is at the very least redoubled; for if we as readers find ourselves on this terrain, does it not therefore mark our own consanguinity with these lawless apparitions, rendering us at the same time agents and victims of chaos?

It is this phenomenon which has led me to adumbrate what I have called the 'law of the orphan'. The orphan is without role models: he or she is 'free', in the sense in which Toni Morrison uses the term of Cholly Breedlove, free to wreak disaster without knowing what rules it is against which we offend. Therefore the existence of the Gothic stands as a limit on the rule of law, and on the transmission of culture, and here lies one of the first paradoxes of Gothic: that just where it appears most beholden to the past, to be indeed a re-creation of a past, however inaccurate or unimaginable that past, just there is where we sense the very notion of *any* recollectable past swing before us and dissolve.

The law of the orphan is intimately related in Gothic to the law of the aristocrat: not merely in the early works, nor in their Victorian successors, but in the endless rule of the corporate aristocrats in Gibson, in the aristocratic figure of the single-named Sharrow in Banks's *Against a Dark Background* (1993), in the ludicrously privileged worlds of Bret Easton Ellis, Dennis Cooper, Donna Tartt.[3] There is a parallel here, and it consists in exemption: it is those conditions which place us below or above the rule of law that form the breeding-ground – or the killing-ground – of Gothic.

The lawyers, the law-makers and law-givers, remain with us also across the trajectory of Gothic: again not only in the variously demonic and insanely comical figures from the eighteenth century, but in Banks's World Court, in Will Self's hilariously Churchillian Fat Controller, in the figures of control and power which dominate the interiorised worlds of the mad heroines and heroes of Janice

Galloway, Yannick Murphy and so many others.[4] Somewhere out there is a lawyer; the relation between the lawyer and any visible notion of justice is always problematic, but all the more so when seen from beyond the glass, from the other side of the mirror.

And through that one-way mirror the characters of Gothic scream and shriek to make their case; for this is the most primal anxiety of all, the 'original' scene of injustice, the sense that however loud we shout, however graphically we portray the distorted world which has become, unjustly, mysteriously, our home, nevertheless our case cannot be heard; it cannot be put. It cannot be put because, in this stance, we are orphans; we have no name, and no credentials. Besides, what we have to say cannot be believed; there is no outside corroboration.

There can be no corroboration because the story we have to tell is all our own; it does not emerge into the world where fixed points can be pinned down and used to guide others through our maze. In the dialogue of the characters in Ellis's *The Rules of Attraction* (1987) as in his *American Psycho*, no discriminations are possible, between the voices of the characters, between the timings of their conversations.[5]

What, then, might be a *crime passionnel*, a 'crime', if such a thing can be, committed in a moment of 'madness' and also within the confines of an intimacy so profound that its contours cannot be mapped? Gothic abounds in such 'crimes', or perhaps we should more simply say in such 'events', the provenance of which is beyond our comprehension for lack of evidence. What exactly would 'evidence' consist of in the narratives of Poe, or of John Banville, whose very texts fracture under the weight of an enormously powerful symbolism which is thoroughly beyond the reach not only of the reader but also of the characters who are embroiled in these painful scenarios of rage and despair?[6]

I suggest further that this question of evidence is another facet of Gothic which renders it emblematic: emblematic of writing, emblematic of the human predicament. For if there is no reliable evidence, what then are we to say of the category of 'experience' itself? Familiar, and in some cases highly respectable and progressive rhetorics, offer us recourse to an unassailable category of 'experience';[7] but Gothic comes to relativise that, to whisper to us that we do not know the truth of what has been, or still is, going on. We know that something is going on; but we do not know what it is, such a certainty would be beyond our impoverished epistemological means.

And so, in Gothic, we find ourselves on a terrain of loss, with all the contradictions that implies. Whatever experience there has been, and with whatever panache we recount it, we cannot bring it back into being: like the King of Singers, like Liu Suola's B himself, it is always already gone, always lost in mists of uncertainty, always referred to some dim, decaying house on the Rhine, or to the recesses of, for example, Peter Ackroyd's House of Doctor Dee, where the past plays out its innumerable tapes around us, inside us, lost in the mists that Ackroyd also incarnates so brilliantly as the scenario for unimaginable crimes in *Dan Leno and the Limehouse Golem* (1994).[8]

This sense of loss, then, we may interpret as a kind of textual deficit; as the impossibility of sealing up the fragments of the 'lost' manuscript (which is clearly, in its very textual incarnation, no longer lost, yet which remains haunted by its own provisionality). Or we may interpret it as loneliness, as the primal ground of the law of the orphan, as the sense encountered in Stephen King's *It* (1986), in Gibson, in Don DeLillo's *White Noise* (1984), that there may be powerful forces moving dimly behind the scenes, mysteriously 'toxic' events, but we are not privy to them.[9] We may find ourselves, in Gothic, excluded from the warm world, from the lit room, but that does not mean that we are thereby privileged to encounter some kind of supernal knowledge, rather that we come to share in the great incomprehension which surrounds that world and which is not even sufficiently concerned with it to ask it questions.

We may also interpret this sense of loss as a type of debt; as a knowledge – perhaps made most alert by the possession of a decent and accountable family tree, at its deepest but least explicable when orphanage has made such credentials for ever unavailable – that something is *owed*, that there is something that we must 'pay off' before... before what? Before we can live? Before we can begin? Or perhaps the debt is, in an obscure way, a debt to ourselves; a necessity under which we are placed of gathering up the fragments and puddles of our spilt personalities before we can again be accepted into the world of conventions, rules and restraints.

I would therefore suggest that we see, in Gothic, work in mourning. Our status as victims, riddled and ridden by anxiety, by the nightmare, is haunted not only by the fantastic and terrifying imagery of further dissolution but also by images of a whole, sealed self which now seems forever beyond our grip, and yet, of course, in saying this we are only saying, as I again tried to do at the beginning of this book, that Gothic is merely narrative in general writ large, granted the 'truth' of melodramatic emphasis. For however narrative attempts to deny its own narrative status, however it attempts to provide us with images of the whole personality, we secretly know that this is not narrative's role at all, that narrative itself could not exist without the sense of the debt to be repaid, the wound to be healed, the fragments to be collected and, at the very least, stored, even if they can never re-emerge into a functioning psychic frame.

On the site of this mourning, as on the site of our victimisation, we are abject; or rather, we are brought to see our own abjection, we are made to confront images of what it is to be lost, orphaned, uncomprehending. This is not to say that this abjection may be felt directly as such, for it can be argued that abjection never exists, never has existed. Abjection we may figure simply as the spur to psychic defences; and thus it will not simply be a still small voice crying in the wilderness that we encounter in Gothic but rather the massive panoply of defences, the great armoury, the 'use of weapons', which is the mark of a secret abjection which must always be concealed from the world.[10]

And this is the genesis of two figures which haunt the Gothic, the monster and the terrorist. Frankenstein's monster as victim, or as agent, of chaos; there is clearly no way of distinguishing between these two faces, any more than there is, at least by the end, of distinguishing between the creator and the created. The monster comes to transcend the law: the monster owes no allegiance to a society in which it is always an orphan, but the monster is also a figure for our own need to deal – powerfully, violently – with our sense of abjection, to become a serial killer, a child abuser, an absolute ruler of a kingdom of death and decay. This monster is not in the end a figure of terror, but a figure of the terrorised; its very physicality, its obdurate and egregious body, is precisely an extrusion of abjection, doomed always to reappear and always again to be slain.

The terrorist has a similar function, but in the kind of chimera the terrorist is we can detect a different lineament: where the monster presents us, and presents the world, with a seemingly irreducible body which is none the less doomed to extinction, the terrorist confronts us with an excess of control, with the notion that the springs of the world can be unwound, that the ramifications of the law can be eluded by a mere effort of mind. This, we might say, is the 'rational' recourse from abjection: an excess of planning to counter the mind-forged anarchy that we have come to perceive as ruling the world.[11]

The monster and the terrorist have no family; they have no family history, no family tree, and thus they are exiled; as we as readers are also exiled when in the presence of these representations of our own despair at making manifest to the world our own past or present condition. They exist in the moments when we know it is hopeless to try to communicate, moments which have now sunk in so far as to become the entire scenario for the narratives of non-communication that Ellis, Cooper and others now so graphically write.[12] Behind all this, of course, lies the figure of Heathcliff, the orphan who is welcomed in; and who thereby points up all the ambivalences and impossibilities of family histories, the ways they redouble and loop back on themselves, defy our pathetic attempts to sort out the past into a neat order.

What is the secret of the family tree? Incest, says Freud.[13] Aristocratic incest, say Poe and the early Gothic writers; a self-serving wish to keep everything within the line, a selfishness which ends up in the madness of the empty corporate cores of the empire of the Tessier-Ashpools, with a forgotten robot manufacturing unintelligible art-works from the floating scraps of the past, the final Gothic artist.[14] At all events, whether it 'is' incest or not, this provides the connection to the Gothic theme of secrets, those secrets that Caleb Williams came to know and which threatened his security, the boundary between the public and the private, from that moment on.

> Should a child have parents 'with secrets',... the child will receive from them a gap in the unconscious, an unknown, unrecognised knowledge – a *nescience*...
>
> The buried speech of the parent will be (a) dead (gap) without a burial place in the child. This unknown phantom returns from the unconscious to haunt its host and may lead to phobias, madness, and obsessions. Its effect can persist through several generations and determine the fate of an entire family line.[15]

We want to know secrets, but we do not want to know secrets: to know them is to compound the debt, to bring us even more rigidly under a tyrannical law which we thought to evade (which we dream of evading). Thus the ambivalences about the seekers after secrets, the Rosicrucians, the Freemasons, the *illuminati*: what is it like if a secret is made manifest, if it ceases to be a secret? What, even worse, would it be like if the rule of law were finally and totally to prevail and all our own secrets were displayed as exhibits in a court of law?

Well, one thing it would be like – perhaps the only real model we have for it – would be the discovery by our mother and father of our secrets. Perhaps they might even discover the secret of our gender; or, most infamous of all, perhaps they have always already known it – these days, even within the womb. What hope of privacy can there be in the face of this most devastating of penetrations, which has always already happened; unless, of course, we choose the recourse – which is not to say that such a choice would be conscious – of rebutting our parents' physical knowledge of our body by adopting a sexuality plainly at odds with the biological evidence. Such a recourse is, of course, common; it is common in the Gothic, and its very existence immediately problematises the notions of 'female' or 'male' Gothic, because in Gothic precisely such gender identities are placed in motion, become fluid, even from the moment of the first monk's habit.[16]

The era of the secret, psychologists tell us, is the period of latency.[17] Animals do not have secrets: they do not have a lacuna in their emotional and sexual development which it is necessary to fill with objects in the inner world which have no visible equivalent in the outer. But human beings do; the path to maturation (like the path to the end of the story) is indirect and encounters stoppages and blockages, periods when no development is going on, moments when we are in need of assistance from adjuvants both benevolent and malign. Previous knowledges, particularly carnal, need to be buried, not for the good of ourselves as individuals, but for the good of the species, because, as the biologists claim, unless there were this hiatus on the path, then there would be no time for us to acquire the power of brain which has made us 'masters of the universe'.[18] Latency is our recourse against the tiger, but it also renders us in need of protection against vulnerability and it also provides a place where we locate a storehouse in which to build up internal figures, which are not precisely memories, nor indeed are they evidently images: they are secrets.

Gothic reminds us of that of which we scarcely need reminding: that some of these secrets are 'guilty' ones. To say that is not to succumb to an essentialist legal rhetoric of guilt, but rather to point out the way in which the colouring of guilt is automatically applied to certain classes of secret; and these are particularly the ones in which Gothic deals. This colouring is dark: it produces what I have referred to as the 'dark imagination', in the context of which anything in the outer world that resonates with these secrets is likely to be internalised and become the focus for a dark identification. This, I have argued, is the essential context within which the problems of 'cultural pollution' should be considered.

It is also, as again I have argued, an essential context within which child abuse must be considered. For Gothic has been telling us about child abuse from the very beginning: it has been telling us stories, fairy-tales for modernity, of evil mothers and stepmothers, of wicked barons, of strange incursions into bedrooms, of impossible family trees where every cousin is simultaneously at least a nephew if not a great-great-grandson. These involutions cannot be ignored; they too have to do with the law of the orphan, just as in Dickens, perhaps most emblematically of all, the choice between wicked parents and no parents at all is constantly and starkly presented.[19]

In this dark space of the imagination, populated with secrets which, it must be stressed, may in some cases not even be known to *ourselves* let alone to anybody else, there is a psychic figure: his name is Satan. When we read of 'satanic abuse', we have to realise that we are dealing here in psychic space; that there is a Satan awaiting awakening in the imagination, although of course it is for professionals to discover the aetiology and conditions of such awakenings, which are clearly not restricted to the childhood years (as they would of course not be if, as we must assume, latency too leaves its own curiously 'latent' traces).

The figure of Satan in the sense in which I mean it is very much as Blake conceived him: not an instigator of evil, but a cosmic blocker.[20] What Satan hates most of all, we might say, is transitional space, the easy flow through stages of development. Satan detests teddy bears; just as Montoni, for no reason ever adequately explained in the text, detests Emily, and even manages to convey some of the energy of this despisal textually by making us as readers irritated with her teddy bear status. Satan blocks off the path of maturation; he is not even keen on the moodiness and grumpiness of adolescents (a surliness shared by so many Gothic heroes), although it can be made to serve his purpose better than many other moods: especially with technological/addictive assistance.[21]

In place of this transitional space, which Satan must close down at all costs, a surrogate is needed; and it is here, I think, that Gothic plays an intriguing double game. For on the one hand, Gothic shows us the deep spaces beyond the law, which are also in themselves beyond Satan and beyond figuration of any kind; but it is also greatly involved in ritual, ceremonial, and here it connects with other blocking factors on maturation.[22] All ritual, all ceremonial, is of the nature of a refusal, a refusal of change (as Jack Gladney comes to see in a pure Freudian dénouement at the end of DeLillo's *White Noise*[23]); it thus has a complex relation to mourning, which it can assist or inhibit. But the unnatural (whatever that might mean) extension of ritual, like the excessive extension of mourning, is clear in its action: it destroys development, and Gothic shows us a panoply of images of this 'arrested' development.

These images of arrested development are, of course, familiar to us in many ways: among other things because we see them presented to us in courts of law. For the law, while it serves in itself to arrest development, cannot abide the thought of another agency which may do so, however fantastic its (satanic) aspirations; and therefore this evil must be punished, says the law, without contemplating the possibility that the evil that is to be punished is, in many respects, akin to the 'evil' associated with the law itself (prisons, chains, permanent disablements of various kinds). The law, however, finds itself more at home in what I have chosen to call a 'culture of horror' than in a 'culture of therapy'; for the law and horror, as the eighteenth-century writers saw all too clearly, confront each other as equals, as rivals, as enemies, as duellists over the static body of the victim, while the culture of therapy is exiled to the waiting room.

With all of these matters, then, the Gothic has to do: as a store of images, as an evolving set of narratives, as a repository of resistance. It also has its function in resisting over-simple notions of memory; for Gothic is the terrain on which we are never sure what – if anything – we have remembered; our sense of certainty is being forever broken down as forces different in kind from ourselves make an assay of our evidence and find it, inevitably, lacking, find it the very soul of deficit. Among these lost images, images which can occur only under the sign of loss, only as 'erased', pre-eminent is the primal scene: in most Gothic fictions there is such a scene, but it is *sous rature*, by which we might choose to understand 'awaiting ratification' as much as 'under erasure'. We cannot know that it happened, whatever it was; only that something happened, and that we are now in the *wake* (the term Barthes uses in this context) of its effects. As we strive to survive this tumultuous onslaught of a barely remembered past, we adopt a variety of stratagems, but many of them can be summarised under the ambiguous headings of recollection and reconstruction; terms which are not so much opposed as complementary gestures at the impossibility of knowing which we discover when we engage with memory – for, of course, to say this is only to recapitulate the doubts previously expressed about the 'integrity' of experience.

Yet was there ever a primal scene, or rather, what kind of epistemological gesture would we be making if we were even to venture to take sides in this argument? Borch-Jacobsen, I have suggested, is useful to an analysis of Gothic because he provides us with a notion which seems closely to approximate to the uncertainties of memory which Gothic encapsulates, incarnates: namely, a notion of primary identification which undercuts and underlies later Oedipal structures. In Gothic, we do not directly ask, What happened? We ask, Where are we, where have we come from – not in the sense of a birth question, but as a question of how it is that we have 'come adrift', what the lingering, haunting sense of oneness is that relegates all our present actions to simulacra, fragments, ghosts.[24]

Borch-Jacobsen also seems relevant to this argument in his emphasis on somnambulism as a feature of the psyche. It is well known, of course, that Gothic trades on the sense that 'we have been there before'; this very sense of *déjà vu* (a sense which functions as an identifiable disease in *White Noise*)[25] is what makes all our attempts to give a 'legal' acount of ourselves pointless and desperate, for we do not know, we cannot remember, where it is we have 'been', or indeed, as Heidegger might say, when 'being' happened. In the gap of consciousness that thus opens up, we move not as though willed or willing but rather as though we are driven to occupy spaces in an already established panoply (ritual, ceremonial), as though, for example, we already know the 'rules of attraction'; we are sleep-walkers, finding ourselves constantly in places which are neither familiar nor unfamiliar (like Will Self's Land of Childhood Jokes),[26] which are therefore, to use a term to which I shall return below, 'uncanny'.

There is thus a hypnotic quality to Gothic, and I have been taking this hypnotic quality to link with a whole series of psychological and clinical terms which attempt to describe phenomena where we are no longer in control of ourselves: possession, habit, addiction, compulsion, obsession. From one point of view, all of these terms can be seen as apposite to the concept of the 'mechanical syndrome' as adumbrated by Freud;[27] that is, to the image of being 'taken over' (or rather, as it might be, 'taken from under') by something machine-like which rises from the waves (of undifferentiation, of 'memory') and destroys our self-control. For the possessed, the addicted, the compulsive and the obsessive are, as Burroughs knows only too well, cardinal figures in the proliferation of control: they stand simultaneously as ultimately resisting and also as those who have already given way, who have abandoned the struggle for individuation, to put it in Jungian terms, and who thus demonstrate the limits on the extent to which such individuation is possible: ever, of course, but also under specific socio-political circumstances which will, from time to time, occupy the space of the paranoigenic force that offers us its versions of control as palliatives for the failures of development.

One image thrown up amid this plethora of mechanisms is that of the 'collector', who may possess or be possessed by his/her collection; hence again the imagery of serial killers in contemporary Gothic,[28] but hence also the apparently endless but fundamentally repetitive desires of earlier Gothic protagonists. When would Manfred consider he had achieved his 'ends'? What would he have had to bring into his 'collection'? What bodies, what component parts? What bodies considered *as* component, we might more appositely ask, which will also serve to remind us of the consanguinity between Gothic and pornography, of which so many recent films also remind us.[29]

The scene of pornography is repetition, interchangeability, the reduction of the body to a series of divisible but repetitive parts, differentiated from each other only by the crudest of arithmetical measurements: a means of bringing under control that which cannot be controlled, and it should not be underestimated that the body which is being brought under control here, evidenced in the bodies of those who are socially weak (most typically the bodies of women) is in fact an emblem for the weakness of the body of the masturbator himself, which seeks through endless repetition to discover a bulwark against dissolution. And the dissolution of the body, the final re-solution of the body into its component parts and its disappearance from a troubling and troubled landscape which contains psychic materials and emotional, passional involvements, is what is most firmly desired on this terrain of crumbling, dissolving, vanishing into a series of meaningless component parts, those very component parts which in recent cyber-fiction are often all that is left of the body while the psyche goes on to seek its own aristocratic, corporate, endlessly wealthy immortality.[30]

When the body dissolves, we find ourselves staring into what I have described as the 'hairline crack in the real'. If the body can dissolve (and we all know that it can and does) then we find that the safe place on which we think we have been standing (a bridge over an infernal abyss, let us say, or even an upstairs room in a country house with a peculiar tree outside the window)[31] reveals itself as not a safe place at all but rather a threshold; and it is at this point that we see the full interplay between the notion that the world might be 'cracking up' and the persuasion that we might be 'cracking up' ourselves, for in this situation we are – as readers? – the gap, the hiatus through which the chill air washes in.

In trying to draw attention to the body as a *topos* within Gothic, to the ways in which Gothic incarnates bodies, even if only to dispose of them in the most gruesome of ways, I have wanted also to call attention to the connection between the Gothic and proliferation. It is necessary for the law to operate under the sign of unity: it can work only if there is a single source of authority, which is why divisions of church and State are so endlessly problematic. One of the ways in which Gothic resists the role of the law is in its addiction to the copious, the multiple, the proliferative: all that Deleuze and Guattari would place under the sign of the rhizome.[32] The Gothic, like some of its own ghosts, is headless; it does not submit easily to canons, any more than it admits abjection before a monotheism. In Gothic we inhabit the land of many gods, perhaps of small gods, powerful but limited in their functioning, and it is the criss-crossing, the latticing, of their purposes and desires which provides one possibility for the mapping of a phantasmatic chaos.

This proliferation, then, flows from the 'spillage' of the personality I have referred to above; and we can also consider Gothic as a process of endless deferral, whether we call to mind the obvious deferrals of Maturin or the belated interlocking of characters in Ellis, Anne Rice and others.[33] What is being deferred here? The re-sealing of the psyche, I would say; the thanatic desire which Gothic in part obeys does not want to return to the fold, to fold into a return, but rather wants to continue to exist amid the spilt, fragmented parts of body and psyche. Although it is anxious about this dispersion, it has its anxieties also as to what re-sealing might entail: if the room were locked with us inside, what else might we find to be there, how should we comport ourselves in the face of forms of fear which no longer have the vast resources of the night and chaos in which to expend themselves, reminding us of their presence only through the ceaseless flow and chatter of their voices?

The very notion of text, of course, has, through its associations with weaving, an intimate connection with at least the possibility – although it may only be that – of this process of re-sealing; or of healing the wound, settling the scar. And it cannot of course be denied that many Gothic fictions do come as close to such a re-sealing as is textually possible, as partly do their realist counterparts; but then again, there is perhaps always something left over, some excess, some 'unexplained' even in the midst of the most 'explained' of the supernatural. This, as Ellis reminds us, is not an exit.[34]

It is not an exit at least partly because it leaves unexplained a certain pathology; or perhaps we might better say, the 'certainty' of pathology. It leaves unexplained how a 'certain' version of criminality can exist independent of any law, as a kind of free-floating signifier, as a sign of pure evil of a kind which not even Satan would much like to touch. Events may be 'wrapped up'; and so may the killer, the robber baron, the evil monk. But the question of how this figure came to be there in the first place, the question of provenance and origin, the question of how the (distorted) family tree which could produce such monstrous growth had arisen in the first place, is not, cannot be, solved; there is something left over.

What is left over, we might say, is the psychopathic. Here we deal in a residual 'legal' category, a category before which the law bows its head and is forced, *in extremis*, to call in, or call on, a further expertise, a further tranche of professionalism,[35] although not for purposes of therapy, rather for purposes of further and indefinable incarceration: the State Hospital, in the resonant Scottish term, which remains as the final outpost of those whose very humanness has been placed under an enduring question mark.

What is to be done with these extreme examples? Is it possible to bring even these under the regime signalled by the panopticon, or will they not rather, like the terrorist and the monster, destroy the glass, the mirror, the telescope, the looking-glass, the microscope, under which they are placed; or, thwarted of that ambition, which is an ambition common to us all, which is to retain their secret on pain of madness or death, will they not simply die? Or kill? Before this scenario, the law flinches; but, as with all institutions, it passes on this movement of weakness. In this case it passes it on, increasingly as the twentieth century draws to its close, to the perceived 'weakness' of psychotherapy, by which is meant the 'weakness' of all psychic explanation and of all notion of the 'cure'; in this process of transference, all that is weak, vulnerable, timid, victimised is passed beyond the law, violently extruded, into a different professionalisation; and perhaps the gender differentials here are too obvious to be pointed out.[36]

Perhaps the panopticon provides one explanation of paranoia, or at least one contribution to an ongoing debate; but I would contend that the scenario of the 'case which cannot be heard' is at least as relevant and symbolic a way of approaching the difficulties of a *topos* which I have previously tried to describe in terms of the 'paranoid Gothic'.[37] In addition to the trope of the 'case', however, I would like to advance its complementary half: the notion of what it might be like to 'be read like an open book'. In this scenario, nothing is hidden; no secrets are possible. One thinks of physiognomy, of the possibility, pre-telepathic, of telling all that can be 'told' from the face, from the 'open face'; one thinks also of cowls, cauls, habits, addictions, the string of metaphors by means of which the 'human' face can be draped, concealed, returned to an unassailable interiority, placed indeed under erasure. Is it possible to erase faciality, or must we 'face' the possibility that we are always and instantly betrayed by our very countenance, by, for example, the thin lips of cruelty, the large eyes of lust? If so, then all of our psychological probings will be of no avail; the judge will screw his eyes up, stare down into the depths of our soul and, without utterance, don the black cap. We are all condemned by the accidents of our birth; or, if you like, by the fruits of the family (poison) tree.

Perhaps more troublingly: if we can be read like an open book, then the question of censorship, always highly germane to the Gothic but particularly so now, becomes pointless. We already know our own, and others', predilections: we know that certain kinds of material should be made available or disallowed to this boy, that girl. And this, indeed, is a common-sense model of how society operates; but it operates, as usual, in complete blindness, and one of its principal blindnesses here is in the area of catharsis. The notion that chaotic fictions might be cathartic cannot be fitted readily into the system of pre-judgment which is essential to any notion, however liberal, of censorship, and thus we are returned again to the world of injustice, to the notion that by accident of family (class, race) one is already guilty; or not guilty.

What might the alternative to this be? One possibility is to project all blame and guilt onto the human race as such: we might call this strand 'eco-Gothic'.[38] According to its mythology, there are terrors still around in the chaos; but those terrors are of our own making, not in the psychological sense but according to a planetary or galactic perspective. The projections of the law are themselves limited by a further 'law', which we are to figure not under the guise of domination but rather as an intuition of harmony, which owes more to Eastern than to Western religions, although it remains under the permanent danger of falling back into a monotheism, even if this monotheism has feministic credentials.

And this terrain of the 'mythological', as I have also contended above, is also the terrain of the Gothic: for its very haunting of past places of understanding, in the dim hope of acquiring thus some way of comprehending the situation outside the law, signifies its acquiescence in a mythological principle. I have tried to suggest some possible sites and contexts for this mythic apprehension, and in particular I would recall three deities who might be 'interested', in the strong sense, in the Gothic: Hades, Hephaestus and Eros. All three have secrets (but so did most of the gods, and many of the goddesses too); but these three in particular can be crystallised into a signifying system of their own, whereby Eros, of course, represents desire; Hades the end of desire; and Hephaestus, the halt, the victim, yet the source of strength, sheltering under Olympus yet in some sense holding it up by his indefatigable labours at the forge, a kind of midpoint where desire is being forever moulded yet burned away; in the forms of writing, in the shapes of art and of craft.

To speak of mythology in this way – that is, as an indispensable aspect of psyche – is to return us momentarily to the thought of James Hillman; and thus to the notion of anima, the plurality of the (female) intellect which haunts all thoughts of system, project and self-aggrandisement. There are many representations of anima (anima can only be known in the 'manifold' of her representations) in Gothic; but I mean here to connect also anima ('soul') to other terms which spring from her name: animation, the animal.[39] Gothic is to do with animation, with the animation of the living body; it is also to do with the animal, with the physical, bodily within humanity but also in the sense in which projections outward from the human come to rest in the 'animal', in all that is conceived as having not to do with the psyche, with the intellect, and which thus returns to haunt us; after hours. But animation has also a much more obviously frightening aspect: it is to do with a certain version of incarnation, or perhaps better reincarnation, but one which is frequently conceived in Gothic as according to a devolutionary dialectic rather than as according to the 'law' of evolution and progress.

Such reincarnations are likely to be troublesome, psychically and textually; at their heights they may raise us towards the sublime (in the sense that this stripping away of the merely contingent may be seen as offering us transcendence) or they may be considered as those forms which arise only on the terrain of the ruined, as the ghastly reanimated forms of the 'remains'. Ruins and remains; from its very 'origin', Gothic has reminded us that there never was a time when all was not ruined, that it is from ruins that we make our way, as it is the case that the phenomenon of the 'Gothic' Dark Ages in some sense 'remakes' the myth and problem of latency within the individual; all that we have forgotten (but we do not know that we have forgotten it, we have no memory of forgetting).

Amid these remains and ruins we are, I think it is fair to say, alarmed; we sense that all is not as it might be, might have been, once was. This alarm creates in us states of emergency, and it is these states of emergency to which Gothic continually, and to our annoyance, irritation, anger and often pleasure, reintroduces us. Gothic fiction does not (usually) offer us the time in which to re-seal, to heal ourselves; rather, it is a fiction in which we are always embarking on the journey without our luggage, setting off through the dark night of space with the airlock still vestigially open. There is the minutest seepage of breath from the outer, the hairline crack which can – but, better, we know it *will* – 'seal' our doom.

We may refer these intimations to the gap in the construction of the house. The house, the castle, is everywhere; from Udolpho to the castle on the Rhine, from Bloch's suburban castle to Banks's Sea House, these vast decaying symbols, themselves always relics, always in the process of being remade or holding out against, resisting, the possibility of being brought (back) within the fate of time and space, are constantly with us in Gothic, undiminished by the years, sometimes transmuted onto a different planet, sometimes inhabited by precisely the same indecipherable monks who inhabited the original buildings; they follow us about, beseeching, secretive, offering up unknown prayers to undecidable effect. Prisons, gaols, monasteries, temples, they are the physical incarnation of the notion of 'institution' itself, and as such they reflect the vicissitudes of 'instituting', according, of course, to a historical logic, but to one which seems curiously indifferent to temporary fluctuations of power.[40]

For we are here in the presence of the dream-house, which is also the house of the body, the house which is the body: in it, the events which happen are what Borch-Jacobsen calls 'dramatisations of the ego', but for what audience? Dramatisations are not exactly carnivalesque, they take place under conditions of 'blind mimesis'; we are in no position to see what we *are*, or are becoming. Yet perhaps nevertheless we can sense here a further tension; for in the castles, the labyrinths, the maddening locations of Gothic we are not only in the presence of a crumbling down to ruin but also and simultaneously immersed in some kind of work of reparation, of trying to see some sense in the damage done, of trying to find a way in which to re-express our guilt and sorrow for previously fantasised demolitions.[41]

And thus the panoply of the so-called 'perversions' is conjured up with ambiguous intent: sadism, masochism, necrophilia. There is no space here to attempt a full relating of these perversions, these psychic formations, to the Gothic; but we can say that Gothic tends very frequently, and possibly especially now, to effect a new relativisation of these structures.[42] For at the end of the day, it seems frequently to be the case not that these 'distortions' are perceived as a root of fracture and disablement; rather, they provide at least a series of possible recourses, built on a great deal of pain and often with enormous psychic energy, against the real enemy, which is precisely the 'perversion' of constricting, normative, male-dominated heterosexuality. Cruelties and obsessions in the Gothic are certainly real, as are the dead female bodies of which Bronfen speaks; but there is a further sense in which at least these fluctuations, twistings, squirmings of the body provide some evidence of resistance, the legacy perhaps of the old myth of de Sade's influence on the Gothic, against the legalised violence of that instrument or regime of oppression which is now known by the name of the corporate State.

In moving towards the conclusion of these remarks, I am aware of trying to inhabit a difficult middle ground between two approaches, which we might loosely call psychoanalytic and deconstructive. I am aware, of course, of the multiple involutions of these terms, of their constant intertwinings such that no deconstructive account seems complete without a prior involvement of the 'Freudian text', no psychoanalytic development, at least on the broad terrain of cultural studies, may be attempted without an emphasis on the linguistic, textual base of the analytic transaction. Nevertheless, it seems to me imperative that this mutual imbrication be seen to hold within it, as something in amber which is in (purposeless, obsessive?) need of perpetuation, preservation, a contradiction; for at root there is here an incompatibility, and one which I have tried to point out in Shelley's *Zastrozzi* among other texts: namely, that the root in (the route back through) the body must remain held in namelessness, in the unrecollectable fact of primal undifferentiation even while at the same time we strip bare the linguistic motifs which hold within themselves the other, inseparable, root of textuality.

We might figure this essential contradiction, over which the Gothic stumbles all the time as over the irrefragable bones of the dead,[43] in another way: as a constant disturbance, a troubling which would upset the Foucauldian notion of historical regimes – or indeed of Bakhtinian units of discourse. These may surely be seen precisely as defences: the insistence on a limit to historical contamination, the insistence that there are clear unitary discourses of which others are comprised, what are these but insistences on a clear hierarchy to be established and perpetuated in discursive prose?

Gothic comes to say that these apparent certainties are themselves fictions, fictions of a high order but simultaneously vulnerable to dispersion, and a dispersion which implies that modernity is always alien to itself.[44] This dispersion is figured in Gothic in many ways: indeed, the central figure of Gothic, the haunting of the present by its own past which may be no more than a construct of a yearning in the present, or indeed may be a premonition of even greater deficit in the future, may be seen as the very penumbra which surrounds these gestures of certainty. Haunting; the

phantom; the spectre; contamination; these are all data in which
Gothic deals, and which endlessly convolute the possibility of neat
guiding lines, threads of Ariadne's making which might guide us
through the labyrinth and back to a sunlit world outside; a break in
the chain of evidence which, of course, the myth goes on to confirm
in the final misaddressing of the all-important signal, which is
turned – by 'accident' – into one of death.

Gothic comes also to ask: to whom do these intimations belong?
Who or what is the body, the text, which carries these symptoms?
Is it possible to perform an act of isolation which will quarantine
this world of uncertainties, troublings, or do we find as we look at
it more closely that its symptoms have already spread everywhere,
that everyone, as in *American Psycho*, will willingly conceal, provide
an alibi for, the most heinous of crimes because we already recognise that all these manifestations of disorder, violence, cannibalism,
are our own?[45] One tactic in the face of this kind of evidence is to
consign such thoughts to the crypt; but we have also to ask ourselves whether Abraham and Torok's formulations measure up to
the inevitability of seepage, the inglorious but indisputable fact of
slime. The crypt may be inscribed, but the inscription slips away;
the crypt may seem to enclose and inoculate a condign secret, but it
remains only interesting in so far as it can be breached, the secret
can be broached; the insides can present themselves for examina-
tion, we can wander among the decaying corpses therein contained
yet not contained.[46]

When we enter the crypt (and we always do; there are no fictions
in which the opportunity to enter it is laughingly passed up, we do
not find that such narratives of missed opportunities have a hold
on our imagination), what we find there is not a secret which
cannot be told to anybody until after our death; what are the endless attempts on the psyche of the Wolf-Man but attempts at
betrayal, and as such paradoxical reinforcements of the crumbling
nature of the crypt's external portals, a dissolution of thresholds?
What we find there is indeed unfamiliar; but as in classic defini-
tions of the uncanny, it is familiar as well. We walk along the
corridor between the neatly stacked coffins as we might wander
through Bates's motel, or the similar locations which figure in so
many other modern Gothic fictions;[47] this is the shape of our
dream-house, although it confronts us, as even the most familiar
of scenarios do, with a remaining question, a question of remains:
do we own (possess) these locations, or are we merely tenants in

them, are we possessed in our habitation of them by our own unacquitted debts? The same question is one which we address to our own bodies.

The two images which seem to me most helpful here are those of the 'filled shell' and of the foreign body. There is a sense in which we might figure the relation of Gothic to realist fiction as the relation of the exoskeletal to the endoskeletal. In realist fiction, there is an internal structure to events which it is the task – even the duty – of the reader to ascertain; there is an internal meaning to be perceived in the interactions of these various simulated lives, and our readerly apprehension of this internal structure serves to liberate us, as indeed the liberation of the characters themselves through their own perception of this 'skeleton' forms the major plot motif. With Gothic, the situation is different: the skeleton (although this is already a misnomer) is already visible, it is what confronts us when we approach the fiction, on the book cover, in the opening words, along the horizon of expectations with which we approach such works: the questions are about what is contained within, whether we are viewing, for example, an 'integral' creature or a hermit crab, something which occupies a 'natural' living space or which has crawled into 'somewhere else' to make its home.

The notion of the foreign body comes to remind us that we have always crawled into somewhere else to make our home; for, according to the law of the orphan, there is nothing else to do. We do not emerge from the womb imbued with a sense that here, and nowhere else, is where we must reside; we emerge – so Gothic tells us – with no idea of what even the notion of residence, of inhabitancy, might mean, and we proceed to construct it from scratch. It is not that we evict other beings in order to make our home; it is that we only know that other beings are sentient when we have already evicted them, when we sense that we are haunted by previous (familial?) inhabitants of spaces we thought to have become our own 'familiars'. Thus we become increasingly aware that our apprehension of foreign bodies, of strange intimations that all is not well with our occupancy (of the world, of our body) is at a deeper level predicated on our growing awareness that we ourselves are the foreign body; perhaps, we might go so far as to say, this is what brings about our death, the growing insupportability of our awareness of the unnatural.

In bringing forward these notions of the filled shell and particularly the foreign body, although these concepts, and especially the latter, are familiar to deconstructive and psychoanalytic discourses, it seems to me that we shall not firmly establish our dealings with them until we also reclaim a discourse which is largely 'foreign' to both of them, the discourse of 'soul'. I have written elsewhere about the nature of soul as to do with an experience of friction, of homelessness, of disanimation which encourages a notion of animation on a 'different' site;[48] I have tried in this book to bring forward a possible approach to the question of soul by looking, especially in connection with *Wuthering Heights,* at a way of reading which might involve accepting different depths, different sinkages, which would produce in us a sense of a root of soul.

This is surely what is also at stake in what I take to be (and am implicitly taking to be in this concluding chapter) the most recent, and immediately contemporary, manifestation of Gothic: namely, cyber-fiction, and its paramount concern with man/machine chimeras, cyborgs, unnatural unions of animation and disanimation, all of which, I think, are gestures towards transcendence, reincarnation, the sublime.[49] What we have here is a querying, a reworking, of soulstuff, a violently extruded will to deal with the passional. The blankness of much of the fiction needs to be read also for its inverse, for the desperation with which it promotes encounters with what it might mean to enter in full into the notion of animation; for the despair with which we encounter the possibility that the body, the body we inhabit, might be seen to have been 'inorganic', disanimated from root, a mere stuff of neurochemistry.

Science and soul; technology and the spiritual; these ancient dilemmas continue to provide much of the 'animation' of Gothic, continue to secure for it the cultural centrality which it has, paradoxically, had for the last three centuries. The great house under the sea continues to exert its magical pull; the question of whether machines dream, and of whether of what they dream is us, continues to exercise us. Is what we are, after all, an artificial intelligence? Are we here to deal with the artifice of intelligence? And if that is the task, then how shall we account for ourselves, multiple, inchoate beings who stretch into space, into soulspace, into cyberspace, before the law, which will have none of these ambiguities, which is there to prohibit, to censor, such ambiguities?

It is on these continuities that I would finally wish to 'rest my case' (and wonder whether, and according to what distortions, it will be heard); a case which might seem peculiar in its resolute refusal to accept legal boundaries. But we do seem to be confronted

with a 'situation' (legal, physical, textual) where the acceptance of
boundaries, historical and geographical, is at the forefront of our
attempts to define and develop the human; and what Gothic shows
us is some of the ways in which this set of problems can be seen
best not by remaining within the licit, endoskeletal assumptions of
the law, according to which foreign bodies do not exist, but according to a different set of distortions, by means of which we are only
too aware of how we inhabit, and are inhabited by – as Gothic has
been since the 'beginning' (which was never a beginning) – a
foreign space.

Notes

1. GOTHIC ORIGINS: THE HAUNTING OF THE TEXT

1. Robert Duncan, 'The Song of the Borderguard', in *Selected Poems*, ed. Robert J. Bertholf (Manchester, 1993), p. 22.

2. For the best recent accounts of these 'origins', see Coral Ann Howells, *Love, Mystery and Misery: Feeling in Gothic Fiction* (London, 1978); Elizabeth McAndrew, *The Gothic Tradition in Fiction* (New York, 1979); Robert Miles, *Gothic Writing 1750–1820: A Genealogy* (London, 1993); Eve Kosofsky Sedgwick, *The Coherence of Gothic Conventions* (New York, 1980); Joseph Wiesenfarth, *Gothic Manners and the Classic English Novel* (Madison, Wisc., 1988).

3. The phrase is from Coleridge's *Table Talk* (1835), and in using it I follow the useful observations of Peter Davidson, Jane Stevenson and Valeria Tinkler-Villani in their Introduction to *Exhibited by Candlelight: Sources and Developments in the Gothic Tradition*, ed. Tinkler-Villani and Davidson (Amsterdam, 1995), pp. 1–5.

4. See, e.g., H.P. Lovecraft, 'The Dreams in the Witch-House', in *At the Mountains of Madness, and Other Novels of Terror*, ed. August Derleth (London, 1966), p. 114; and on contamination in the sense in which I mean it here, see C.G. Jung, *The Psychogenesis of Mental Disease*, in *The Collected Works*, ed. Herbert Read *et al.*, 19 vols (London, 1953–67), III, 22–5, and *The Practice of Psychotherapy: Essays on the Psychology of the Transference and Other Subjects*, in *Collected Works*, XVI, 292–4.

5. On the general issues of textuality, loss and creativity, see, e.g., Marion Milner, 'The Role of Illusion in Symbol Formation', in *The Suppressed Madness of Sane Men* (London, 1987), pp. 83–113.

6. Cf. some of the wordings in Maurice Blanchot, *The Space of Literature*, trans. Ann Smock (Lincoln, Nebr., and London, 1982), and especially his discussions of Rilke at pp. 128–38.

7. Or we might similarly see it as

> a system of rules, the unity of the system being due to the rule of recognition.... the validity of each law refers back to some other rule that authorises an official or an official body to establish that law, and so on until the rule of recognition is reached. We thus have the picture of a legal system as a network of chains of validity...
> (Theodore M. Benditt, *Law as Rule and Principle: Problems of Legal Philosophy* [Brighton, 1978], p. 73)

But if we do, then surely we are again in the kind of infinite regress that haunts all discourse of authority and origins.

8. For some intriguing commentary on this 'pure line', construed as the notion of the 'rule', see Mark Kelman, *A Guide to Critical Legal Studies* (Cambridge, Mass., and London, 1987), pp. 55–63.

9. See G.W.F. Hegel, *Philosophy of Right*, trans. T.M. Knox (Oxford, 1945), pp. 209–11; John Berger *et al.*, *Ways of Seeing* (London, 1972), pp. 94–7, and John Berger, *Art and Revolution: Ernst Neizvestny and the Role of the Artist in the USSR* (London, 1969), pp. 128–33; Jacques Derrida, *Marges de la Philosophie* (Paris, 1972), p. 354.

10. See Slavoj Žižek, *Looking Awry: An Introduction to Jacques Lacan through Popular Culture* (Cambridge, Mass., 1992).

11. For some of the more interesting recent comments on Gothic film, see Will H. Rockett, *Devouring Whirlwind: Terror and Transcendence in the Cinema of Cruelty* (Westport, Conn., 1988), and Vera Dika, *Games of Terror: 'Halloween', 'Friday the 13th' and the Films of the Stalker Cycle* (Madison, Wisc., 1990). See also Jonathan Lake Crane, *Terror and Everyday Life: Singular Moments in the History of the Horror Film* (Thousand Oaks, Calif., 1994).

12. The reference is to Greg Bear, *Queen of Angels* (London, 1990), in which the 'hellcrown' carries the interesting double role of torture machine and unit of international currency.

13. See Jacques Derrida, *Of Grammatology*, trans. Gayatri Spivak (Baltimore, Md., and London, 1976), p. 158.

14. See Herbert Morris, *On Guilt and Innocence: Essays in Legal Philosophy and Moral Psychology* (Berkeley, Calif., 1976), pp. 59ff., 89–110; Leo Katz, *Bad Acts and Guilty Minds: Conundrums of the Criminal Law* (Chicago and London, 1987), *passim*; and on this as well as many other issues throughout, Jacques Derrida, 'Force of Law: The "Mystical Foundation of Authority"', in *Deconstruction and the Possibility of Justice*, ed. Drucilla Cornell, Michel Rosenfeld and David Gray Carlson (New York and London, 1992), pp. 3–67.

15. See the complex arguments in Jacques Derrida, 'Devant la loi', in *Philosophy and Literature*, ed. A. Phillips Griffiths (Cambridge, 1984), pp. 173–88; also Irene E. Harvey, 'Derrida and the Issues of Exemplarity', in *Derrida: A Critical Reader*, ed. David Wood (Oxford, 1992), pp. 193–217.

16. See C.R. Maturin, *Melmoth the Wanderer*, ed. Douglas Grant (Oxford, 1968), pp. 306ff.; the passage begins: 'Another amusement of these people, so ingenious in multiplying the sufferings of their destiny, is what they call law.'

17. On the 'case', see, e.g., James K. Chandler, 'Scott's Historical Casuistry', paper delivered at Scott in Carnival: The Fourth International Scott Conference, Edinburgh, 1991.

18. And, as Nicholas Royle has reminded me, 'what falls (*cadere*) as by chance (*casus*)'.

19. On the 'container/contained' relationship, see particularly Wilfred R. Bion, *Elements of Psychoanalysis* (London, 1963), pp. 3, 26–7, 31–2, and *Attention and Interpretation* (London, 1970), pp. 72–82, 106–24.

20. See Jane Austen, *Pride and Prejudice*, ed. Pamela Norris (London, 1993), pp. 147–52.
21. See Vivian C. Seltzer, *The Psychological Worlds of the Adolescent: Public and Private* (New York, 1989), pp. 158–9; Irving B. Weiner, *Psychological Disturbance in Adolescence* (New York, 1970), pp. 41ff.
22. J.L. Austin, in his classic *How to do Things with Words* (Oxford, 1962), claims that, for example, 'my success in apologising depends on the happiness of the performative utterance "I apologise" ' (p. 47). This, I suggest, is unlikely to be the whole of the story.
23. Or, to put it another way:

    . . . lack is not solely negative: it attests to the stirring of an impetuous power through which desire begins to be more than itself.

    Although this comment might well have been made by Jacob Boehme, it is in fact from William Desmond, *Desire, Dialectic and Otherness: An Essay on Origins* (New Haven, Conn., 1987), p. 18.
24. See Mary Shelley, *Frankenstein*, ed. D.L. Macdonald and Kathleen Scherf (Ontario, 1994), p. 84; and Mikkel Borch-Jacobsen, *The Emotional Tie: Psychoanalysis, Mimesis and Affect* (Stanford, Calif., 1992).
25. See Gilles Deleuze and Claire Parnet, *Dialogues* (1977), trans. Hugh Tomlinson and Barbara Habberjam (London, 1987), p. ix.
26. See Martin Heidegger, particularly 'Hölderlin and the Essence of Poetry', in *Existence and Being*, ed. Werner Brock (London, 1949), pp. 291–315, or his summary comment in *Being and Time*, trans. John Macquarrie and Edward Robinson (Oxford, 1973), p. 205; and Jacques Derrida, *The Post Card: From Socrates to Freud and Beyond*, trans. Alan Bass (Chicago, 1987), and 'Différance', in *Margins of Philosophy*, trans. Bass (Chicago, 1982), pp. 1–27.
27. And what can be said would presumably centre on a text like *L'Innommable* (1952) and its involvement in a specific elaboration of a repetition machine, and what this might imply for the dissolution of history and memory.
28. See Maturin, p. 502.
29. See Charles Dickens, *The Old Curiosity Shop*, ed. Paul Schlicke (London, 1995), p. 215; and, of course, the famous instance of dismay at Nell's death recounted by Schlicke in his Introduction, p. xvii.
30. For further consideration of this point, see pp. 108–9, 120 below.
31. On John Martin, see T.S.R. Boase, *English Art 1800–1870* (Oxford, 1959), pp. 105–8; Hugh Honour, *Romanticism* (London, 1979), pp. 56–8 and other occasional references; William Feaver, *The Art of John Martin* (Oxford, 1975); Ruthven Todd, 'The Imagination of John Martin', in *Tracks in the Snow: Studies in English Science and Art* (London, 1946), pp. 94–122.

32. Bowsprit cracked with ice and paint cracked with heat.
     I made this, I have forgotten
     And remember.

The rigging weak and the canvas rotten
Between one June and another September.
Made this unknowing, half conscious, unknown, my own.

('Marina', in T.S. Eliot, *Collected Poems 1909–1962* [London, 1963], p. 116)

33. See Bret Easton Ellis, *American Psycho* (London, 1991), p. 399.
34. See pp. 144ff. below.
35. On the Gothic and ceremony, see my 'Ceremonial Gothic', a paper delivered to the Second Conference of the International Gothic Association, Stirling, 1995, and to be published in a volume of the conference proceedings in 1998.
36. I am thinking of the half-convinced re-enactments of a putatively violent history that make up contemporary British street anarchism.
37. Cf. Freud on the general theory of the complexes in his disappointingly slight paper, 'Psycho-Analysis and the Establishment of the Facts in Legal Proceedings' (1906), in *Standard Edition of the Complete Psychological Works of Sigmund Freud*, ed. James Strachey *et al.*, 24 vols (London, 1953–74), IX, 99–114.
38. For a discourse of ruins and how they might influence all our interpretations, see most helpfully Bill Readings, 'Dwelling in the Ruins', in *The University in Ruins: Essays on the Crisis in the Concept of the Modern University*, ed. Timothy Clark and Nicholas Royle (Stirling, 1995), pp. 15–28.
39. 'Thus a ceremonial starts as an *action for defence* or *insurance*, a *protective measure....* It may thus be compared to an unending conflict; fresh psychical efforts are continually required to counterbalance the forward pressure of the instinct' (Freud, 'Obsessive Actions and Religious Practices' (1907), in *Standard Edition*, IX, 123–4).
40. On the Gothic and transgression, see, e.g., Ann McWhir, 'The Gothic Transgression of Disbelief: Walpole, Radcliffe and Lewis', and Coral Ann Howells, 'The Pleasure of the Woman's Text: Ann Radcliffe's Subtle Transgressions', both in *Gothic Fictions: Prohibition/Transgression*, ed. Kenneth W. Graham (New York, 1989), pp. 29–47 and 151–62; also Michelle A. Massé, *In the Name of Love: Women, Masochism, and the Gothic* (Ithaca, NY, 1992).
41. See Stephen King, *Christine* (London, 1983), pp. 5, 205, 447; the discourse of assemblages is developed in Gilles Deleuze and Félix Guattari, *A Thousand Plateaus: Capitalism and Schizophrenia*, trans. Brian Massumi (London, 1988), e.g., pp. 331–4, 398–403, 510–14.
42. The most obvious reference is to Keith Jeffery and Peter Hennessy, *States of Emergency: British Governments and Strikebreaking since 1919* (London, 1983); but the notion of the 'state of emergency' as both product and precondition of the bourgeois State can be found in thinkers as diverse as Althusser, Gramsci, Nairn and Eco.
43. Some of these 'interests' are those explored by Terry Eagleton in *Myths of Power: A Marxist Study of the Brontës* (2nd edn, London, 1988), pp. 97–121.

44. See Martin Amis, *London Fields* (London, 1989), p. 420.
45. I take this to follow from Freud's remarks in 'The Economic Problem of Masochism' (1924), in *Standard Edition*, XIX, 157–70, and in *New Introductory Lectures on Psycho-Analysis* (1933), in *Standard Edition*, XXII, esp. 104–7.
46. See Emily Brontë, *Wuthering Heights* (1847), ed. David Daiches (Harmondsworth, Middx., 1965), p. 217.
47. See John Forrester, *The Seductions of Psychoanalysis: Freud, Lacan and Derrida* (Cambridge, 1990), e.g., pp. 62–82.
48. See, for example, Janice Galloway, 'Blood'; Scott Bradfield, 'Didn't She Know'; Yannick Murphy, 'The Fish Keeper'; Lynne Tillman, 'A Dead Summer'; Emma Tennant, 'Rigor Beach', all in *The New Gothic*, ed. Patrick McGrath and Bradford Morrow (London, 1992), pp. 85–94, 95–111, 129–34, 135–45, 231–8.
49. On the uncanny, see of course Freud, *The 'Uncanny'* (1919), in *Standard Edition*, XVII, 217–56. But basic to my argument throughout is that uncanny phenomena have to do with *projection*, probably in the way James Hillman sees it: 'what psychology has had to call *projection* is simply *animation*, as this thing or that spontaneously comes alive, arrests our attention, draws us to it' (*A Blue Fire: The Essential James Hillman*, ed. Thomas Moore [London, 1990], p. 99).
50. Jacques Derrida, 'Me – Psychoanalysis: An Introduction to the Translation of *The Shell and the Kernel* by Nicolas Abraham', *Diacritics*, 9.1 (1979), 12.
51. The 'barbarian' in the somatised world of Iain Banks's *The Bridge* (London, 1986) is in some ways emblematic of this condition, perhaps especially in relation to the dramatisations of the heroic ego; see, e.g., pp. 139–47.
52. See Mary Shelley, pp. 229ff.
53. In *The Literature of Terror*, reissued in two revised volumes, *The Gothic Tradition* and *The Modern Gothic* (London, 1996).

2. THE GOTHIC AND THE LAW: LIMITS OF THE PERMISSIBLE

1. Nicholas Royle, 'This is not a Book Review. Esther Rashkin: *Family Secrets and the Psychoanalysis of Narrative*', *Angelaki*, 2.1 (1995), 34.
2. See Daniel Defoe, *Captain Singleton*, intro. James Sutherland (London, 1963), p. 2.
3. See Daniel Defoe, *Moll Flanders*, intro. Kenneth Rexroth (New York, 1964), pp. 11–12.
4. See Tobias Smollett, *The Adventures of Roderick Random*, ed. Paul-Gabriel Boucé (Oxford, 1979), pp. 4, 1.
5. Oliver Goldsmith, *The Vicar of Wakefield*, intro. Austin Dobson (London and New York, 1900), p. 19.
6. See Fanny Burney, *Evelina*, intro. Edward A. Bloom (London, 1968), p. 15.

Notes

7. See Ann Radcliffe, *The Italian*, intro. Frederick Garber (London, 1971), p. 2.
8. See Samuel Richardson, *Pamela*, intro. M. Kinkead-Weekes, 2 vols (London, 1962), I, 420–1, 164–9.
9. See Henry Fielding, *The History of Tom Jones*, ed. R.P.C. Mutter (Harmondsworth, Middx., 1966), esp. pp. 840–3; William Beckford, *Vathek*, ed. Roger Lonsdale (London, 1970), pp. 109–20; William Godwin, *The Adventures of Caleb Williams*, intro. Walter Allen (London, 1966), pp. 349–60.
10. See Fielding, *Tom Jones*, p. 778.
11. See Tobias Smollett, *The Expedition of Humphry Clinker*, ed. Angus Ross (Harmondsworth, Middx., 1967), pp. 241–2.
12. Defoe, *Moll Flanders*, p. 220; 'hedge solicitors' were particular objects of scorn.
13. Jonathan Swift, *Gulliver's Travels*, intro. Michael Foot (Harmondsworth, Middx., 1967), p. 297.
14. Henry Fielding, *Joseph Andrews*, intro. A.R. Humphreys (London, 1962), p. 44.
15. Fielding, *Tom Jones*, p. 161.
16. See Tobias Smollett, *The Adventures of Peregrine Pickle*, ed. James L. Clifford (London, 1969), pp. 68–71; *Clinker*, e.g., pp. 207–12. Smollett, of course, spent time in gaol himself.
17. Fielding, *Joseph Andrews*, p. 227.
18. See Smollett, *Pickle*, p. 684; obviously this is partly a joke.
19. See Robert Bage, *Hermsprong, or, Man as he is not*, ed. Peter Faulkner (Oxford, 1985), p. 80.
20. There is now an extensive literature on the 'foreign body'; see, e.g., Nicholas Royle, *After Derrida* (Manchester, 1995), pp. 143–58.
21. See Swift, pp. 104–6; Laurence Sterne, *Tristram Shandy*, ed. Gerald Weales (New York, 1960), pp. 37–40.
22. Tobias Smollett, *The Adventures of Ferdinand Count Fathom*, ed. Damian Grant (London, 1971), p. 175.
23. See my *Literature of Terror*, I, 40–3.
24. See Robert Robson, *The Attorney in Eighteenth-Century England* (Cambridge, 1959), p. 11.
25. Brian Abel-Smith and Robert Stevens, *Lawyers and the Courts: A Sociological Study of the English Legal System, 1760–1965* (London, 1967), p. 20.
26. See Fielding, *Tom Jones*, e.g., p. 327.
27. Abel-Smith and Stevens, p. 9.
28. Fielding, *Tom Jones*, p. 327; this passage is quoted by Abel-Smith and Stevens, p. 10.
29. Fielding, *Tom Jones*, p. 109.
30. Fielding, *Tom Jones*, p. 184.
31. See Fielding, *Tom Jones*, pp. 410–11.
32. See Tobias Smollett, *The Life and Adventures of Sir Launcelot Greaves*, ed. David Evans (London, 1973), pp. 86–94; *Clinker*, pp. 205–6.
33. See Horace Walpole, *The Castle of Otranto*, ed. W.S. Lewis (London, 1969), e.g., p. 91.

34. Abel-Smith and Stevens, p. 14.
35. See Clara Reeve, *The Old English Baron*, ed. James Trainer (London, 1967), p. 124.
36. See, e.g., Frank Milton, *The English Magistracy* (London, 1967), p. 13.
37. Charles Brockden Brown, *Wieland, or, The Transformation* (Garden City, NY, 1973), p. 256.
38. See my *Literature of Terror*, I, 114–39.
39. Michael Ignatieff, *A Just Measure of Pain: The Penitentiary in the Industrial Revolution, 1750–1850* (New York, 1978), p. 28.
40. Reported in J. Latimer, *Annals of Bristol: The Eighteenth Century* (London, 1893), p. 454; see Ignatieff, p. 31.
41. See Ignatieff, p. 31.
42. Ignatieff, p. 37.
43. See Goldsmith, p. 226.
44. There is a clear brief statement of the development of the inner world in Melanie Klein, 'On Identification' (1955), in *Envy and Gratitude, and Other Works 1946–1963* (London, 1975), pp. 141–2, based around the complex interaction between persecutory and depressive anxieties.
45. John Fielding, according to Ignatieff, p. 33.
46. See Henry Mayhew and John Binny, *The Criminal Prisons of London* (London, 1968), p. 592.
47. See Defoe, *Flanders*, pp. 286–7.
48. See Smollett, *Roderick Random*, pp. 170–6; Reeve, pp. 98–102; Matthew Lewis, *The Monk* (London, 1973), pp. 276–80, 333–41; Brockden Brown, pp. 185–98, 201, 224–44.
49. See Smollett, *Peregrine Pickle*, pp. 709–32, and nn. thereto.
50. See Smollett, *Clinker*, pp. 179–83 (Jery's account of the proceedings).
51. See, e.g., Lewis M. Knapp, *Tobias Smollett: Doctor of Men and Manners* (Princeton, NJ, 1949), pp. 227–47; and my 'Smollett and the Logic of Domination', *Literature and History*, No. 2 (1975), pp. 60–83.
52. See below, pp. 213–18ff.
53. See Bage, pp. 220–8.
54. See Radcliffe, *The Italian*, e.g., pp. 200–7, 305–67, 389–405.
55. Certainly in *Evelina* the law seems to be regarded as beyond reproach; see, e.g., p. 171.
56. See, e.g., Ignatieff, pp. 44–5.
57. Swift, p. 325.
58. See Swift, pp. 236–7; Bage, *passim*. Miss Fluart's rare rationality is especially marked by her mockery of litigiousness; see, e.g., Bage, p. 153.
59. Lewis, p. 39.
60. Donald Bruce, *Radical Doctor Smollett* (London, 1964), p. 83.
61. See Defoe, *Flanders*, pp. 291–301.
62. See Goldsmith, pp. 238–9; this, obviously, connects with the more general eighteenth-century interest in criminal physiognomy.
63. See Ann Radcliffe, *The Mysteries of Udolpho*, ed. Bonamy Dobrée (London, 1970), p. 218.

Notes

229

64. Defoe, *Singleton*, p. 25. This version of pirate community is in a recognisable tradition; see Maximillian E. Novak, *Economics and the Fiction of Daniel Defoe* (Berkeley, Calif., and Los Angeles, 1962), pp. 103–27; Peter Earle, *The World of Defoe* (London, 1976), pp. 60–6.
65. See Friedrich Schiller, *Die Räuber*, ed. C.P. Magill and L.A. Willoughby (Oxford, 1972), *passim*; Francis Lathom, *The Midnight Bell: A German Story...*, intro. Devendra P. Varma (London, 1968), pp. 144–55.
66. See Goldsmith, pp. 243–6; Godwin, *passim*; Bage, e.g., pp. 45, 49, 92, 213; Radcliffe, *The Italian*, pp. 121–2, 173.
67. Abel-Smith and Stevens, p. 17.

3. LAWS WHICH BIND THE BODY: THE CASE OF THE MONSTER

1. Ted Hughes, 'Ghost Crabs', in *Selected Poems 1957–1981* (London, 1982), p. 67.
2. See Samuel Weber, 'In the Name of the Law', in ed. Cornell, Rosenfeld and Carlson, pp. 232–57; 'the "people of today" is... determined by the laws of the past, but at the same time – which is therefore determined as a time of the past – this people of today is not bound by those laws...' (p. 247).
3. See H.G. Wells, *The Island of Doctor Moreau*, ed. Brian Aldiss (London, 1993), e.g., pp. 55–62; William Blake, *A Descriptive Catalogue* (1809), in *Complete Writings*, ed. Geoffrey Keynes (London, 1966), p. 585.
4. Or perhaps by the 'phantom body of the police' (Derrida, 'Force of Law', p. 45); see also Agnes Heller's powerful essay, 'Rights, Modernity, Democracy', in ed. Cornell, Rosenfeld and Carlson, pp. 346–60, and Franz L. Neumann, *The Rule of Law: Political Theory and the Legal System in Modern Society* (Leamington Spa and Heidelberg, 1986), pp. 11–24.
5. Among many approaches of this kind, see, e.g., *Monster Theory: Reading Culture*, ed. Jeffrey Jerome Cohen (Minneapolis, 1996).
6. See Michel Foucault, e.g., *The Birth of the Clinic: An Archaeology of Medical Perception*, trans. A.M. Sheridan Smith (London, 1973), pp. 124–48; *Discipline and Punish: The Birth of the Prison*, trans. Alan Sheridan (Harmondsworth, Middx., 1971), pp. 3–31; *Power/Knowledge: Selected Interviews and Other Writings 1972–1977*, ed. Colin Gordon (Brighton, 1980), pp. 55–62.
7. But perhaps it would be equally correct to say that it is the offices of the law that enforce the social formation of 'monsters' (those 'shown off' as deterrents?). I am thinking of the conclusions reached by the Commission for Racial Equality enquiry reported in Roger Hood, *Race and Sentencing* (Oxford, 1992).
8. On the history of the labyrinth, useful sidelights are shed by Penelope Reed Doob, *The Idea of the Labyrinth from Classical Antiquity through the Middle Ages* (Ithaca, NY, 1992).

230 Notes

9. See Toni Morrison, *The Bluest Eye* (London, 1979), pp. 125–6; *inter alia* 'free', we note, 'to live his fantasies, and free even to die'.
10. See in particular Chris Baldick, *In Frankenstein's Shadow: Myth, Monstrosity, and Nineteenth-Century Writing* (Oxford, 1987); but also on the subject of the exhibition of the body Paul Semonin, 'Monsters in the Marketplace: The Exhibition of Human Oddities in Early Modern England', in *Freakery: Cultural Spectacles of the Extraordinary Body*, ed. Rosemarie Garland Thomson (New York, 1996), pp. 69–81.
11. See, e.g., Christopher Norris, *Deconstruction: Theory and Practice* (London and New York, 1982), pp. 56–73.
12. Friedrich Nietzsche, *Beyond Good and Evil: Prelude to a Philosophy of the Future*, trans. R.J. Hollingdale (Harmondsworth, Middx., 1973), p. 19.
13. See, e.g., Robert C. Solomon, *The Passions: The Myth and Nature of Human Emotion* (New York, 1976), p. 126.
14. Jerome Kagan, *The Nature of the Child* (New York, 1984), p. xiv.
15. See Sandor Ferenczi, *Final Contributions to the Problems and Methods of Psycho-analysis*, ed. Michael Balint (London, 1955), e.g., p. 246.
16. We can perhaps see a useful refraction of this issue in the notorious 'debate' between Derrida and John R. Searle; see Searle, 'Reiterating the Differences: A Reply to Derrida', *Glyph*, I (1977), 198–208; Derrida, *Limited Inc*, ed. Gerald Graff (Evanston, Ill., 1988).
17. This is the basis of my previous discussion of *Frankenstein* in *Literature of Terror*, I, 106–11.
18. See James Hillman, *The Dream and the Underworld* (New York, 1979), esp. pp. 23–67; Nicolas Abraham and Maria Torok, *The Wolf Man's Magic Word: A Cryptonymy*, trans. Nicholas Rand (Minneapolis, 1986).
19. On the difficulties of the concept of the 'name-of-the-father', cf. Elizabeth Grosz, *Jacques Lacan: A Feminist Introduction* (London and New York, 1990), pp. 70–1, 103–5, 188; Madelon Sprengnether, *The Spectral Mother: Freud, Feminism, and Psychoanalysis* (Ithaca, NY, 1990), pp. 8, 196ff.
20. See Hillman, *Dream and the Underworld*, pp. 33–45; also *A Blue Fire*, p. 174.
21. See *A Blue Fire*, pp. 13–91; Hillman, *Dream and the Underworld*, pp. 191–202.
22. See Byron, *Don Juan*, Canto XIII, stanza 40, l. 2, in *Byron*, ed. Jerome J. McGann (Oxford and New York, 1986), p. 775.
23. See Apollodorus, *The Library*, II, v, 12; also Hillman, *Dream and the Underworld*, pp. 28, 185, 110–17.
24. For just one of many recent dealings with this question, see Vanessa D. Dickerson, 'The Ghost of a Self: Female Identity in Mary Shelley's *Frankenstein*', *Journal of Popular Culture*, 27.3 (1993), 79–91.
25. See Blake, e.g., *Vala, or, The Four Zoas* (1795–1804), Night the Ninth, ll. 692–794, and *Milton* (1804–8), 27, 1–41, in *Complete Writings*, pp. 375–8, 513–14.

26. Cf. Jane Gallop, *Reading Lacan* (Ithaca, NY, 1985), pp. 157–85, and Grosz, pp. 67–74.
27. See Otto Rank, *The Don Juan Legend*, trans. D.G. Winter (Princeton, NJ, 1975).
28. See Rank, e.g., p. 95.
29. See further on this my '*Don Juan*, or, The Deferral of Decapitation: Some Psychological Approaches', in *Theory in Practice: Byron's 'Don Juan'*, ed. Nigel Wood (Buckingham, 1993), pp. 122–53.
30. See Hermann Diels, *Die Fragmente der Vorsokratiker*, ed. Walther Kranz (Berlin, 1934–8), 22 B 123.
31. See Christine Berthin, 'The Poetics of Concealment: Cryptonyms, Phantoms and Family Secrets in Gothic Fiction', paper delivered at the conference of the European Society for the Study of English, Bordeaux, 1993.
32. As might be the general condition of all writing:

> The work requires of the writer that he lose everything he might construe as his own 'nature', that he lose all character and that, ceasing to be linked to others and to himself by the decision which makes him an 'I', he becomes the empty place where the impersonal affirmation emerges.
>
> (Blanchot, p. 55)

Does this take us the essential step *beyond* a relapse into mere 'negative capability'?

4. RE-ENACTMENTS OF THE PRIMAL SCENE: THE EXAMPLE OF *ZASTROZZI*

1. Tadeusz Rachwał, *Word and Confinement: Subjectivity in 'Classical' Discourse* (Katowice, 1992), p. 29.
2. Or, perhaps, the 'sequence of scenes' described by Jean Laplanche; see his *New Foundations for Psychoanalysis*, trans. David Macey (Oxford, 1989), pp. 109ff., in which he spells out the implications for seduction theory of various views of the epistemological status of the primal scene.
3. See Blake, e.g., *Vala, or, The Four Zoas*, Night the Fourth, ll. 63–110, in *Complete Writings*, pp. 299–300.
4. See Eustace Chesser, *Shelley and Zastrozzi: Self-Revelation of a Neurotic* (London, 1965), p. 33.
5. See my *Literature of Terror*, I, 138.
6. See John Donne, 'A Nocturnal upon St Lucie's Day, being the shortest day', in *John Donne*, ed. John Carey (Oxford, 1990), pp. 116–17.
7. See Freud, *On the Sexual Theories of Children* (1908), in *Standard Edition*, IX, 220–2; also *From the History of an Infantile Neurosis* ['The Wolf-Man'] (1918), in *Standard Edition*, XVII, 7–122.

8. See Carl Jung, *Psychology and Alchemy* (1944), in *Collected Works*, XII, 193, 213.
9. See Edward Trelawny, *Recollections of the Last Days of Shelley and Byron* (1858), ed. Edward Dowden (London, 1906), pp. 39–40.
10. See Hillman, *Dream and the Underworld*, pp. 23–67; also Homer, *Odyssey*, XI, 38ff.
11. Cf. Marie Roberts, *Gothic Immortals: The Fiction of the Brotherhood of the Rosy Cross* (London, 1990), e.g., pp. 208–13.
12. The Wendigo is the 'evil spirit' of the Algonkian Indians; or perhaps it is 'the phantom of hunger that stalks the forests in search of . . . victims to satisfy its craving for human flesh'; at any rate it moves with impossible, consuming, dream-like speed. See J.R. Colombo, *Canadian References* (Toronto, 1976), p. 558.
13. See Jung, *Psychology and Alchemy*, in *Collected Works*, XII, 285–6.
14. See Lewis, e.g., pp. 210–21; also Russell Hoban, *The Medusa Frequency* (London, 1987), e.g., pp. 93–102.
15. See Propertius, *Elegies*, IV, 9; Ovid, *Fasti*, I, 543ff.; Livy, I, 7; Virgil, *Aeneid*, VIII, 193ff.
16. See Hillman, *Dream and the Underworld*, pp. 110–17.
17. See Edward Trelawny, *Records of Shelley, Byron and the Author*, 2 vols (London, 1878), I, 158.
18. See Freud, *Totem and Taboo* (1913), in *Standard Edition*, XIII, 140–6; and *Moses and Monotheism: Three Essays* (1939), in *Standard Edition*, XXIII, 80–92.
19. See Freud, *Fragment of an Analysis of a Case of Hysteria* [Dora] (1903), in *Standard Edition*, VII, 3–122.
20. See Freud, *Analysis of a Phobia in a Five-Year-Old Boy* [Little Hans] (1909), in *Standard Edition*, X, 25, 119–27, 137–41.
21. See Ned Lukacher, *Primal Scenes: Literature, Philosophy, Psychoanalysis* (London, 1990), e.g., pp. 12, 22–4.
22. See Abraham and Torok, e.g., pp. 39–40.
23. See Sylvia Plath, 'Daddy', in *Ariel* (London, 1965), pp. 54–6.
24. See, e.g., my *Literature of Terror*, I, 49–52, 137. Note also that other editions of *Zastrozzi* offer us different permutations of this omission.
25. See Jung, *Transformation Symbolism in the Mass* (1954), in *Collected Works*, XI, 236–7.
26. See Freud, *The Interpretation of Dreams* (1900), in *Standard Edition*, e.g., IV, 193–7, 231–2; V, 469–70.
27. See Freud, *Civilisation and its Discontents* (1930), in *Standard Edition*, XXI, 69–71.
28. See, e.g., Victor Sage, *Horror Fiction in the Protestant Tradition* (London, 1988).
29. On lines of flight and their relation to the body and the law, see Deleuze and Guattari, pp. 88–9, 121–2, 133–4, 422–3.
30. See Bertolt Brecht, *The Caucasian Chalk Circle*, in, e.g., *Parables for the Theatre*, intro. Eric Bentley (Harmondsworth, Middx., 1965), pp. 111–207. We learn of Azdak that he 'denounced himself and ordered the policeman to take him to Nuka, to court, to be judged' (p. 174).

31. See Timothy Marshall, *Murdering to Dissect: Grave-robbing, Franken-stein, and the Anatomy Literature* (Manchester, 1995).
32. For a sophisticated account of the aesthetics of terror, see Terry Heller, *The Delights of Terror: An Aesthetics of the Tale of Terror* (Urbana, Ill., 1987).

5. REGIMES OF TERROR: FROM ROBESPIERRE TO CONRAD

1. Perhaps this is more of a question than it seems.
2. Seamus Heaney, 'Punishment', in *North* (London, 1975), p. 38.
3. See Edmund Burke, *Reflections on the Revolution in France*, intro. A.J. Grieve (London, 1964), pp. 68–9.
4. Stanley Loomis, *Paris in the Terror, June 1793 to July 1794* (London, 1965), pp. 73–4.
5. See Blake, 'On Homer's Poetry and on Virgil' (*c.* 1820), in *Complete Writings*, p. 778, where it is 'the Classics, & not Goths nor Monks, that Desolate Europe with Wars'.
6. Cf. the extraordinary instance of the return of the repressed given by Freud in 'Delusions and Dreams in Jensen's *Gradiva*' (1907), in *Standard Edition*, IX, 35, where 'Sin' takes 'the very place of the Saviour on the cross'.
7. Blake, *Jerusalem* (1804–20), 31, 29–38, in *Complete Writings*, p. 657.
8. Charles Dickens, *A Tale of Two Cities*, intro. Sir John Shuckburgh (London, 1967), p. 249.
9. See Royle, *After Derrida*, e.g., p. 147; it is perhaps indeed a 'para-site'.
10. On related issues, see Massé, *In the Name of Love*; Jeffrey Weeks, *Sex, Politics and Society: The Regulation of Sexuality since 1800* (2nd edn, London, 1989); and various essays in *Body Guards: The Cultural Politics of Gender Ambiguity*, ed. Julia Epstein and Kristina Straub (New York and London, 1991).
11. See F.R. Leavis, *The Great Tradition* (London, 1948), pp. 209–19.
12. The reference is to Richard von Krafft-Ebing, *Psychopathia Sexualis* (1893). One of Krafft-Ebing's main areas of work, incidentally, was in 'judicial psychopathology', for 'Law and Jurisprudence have thus far given but little attention to the facts resulting from investigations in psycho-pathology. Law ... is constantly in danger of passing judgement on individuals who ... are not responsible for their acts' (p. 334).
13. See my *Literature of Terror*, I, 29–37.
14. We need to bear in mind here Reiner Schürmann's remarks that 'transgression occurs at the very heart of legislation, in its essence and its instances. Not that agents always abuse the rule, but always, as it regulates, the rule abuses itself. ... any name laying down the law contains in it its own forces of abandon' ('Conditions of Evil', trans. Ian Janssen, in ed. Cornell, Rosenfeld and Carlson, p. 399).
15. See Wells, *The Holy Terror* (London, 1939), p. 12.
16. See Freud, *Moses and Monotheism*, in *Standard Edition*, XXIII, 75–7.
17. Perhaps Iris Murdoch's most intriguing moment of commentary on her own art is the short, bleak chapter 'Void' in *Metaphysics as a*

Guide to Morals (London, 1992), pp. 498–503, which, in its very frustrations and evasions, calls to mind Hillman's comments on 'the Great Enemy', depression (see *A Blue Fire*, p. 153).

18. Doris Lessing, *The Good Terrorist* (London, 1985), p. 370.

19. On these issues, see Lynn Hunt, *Politics, Culture, and Class in the French Revolution* (Berkeley, Calif., 1984) and *The Family Romance of the French Revolution* (Berkeley, Calif., 1992).

20. Cf. Judith Butler, 'Subjection, Resistance, Resignification: Between Freud and Foucault', in *The Identity in Question*, ed. John Rajchman (New York and London, 1995), esp. pp. 240ff.; and my *The Hidden Script: Writing and the Unconscious* (London, 1985), esp. pp. 97–112.

6. IDENTIFICATION AND GENDER: THE LAW OF LIGEIA

1. Timothy Clark, *Derrida, Heidegger, Blanchot: Sources of Derrida's Notion and Practice of Literature* (Cambridge, 1992), p. 74.

2. See Elisabeth Bronfen, *Over her Dead Body: Death, Femininity and the Aesthetic* (Manchester, 1992), pp. 330–6. All further citations from Bronfen in this chapter are from these pages.

3. Edgar Allan Poe, 'Ligeia', in *Collected Works of Edgar Allan Poe*, ed. Thomas O. Mabbott, 3 vols (Cambridge, Mass., 1969–78), II, 319.

4. Bob Dylan, 'Boots of Spanish Leather' (1964); the lyric interestingly inverts the gendering of its own sources.

5. Cf. Jean Baudrillard, 'Subjective Discourse or the Non-Functional System of Objects', in *Revenge of the Crystal: Selected Writings on the Modern Object and its Destiny, 1968–1983* (London, 1990), pp. 53–6.

6. This is not a point developed by Bronfen; but see, e.g., my 'Narrative and Psychology in Gothic Fiction', in ed. Graham, pp. 1–27. See Klein, 'On the Theory of Anxiety and Guilt' (1948) and 'Some Theoretical Conclusions Regarding the Emotional Life of the Infant' (1952), in *Envy and Gratitude*, pp. 25–42 and 61–93.

7. Mikkel Borch-Jacobsen, *The Freudian Subject*, trans. Catherine Porter (London, 1989), p. 6.

8. See Mikkel Borch-Jacobsen, *Lacan: The Absolute Master*, trans. Douglas Brick (Stanford, Calif., 1991), e.g., pp. 16–19, 116–21.

9. Cf. pp. 206–9 below.

10. See Søren Kierkegaard, *The Concept of Dread*, trans. Walter Lowrie (Princeton, NJ, 1957), pp. 14–50.

11. See Blake, 'The Tyger', in *Songs of Experience* (1789–94), in *Complete Writings*, p. 214; see also Roger Sabin, *Adult Comics: An Introduction* (London and New York, 1993), pp. 57, 175–6; Ernest Cashmore, *Rastaman: The Rastafarian Movement in England* (London, 1983), esp. pp. 156–61.

12. The very structure of Gallop's *Reading Lacan*, to take but one example, is a representation, further refracted through a Lacanian lens, of these struggles.

13. See my 'Edgar Allan Poe: Tales of Dark Heat', in *Nineteenth-Century Suspense: From Poe to Conan Doyle*, ed. Clive Bloom *et al.* (London, 1988), pp. 12–13.
14. On the dream-house in general, see Freud, *Introductory Lectures on Psycho-Analysis* (1916–17), in *Standard Edition*, XV, 153, 159; here see more particularly his remarks on the 'wooden house' as the coffin in *The Interpretation of Dreams*, in *Standard Edition*, V, 454–5.
15. Borch-Jacobsen, *The Freudian Subject*, pp. 38–9.
16. Cf. Paul Ricoeur, *Freud and Philosophy: An Essay on Interpretation*, trans. Denis Savage (New Haven and London, 1970), pp. 130–2, 482.
17. As Lacan says there never can be:

> This reel is not the mother reduced to a little ball by some magical game...it is in the object to which the opposition is applied in act, the reel, that we must designate the subject.
> (Jacques Lacan, *The Four Fundamental Concepts of Psycho-Analysis*, ed. Jacques-Alain Miller [London, 1977], p. 62)

18. Borch-Jacobsen, *The Freudian Subject*, p. 234, quoting Freud, 'Group Psychology and the Analysis of the Ego' (1921), in *Standard Edition*, XVIII, 127.
19. Borch-Jacobsen, *The Freudian Subject*, p. 232.
20. Borch-Jacobsen, *The Freudian Subject*, p. 37.
21. Borch-Jacobsen, *The Freudian Subject*, p. 89.
22. Cf. Baudrillard's remarks on photographic and other images in *The Evil Demon of Images*, trans. Paul Patton and Paul Foss (Sydney, 1987).
23. Borch-Jacobsen, *The Freudian Subject*, p. 73.
24. Cf. Eve Sedgwick, *Between Men: English Literature and Male Homosocial Desire* (New York, 1985), e.g., pp. 21–7.
25. Borch-Jacobsen, *The Freudian Subject*, p. 20, quoting Freud, *The Interpretation of Dreams*, in *Standard Edition*, IV, 267.
26. Borch-Jacobsen, *The Freudian Subject*, p. 22.
27. Borch-Jacobsen, *The Freudian Subject*, p. 45.
28. See my 'Angela Carter: Supersessions of the Masculine', in *The Hidden Script*, pp. 28–42.

7. A DESCENT INTO THE BODY: *WUTHERING HEIGHTS*

1. Baudrillard, *Revenge of the Crystal*, p. 53.
2. Brontë, *Wuthering Heights*, p. 367.
3. Cf. Geoffrey Hartman on the epitaph among various kinds of inscription in 'Wordsworth, Inscriptions, and Romantic Nature Poetry' (1965), reprinted in Hartman, *Beyond Formalism: Literary Essays 1958–1970* (New Haven and London, 1970), pp. 206–30.
4. See, e.g., Donald P. Spence, *The Freudian Metaphor: Toward Paradigm Change in Psychoanalysis* (New York, 1987), pp. 11–16; also Jung, *Mysterium Coniunctionis* (1954), in *Collected Works*, XIV, 333–4.

5. See, e.g., H.J. Rose, *A Handbook of Greek Mythology* (London, 1953), pp. 78ff.
6. Which no doubt connects with Hades' older status as a fertility god; for an interesting sidelight on this connection, see Joseph Campbell, *The Masks of God: Creative Mythology* (New York, 1968), p. 410.
7. See Apollodorus, I, v, 2; Ovid, *Metamorphoses*, V, 438ff., and *Fasti*, IV, 615–20; Pausanias, *Description of Greece*, I, xxxvii, 2.
8. See Jacques Derrida, 'Che cos'a la poesia?', in *A Derrida Reader: Between the Blinds*, ed. Peggy Kamuf (Hemel Hempstead, 1991), pp. 225ff.
9. Cf., e.g., Robert White, 'Missing a Generation: The Rat Man and Hamlet', *Angelaki*, 2.1 (1995), 42.
10. Although, as we may recall, Antony's 'daemon' is 'noble, courageous, high, unmatchable/Where Caesar's is not', none the less 'near him thy angel/Becomes afeard, as being o'erpow'red', or so the soothsayer tells him; see Shakespeare, *Antony and Cleopatra*, II. iii. 20–3 in, e.g., ed. Barbara Everett (New York, 1988), pp. 78–9.
11. See Robert Graves, *The Greek Myths*, 2 vols (Harmondsworth, Middx., 1955), I, 53, 144–5; also Ovid, *Fasti*, V, 493ff.
12. Brontë, *Wuthering Heights*, p. 366.
13. Cf. the position of the judge according to the claims of legal realism, who

> must decide which rules to apply, and this is done in an act of judicial reasoning in which there are no *other* rules telling the judge which rule to apply.... we see that judges are free to reach any result in a case that they wish to reach...
>
> (Benditt, p. 4)

and may thus incarnate precisely this 'disembodied sovereign'.
14. But which, of course, has also its negative, unobserved side, that side of Freud, for example, which we may find exhibited in his dealings with 'Dora'. See, *inter alia*, Jane Gallop, *Feminism and Psychoanalysis: The Daughter's Seduction* (London, 1982), pp. 132–50.
15. See, e.g., Brontë, *Wuthering Heights*, p. 16; also C.P. Sanger, 'The Structure of *Wuthering Heights*', in <u>Wuthering Heights</u>: *Authoritative Text, Backgrounds, Criticism*, ed. William M. Sale, Jr, and Richard J. Dunn (New York, 1990), pp. 331–6.
16. Most strikingly, perhaps, in relation to Eros: see Plutarch, *Amatorius*, 20; but also Virgil, *Ciris*, 134f., and Cicero, *De Natura Deorum*, III, 23.
17. As well as p. 46ff. above, see also Gallop, *Feminism and Psychoanalysis*, pp. 39, 47–9, 71.
18. See James Hillman, *Anima: An Anatomy of a Personified Notion* (Dallas, Texas, 1985), e.g., pp. 147–67; *Insearch: Psychology and Religion* (Dallas, Texas, 1967), pp. 95–102.
19. Cf. the symbolisation of the Empusae: see, e.g., Aristophanes, *The Frogs*, 285ff.; Philostratus, *The Life of Apollonius of Tyana*, IV, 25.
20. See Hillman, *Insearch*, pp. 68–94.

21. As, emblematically, in the case of Sagaris; see Plutarch, *On Rivers*, 12.
22. See Freud, 'Obsessions and Phobias: Their Psychical Mechanism and their Aetiology' (1895), in *Standard Edition*, III, 74ff.
23. The logic of the pseudonym has not as yet been traced; but its beginnings are perhaps implicit in concepts like the 'ambiguity of obliteration', which we find in Philippe Lacoue-Labarthe, *The Subject of Philosophy*, ed. Thomas Trezise (Minneapolis, 1993), pp. 57–98.
24. See Coleridge, e.g., 'Lines written at Shurton Bars' (1795), 'The Eolian Harp' (1795), 'Dejection: An Ode' (1802) and many other poems: in S.T. Coleridge, *Poetical Works*, ed. E.H. Coleridge (London, 1967), pp. 96–100, 100–2, 362–8.
25. See the Homeric Hymns to Hermes; Sophocles, Fragments of *The Searchers*.
26. See, e.g., Homer, X, 133ff.
27. See Donne, 'Nocturnal upon St Lucie's Day', l. 15, in *John Donne*, p. 116.
28. This is, of course, Hades as 'Pluton'; see nn. 5 and 6 above.
29. See, e.g., Rose, p. 79.
30. As perhaps also in the myth of Theseus and Peirithous in the under-world (see Diodorus Siculus, IV, 63; Horace, *Odes*, IV, vii).
31. See *The Tibetan Book of the Dead*, ed. W.Y. Evans-Wentz (Oxford, 1960), pp. 175ff.
32. And again:

> Study me then, you who shall lovers be
> At the next world, that is, at the next spring:
> For I am every dead thing,
> In whom love wrought new alchemy.
> ('Nocturnal upon St Lucie's Day', ll. 10–13)

33. See *Dhammapada: Translation of Dharma Verses with the Tibetan Text*, trans. dGe-'dun Chos-'phel *et al.* (Berkeley, Calif., 1985), e.g., pp. 121, 173, 185.
34. Cf. Baudrillard on the 'object-passion' in *Revenge of the Crystal*, pp. 44–6.
35. See, e.g., Gaston Bachelard, *The Psychoanalysis of Fire*, trans. Alan C.M. Ross (London, 1964), pp. 21–41; also Roch C. Smith, *Gaston Bachelard* (Boston, Mass., 1982), pp. 70–115.
36. See, e.g., Homer, *Iliad*, XVIII, 372ff.

8. *PSYCHO*PATHOLOGY: CONTAMINATION AND THE HOUSE OF GOTHIC

1. William Burroughs, quoted in a report on his wife's death, *New York Daily News* (8 September 1951).
2. Robert Bloch, *Psycho* (New York, 1959), p. 126.

3. Cf. the account of narcissism in Karen Horney, *New Ways in Psychoanalysis* (London, 1939), pp. 88–100.

4. This connection between mourning and revenge is brought out with especial force by Freud in his discussion of 'the Devil as a father-substitute' in 'A Seventeenth-Century Demonological Neurosis' (1923), in *Standard Edition*, XIX, 69–105. See particularly pp. 86–7.

5. Bloch, *Psycho*, p. 126.

6. See Bloch, *Psycho*, pp. 11–12.

7. Cf. p. 46 above.

8. Cf. pp. 110–20 above.

9. See the remarkable insights, some of them left entirely implicit, in Erik H. Erikson, 'The Fate of the Drives in School Compositions' (1931), trans. Inge S. Hoffman, and, with Kai T. Erikson, 'The Confirmation of the Delinquent' (1957), in *A Way of Looking at Things: Selected Papers from 1930 to 1980*, ed. Stephen Schlein (New York and London, 1987), pp. 39–69, 621–30.

10. And it seems only appropriate to read transvestitism itself as a problem of *reading*, as do Arnold Birenbaum and Edward Sagarin in *Norms and Human Behaviour* (New York, 1976), p. 131.

11. Cf. H.K. Fierz, 'The Clinical Significance of Extraversion and Introversion', trans. C. Rowland, in *Current Trends in Analytical Psychology*, ed. Gerhard Adler (London, 1961), pp. 88–97.

12. See Deleuze and Guattari, esp. pp. 149–66:

> The body without organs is desire; it is that which one desires and by which one desires.... Even when it falls into the void of too-sudden destratification, or into the proliferation of a cancerous stratum, it is still desire.
>
> (p. 165)

13. See Patrick Süskind, *Perfume: The Story of a Murderer*, trans. John E. Woods (London, 1986), pp. 261–3.

14. I am suggesting here a much broader definition of addiction (and one that would utter Freud's addictions, for example, at the same time as revealing some of the roots of the Gothic) than that proposed by Avital Ronell in *Crack Wars: Literature, Addiction, Mania* (Lincoln, Nebr., 1992).

15. Cf. Baudrillard on 'the marginal system: the collection' and on 'stereo-porno' in *Revenge of the Crystal*, pp. 43–58 and 146–52.

16. Cf. p. 71 above.

17. See John Fowles, *The Collector* (London, 1963), e.g., pp. 45, 58, 148.

18. Cf. Ackbar Abbas, 'Walter Benjamin's Collector: The Fate of Modern Experience', *Working Papers of the Centre for Twentieth-Century Studies*, No. 3 (Milwaukee, 1986).

19. See Derrida, Foreword, in Abraham and Torok, p. xxxv.

20. As it seems to have been for the Wolf-Man: see Freud, *From the History of an Infantile Neurosis*, in *Standard Edition*, XVII, 61–6.

21. This might suggest an aetiology in terms of inhibitions in playing, which would themselves be connected to wider issues of creativity

and reparation; see Klein, 'The Psycho-Analytic Play Technique: Its History and Significance' (1955), in *Envy and Gratitude*, pp. 124, 129–31.

22. Cf. Elizabeth Wilson, *Adorned in Dreams: Fashion and Modernity* (London, 1985), pp. 117–33.
23. Robert Bloch, *American Gothic* (New York, 1974), p. 206.
24. See Will Self, *My Idea of Fun* (London, 1993), pp. 253–84; '...overall the impression the Money Critic's room gave was of a relief map of currencies, in which the lumpings and moundings of diverse kinds indicated their relative liquidity and value' (p. 282).
25. One of many examples can be found in the early history of the Wolf Man, and marks his (in this instance temporary) submission to an iron law; see Freud, *From the History of an Infantile Neurosis*, in *Standard Edition*, XVII, 16–17. My apparently provocative recasting of this as a 'psychotic' episode would follow Klein.
26. See Xi Xi, *A Girl Like Me, and Other Stories*, afterword by Stephen C. Soong (Hong Kong, 1986), pp. 1–16.
27. See Brian R. Clifford and Ray Bull, *The Psychology of Person Identification* (London, 1978), pp. 96–8, 143, 192–204; also

> The life of our courts, the trial process, is based upon the fiction that witnesses see and hear correctly and so testify, and if they do not testify with accuracy on direct examination, cross-examination will straighten them out... [which] is another fiction.
>
> (J. Marshall, 'The Evidence: Do We See and Hear What Is? Or Do Our Senses Lie?', *Psychology Today*, 2 (1969), 50)

9. LAWS OF RECOLLECTION AND RECONSTRUCTION: STEPHEN KING

1. Meg Harris Williams and Margot Waddell, *The Chamber of Maiden Thought: Literary Origins of the Psychoanalytic Model of the Mind* (London, 1991), p. xiii.
2. See, e.g., King, *Christine.*
3. See Stephen King, *The Shining* (New York, 1977), e.g., pp. 152–66.
4. See, e.g., the hinted character connections that link *Rita Hayworth and Shawshank Redemption* and *Apt Pupil*, both in Stephen King, *Different Seasons* (New York, 1982).
5. See Freud, e.g., 'The Dissolution of the Oedipus Complex' (1924), in *Standard Edition*, XIX, 173–9.
6. See Freud, *From the History of an Infantile Neurosis*, in *Standard Edition*, XVII, 48–60.
7. See Freud, *Analysis of a Phobia in a Five-Year-Old Boy*, in *Standard Edition*, X, esp. 135–6; and *From the History of an Infantile Neurosis*, in *Standard Edition*, XVII, 29ff.
8. Lukacher, p. 42.
9. Lukacher, pp. 42–3.

10. The reference is to Joseph Heller, *Something Happened* (New York, 1966); and on the 'overlordly' tone in which this story is told, see Derrida on Kant in 'Of an Apocalyptic Tone Newly Adopted in Philosophy', in *Derrida and Negative Theology*, ed. Harold Coward and Toby Coshay (Albany, NY, 1992), pp. 30–42.

11. See, e.g., Marcel Detienne, *The Creation of Mythology*, trans. Margaret Cook (Chicago and London, 1986), pp. 33ff.

12. See Stephen King, *The Sun Dog*, in *Four Past Midnight* (New York, 1990), p. 905.

13. Cf. p. 109 above.

14. Bronfen, p. 256.

15. See Bronfen, p. 326.

16. King, *The Sun Dog*, p. 871.

17. The reference is to Roy Fisher, 'The Hill Behind the Town', in *Poems 1955–1980* (Oxford, 1980), pp. 23–4.

18. See Freud, *Leonardo da Vinci and a Memory of his Childhood* (1910), in *Standard Edition*, XI, 86–7.

19. See Hillman, *Dream and the Underworld*, e.g., pp. 59–64; *A Blue Fire*, pp. 38–49.

20. Graves, *The Greek Myths*, I, 58.

21. I am thinking here of the imagery at the beginning and end of Poe, 'The Fall of the House of Usher' (1839), in *Collected Works*, II, 397–8 and 417.

22. I am thinking here not only of the notion of the unconscious but also of the Derridean 'experience of the impossible'; see, e.g., *Experiencing the Impossible*, ed. Timothy Clark and Nicholas Royle (Stirling, 1993), p. 2 and *passim*.

23. See, e.g., Baudrillard's analysis of *The Student of Prague* in *La Société de consommation* (Paris, 1970), p. 395.

24. The references are to Deleuze and Guattari, pp. 158–9, 188–9, 497–9. At p. 498, Deleuze and Guattari equate the 'Gothic line' with the 'nomadic line invested with abstraction'.

25. See Julia Kristeva, *Powers of Horror: An Essay on Abjection*, trans. Leon Roudiez (New York, 1982).

26. See Hillman, *Re-Visioning Psychology* (New York, 1995), pp. 159–61.

27. See Freud, *The Interpretation of Dreams*, in *Standard Edition*, V, 554–64.

28. See Robert Graves, *The White Goddess* (London, 1948); also John B. Vickery, *Robert Graves and the White Goddess* (Lincoln, Nebr., 1972), pp. 34–41.

29. See, e.g., D.W. Winnicott, 'Transitional Objects and Transitional Phenomena' (1953), in *Essential Papers on Object Relations*, ed. Peter Buckley (New York, 1986), esp. pp. 259–60.

30. Cf. Baudrillard, *Revenge of the Crystal*, pp. 182ff.

31. See Stephen King, *Misery* (New York, 1987), p. 364.

32. See Jacques Lacan, 'The Function and Field of Speech and Language in Psychoanalysis' (1953), in *Écrits: A Selection*, trans. Alan Sheridan (London, 1977), pp. 30–107.

33. See Stephen King, *'Salem's Lot* (New York, 1975), pp. 3–12, 470–83.

34. See King, *Secret Window, Secret Garden*, in *Four Past Midnight*, p. 482.

35. See Kurt Vonnegut, *Slapstick, or, Lonesome No More!* (New York, 1976).
36. See, e.g., Paul L. Harris, *Children and Emotion: The Development of Psychological Understanding* (Oxford, 1989), pp. 51–80.
37. See King, *The Shining*, e.g., pp. 283–91.

10. THE BODY SUBLIME: LIU SUOLA'S *KING OF SINGERS*

1. Introduction to *Classical Chinese Tales of the Supernatural and the Fantastic: Selections from the Third to the Tenth Century*, ed. Karl S.Y. Kao (Bloomington, Ind., 1985), p. 2.
2. The original title is 'Xunzhao gewang', and it is collected in Liu, *Ni bie wu xuanze* (*You Have no Choice*) (Beijing, 1986). I am using the translation by Martha Cheung Puiyiu, University of Hong Kong.
3. Liu, p. 4; on the voices and presence of the banditti, cf., e.g., Radcliffe, *Udolpho*, p. 54.
4. Liu, p. 4; and see Edmund Burke, *Philosophical Inquiry into the Origin of our Ideas of the Sublime and Beautiful* (1756), ed. J.T. Boulton (London, 1958), e.g., p. 68. For some further reflections on sublimity and Chinese literature, see aso Wong Kin-yuen, 'Negative/Positive Dialectic in the Chinese Sublime', in *The Chinese Text: Studies in Comparative Literature*, ed. Ying-hsiung Chou (Hong Kong, 1986), pp. 119–58.
5. See Melanie Klein, 'Infantile Anxiety Situations Reflected in a Work of Art and in the Creative Impulse' (1929), in *Love, Guilt and Reparation, and Other Works 1921–1945* (London, 1975), pp. 210–18; one of the very few attempts to look at the practical psychology of the law is *Legal and Criminal Psychology*, ed. Hans Toch (New York, 1961); see also Jeffrie G. Murphy, *Retribution, Justice, and Therapy: Essays in the Philosophy of Law* (Dordrecht, 1979), pp. 77ff.
6. See, e.g., Laurence Sickman and Alexander Soper, *The Art and Architecture of China* (Harmondsworth, Middx., 1971), pp. 182–6, 203–22, 339–52; and, more particularly, the accompanying Plates. Among the earlier masters, it may well be artists like Fan K'uan (*c.* 990–1030) and Li Ch'êng (*c.* 940–67) who are most relevant here.
7. See, e.g., my *Literature of Terror*, II, 189.
8. A cardinal example that comes to mind is Martin's 'The Fall of Nineveh' (1829); see, e.g., Feaver, pp. 99–103.
9. See Bill Readings, 'Sublime Politics: The End of the Party Line', *Modern Language Quarterly* (1992), 409–25.
10. Some interesting and relevant comments, relating to much older literature, can be found in Stephen Chan Chingkiu, 'The Return of the Ghostwoman: A Critical Reading of Three Sung *Hua-pen* Stories', *Journal of the Asian-Pacific Cultural Centre*, XV, 3 (1987), 47–71.
11. See, e.g., Coleridge, 'The Wanderings of Cain', in *Poetical Works*, pp. 285–92.
12. See, e.g., Maturin, p. 195.
13. Cf., e.g., Ralph V. Tymms, *Doubles in Literary Psychology* (Cambridge, 1949).

14. The most relevant analyses are those of Barthes in *The Fashion System* (1967), trans. Matthew Ward and Richard Howard (London, 1985).
15. See Freud, e.g., *Introductory Lectures on Psycho-Analysis*, in *Standard Edition*, XVI, 396–7.
16. See, e.g., Raymond Williams, *The Country and the City* (London, 1973), *passim*; and Pat Rogers, 'The Writer and Society', in *The Context of English Literature: The Eighteenth Century*, ed. Rogers (London, 1978), pp. 14ff.
17. See, e.g., Yang Lian, 'Torches', trans. Sean Golden and John Minford, in *Seeds of Fire: Chinese Voices of Conscience*, ed. Geremie Barmé and John Minford (Hong Kong, 1986), pp. 247–8; and many other poems and extracts in this collection.
18. Adaptation of a Chinese proverb in Leon Wieger, *Chinese Characters: Their Origin, Etymology, History, Classification and Signification*, trans. L. Davrout (New York, 1915), p. 15.
19. See Preface, in Wordsworth and Coleridge, *Lyrical Ballads* (1798), ed. R.L. Brett and A.R. Jones (London, 1963), pp. 248–50.
20. Liu, p. 27; cf. Baldick, pp. 10–29.
21. A frequent trope in the Gothic from Radcliffe to Sheridan LeFanu, and Oscar Wilde, *The Picture of Dorian Gray* (1891).
22. See my *Literature of Terror*, II, 193–6; also my 'Narrative and Psychology in Gothic Fiction', in ed. Graham, p. 11.
23. Cf., e.g., Eric Josephson and Mary Redmer Josephson, 'Alienation: Contemporary Sociological Approaches', in *Alienation: Concept, Term, and Meanings*, ed. Frank Johnson (New York and London, 1973), pp. 163–81; see also Richard Schacht, *Alienation*, intro. Walter Kaufmann (London, 1971); Ignace Feuerlicht, *Alienation: From the Past to the Future* (Westport, Conn., 1978).
24. See, e.g., Milner, 'Psychoanalysis and Art' (1956), in *The Suppressed Madness of Sane Men*, pp. 208–9; and Michael Holstein, 'Keats: The Poet-Healer and the Problem of Pain', *Keats-Shelley Journal*, XXXVI (1987), 32–49.
25. See Hillman, *Dream and the Underworld*, pp. 23–67.
26. See Hugh Blair, 'A Critical Dissertation on the Poems of Ossian' (1765), in, e.g., James Macpherson, *The Poems of Ossian and Related Works*, ed. Howard Gaskill (Edinburgh, 1996), pp. 347ff.

11. GOTHIC AFTER/WORDS: ABUSE AND THE BODY BEYOND THE LAW

1. Sara Guyer, 'Albeit Eating: Towards an Ethics of Cannibalism', *Angelaki*, 2.1 (1995), 67.
2. In this chapter, although I shall allude to other texts as well, I have adopted a central corpus of twelve contemporary fictions as examples of the types of Gothic phenomenon I want to explore. They are Peter Ackroyd, *The House of Doctor Dee* (1993) and *Dan Leno and the Limehouse Golem* (1994); Martin Amis, *Money* (1984); John Banville, *Mefisto* (1986) and *The Book of Evidence* (1989); Dennis Cooper, *Closer*

(1989); Don DeLillo, *White Noise* (1984); Bret Easton Ellis, *The Rules of Attraction* (1987); William Gibson, *Count Zero* (1986) and *Mona Lisa Overdrive* (1988); Will Self, *The Quantity Theory of Insanity* (1991); and Donna Tartt, *The Secret History* (1992).

3. See, for example, the interestingly Euro-named but largely defunct Tessier-Ashpools of Gibson's mythology. The worlds of privilege encapsulated in Ellis's *Rules of Attraction*, in Cooper, in Tartt, give a strong impression of being different perspectives (differentiated mainly in terms of sexual orientation) on a single 'scene', the violent and bleak subtext of which is perhaps most brilliantly manifested in Victor's eventual contribution in *Rules of Attraction*, pp. 229–30.

4. Perhaps a comment is provided by Self in 'The Quantity Theory of Insanity':

> I had no sense of being singled out as unique, or blessed. I had no suspicion that I might be the *ubermensch* [sic]. Quite the reverse. It was painfully clear to me that I was destined to become like my father, constantly striving to stave off chaos through rigorous application to detail.
>
> (*Quantity Theory of Insanity*, p. 99)

5. And the same is emblematically true in Cooper:

> George continued, his lips nearly motionless. Philippe smiled when a pause seemed to warrant warmth, knowing that he could agree with whatever George said. The boy longed to speak, and there was 'nobody else to speak to', in his words, which was some sort of privilege.
>
> (*Closer*, p. 104)

In the case of Philippe, as elsewhere, this knowledge of privilege is equated with death.

6. This notion of evidence connects directly with the meaning-free detail that accumulates in and around these texts:

> Maolseachlainn Mac Giolla Gunna, my counsel and, he insists, my friend, has a trick of seizing on the apparently trivial in the elaboration of his cases. Anecdotes of his methods circulate in the corridors of chancery, and around the catwalk in here. Details, details are his obsession.
>
> (Banville, *Book of Evidence*, p. 73)

7. One particularly influential one, intellectually and practically, has been the Tavistock 'open systems' approach; see the very varied essays in *Exploring Individual and Organisational Boundaries*, ed. W. Gordon Lawrence (Chichester, 1979), and perhaps especially Barry Palmer, 'Learning and the Group Experience', at pp. 169–92.

8. And what, therefore, might 'evidence' constitute on this ambiguous terrain? A question fit to be put by counsel:

> What is the evidence against Mrs Cree, after all? She purchased some arsenic powder for rats. That is the sum of it. If that were

grounds for the charge of murder, half the women of England would be standing in this place.

(Ackroyd, *Dan Leno*, p. 157)

9. The 'airborne toxic event' that dominates *White Noise*, producing its own further interference – or turbulence – in a realm of interference, has its own mythic dimension and produces its own undecidabilities of response:

> The enormous dark mass moved like some death ship in a Norse legend, escorted across the night by armoured creatures with spiral wings. We weren't sure how to react.
>
> (DeLillo, *White Noise*, p. 127)

10. But this abjection may also conduce to ritualisation and paranoia:

> Everything had brought me to this knowledge, there was no smallest event that had not been part of the plot. Or perhaps I should say: had brought me back to it. For had I not always known, after all? From the start the world had been for me an immense formula.
>
> (Banville, *Mefisto*, p. 185)

11. Similarly, we might think,

> The artist who thinks he sovereignly opposes all values and protects within himself through his art the source of all-powerful negation submits to the universal destiny no less than the artist who produces 'useful' works. Perhaps he submits more.
>
> (Blanchot, p. 217)

12. David, in *Closer*, suggests to us one, rather dubious, way in which this non-communication might function:

> I'm talking in circles. That's not a clever ploy, really. Maybe somewhere in the back of my mind I hope speaking like this might hypnotise the world so I can slip away.... No matter how I extend myself I don't get closer to who I am...
>
> (Cooper, *Closer*, p. 36)

13. See Freud, *Totem and Taboo*, in *Standard Edition*, XIII, 1–161; also Joseph Shepher, *Incest: A Biosocial View* (New York, 1983).

14. The image is of the Boxmaker, unconsciously still trying to 'make' amid the shards, if it be only 'an arrangement of brown old maps and tarnished mirror. The seas of the cartographers had been cut away, exposing the flaking mirrors, landmasses afloat on dirty silver...' (Gibson, *Count Zero*, p. 310). Only pages before, the 'Gothicks' have been active...

15. Nicolas Abraham, quoted in Esther Rashkin, *Family Secrets and the Psychoanalysis of Narrative* (Princeton, NJ, 1992), p. 27.

16. See, among many other relevant texts, Mary Walker, 'Between Fiction and Madness: The Relationship of Women to the Supernatural in Late Victorian Britain', in *That Gentle Strength*, ed. Lynda L. Coon, Katherine J. Haldane and Elisabeth Sommer (Charlottesville, Va.,

1990), pp. 230–42; and Judith Butler, *Bodies that Matter: On the Discursive Limits of 'Sex'* (New York, 1993).

17. See, e.g., Anna Freud, *The Harvard Lectures*, ed. Joseph Sandler (London, 1992), esp. pp. 47ff.

18. 'Whereas in the first period of infantile sex development the instinctive demands have been very strong and the force of the ego directed against them was comparatively weak, the instinctive demands now drop, and that gives the child a chance to develop further, to strengthen itself, to accomplish all sorts of other tasks. The most important of these is learning, in the sense of the development of the intellect' (Anna Freud, p. 47).

19. There has been no extended study of the anxiety of orphanage in Dickens; but see Angus Wilson, 'Dickens on Children and Childhood', in *Dickens 1970*, ed. Michael Slater (London, 1970), pp. 195–227.

20. See Blake, *Vala, or, The Four Zoas*, Night the Eighth, ll. 102–6, in *Complete Writings*, p. 343; *Milton*, pp. 489–90.

21. Of kinds explored in almost all our texts, although perhaps *Money* stands as the archetype (see, e.g., pp. 121ff.); later, naturally, we are in a 'gothic cafeteria' (p. 165). Also:

> Without the paternal metaphor holding things together, one was at a loss [sic], one became the artisan of one's own body, fiddling around, experimenting, creating new parts or treating the psyche like an organ, a sick organ. One became a maniacal bricoleur of one's own body.
>
> (Ronell, pp. 74–5)

22. 'Let us now summarise the points in which agreement between taboo usages and obsessional symptoms is most clearly shown... (4) the fact that they give rise to injunctions for the performance of ceremonial acts' (Freud, *Totem and Taboo*, in *Standard Edition*, XIII, 28–9)
        Such acts, of course, are also endemic to Gothic narrative structure, for it is not irrelevant to narrative development (or its reverse) that, for example, 'with the aid of the *Mutus Liber* [sic] I made a crystalline table which was round like a cartwheel and painted upon it certain characters and names in yellow and blue...' (Ackroyd, *House of Doctor Dee*, p. 183), and that such ceremonials punctuate and drive the plot.

23. See DeLillo, *White Noise*, pp. 304ff., but perhaps the most resonant comment in these pages about an afterlife remains: 'The supermarket shelves have been rearranged' (p. 325).

24. 'The ghost touched his lips with a slim forefinger. "I'm something else as well, yes. I do display a bit too much initiative for a mere guide programme. Though the model I'm based on is top of the line, extremely sophisticated. I can't tell you exactly what I am, though, because I don't know"' (Gibson, *Mona Lisa Overdrive*, p. 204).

25. But also as a prophylactic of death:

Most of us have probably seen our own death but haven't known how to make the material surface. Maybe when we die, the first thing we'll say is, 'I know this feeling. I was here before'.

(DeLillo, *White Noise*, p. 151)

But *where*?

26. See Self, *My Idea of Fun*; but also, for example, Banville:

On the hospital steps I stopped. A high gold autumn evening was sinking over the rooftops. Forever after I would think of the city like that, like a waste of magnificent wreckage, going down. My hands shook, stuffed into these unaccustomed pockets. Such space, such distance. I was dizzy.

(*Mefisto*, p. 139)

27. See, e.g., Freud's interesting deployment of mineralogical metaphor in *Introductory Lectures on Psycho-Analysis*, in *Standard Edition*, XVI, 390.

28. An imagery not, however, to be regarded as purely anthropocentric, for cities too, as well as other more expectant locales, have their own desires:

It was almost as if they had been waiting impatiently for these murders to happen – as if the new conditions of the metropolis required some vivid identification, some flagrant confirmation of its status as the largest and darkest city of the world.

(Ackroyd, *Dan Leno*, p. 88)

29. See some of the argument in Molly Haskell's classic *From Reverence to Rape: The Treatment of Women in the Movies* (2nd edn, Chicago, 1987); also E. Ann Kaplan, *Women and Film: Both Sides of the Camera* (London, 1983), pp. 73–82, and Brian McNair, *Mediated Sex: Pornography and Postmodern Culture* (London, 1996).

30. '3Jane was the filament, Tessier-Ashpool the strata, her birthdate officially listed as one with her nineteen sibling clones. . . . The critics [sic] agreed: 3Jane was Becker's trigger. With 3Jane's birth, the focus of the documentary shifted subtly, exhibiting a new intensity, a heightening of obsession – a sense, more than one critic had said, of sin' (Gibson, *Mona Lisa Overdrive*, p. 136).

31. The reference is to M.R. James, 'The Ash-tree', in *Ghost Stories of an Antiquary* (Harmondsworth, Middx., 1974), pp. 52–68.

32. 'Multiplicities are rhizomatic, and expose arborescent pseudo-multiplicities for what they are. There is no unity to serve as a pivot in the object, or to divide in the subject. There is not even the unity to abort in the object or 'return' in the subject' (Deleuze and Guattari, p. 8).

33. See, of course, the endlessly deferred brotherhood of Sean and Patrick Bateman in Ellis at, e.g., *Rules of Attraction*, pp. 139–41, where it figures only as interference in a quite different telephone call and thus as a breach in communicative legality.

34. See the end of Ellis, *American Psycho*; but also that of Banville, *Book of Evidence*:

> It's my story, I said, and I'm sticking to it. He laughed at that. Come on, Freddie, he said, how much of it is true? It was the first time he had called me by my name. True, Inspector? I said. All of it. None of it. Only the shame.
>
> (p. 220)

35. For two very different versions of what might be at stake in the issue of professionalism, see Eliot Freidson, *Professional Powers: A Study of the Institutionalisation of Formal Knowledge* (Chicago, 1986), and Blaise Cronin and Elisabeth Davenport, *Post-Professionalism: Transforming the Information Heartland* (London and Los Angeles, 1988).

36. See, e.g., Norman J. Finkel, *Therapy and Ethics: The Courtship of Law and Psychology* (New York, 1980), which in many ways prefigures more contemporary debates; and various essays in *Psychotherapy and its Discontents*, ed. Windy Dryden and Colin Feltham (Buckingham, 1992).

37. See *Literature of Terror*, I, 114–39.

38. On which DeLillo provides ironic sidelights:

> 'Here it is practically the twenty-first century and you've read hundreds of books and magazines and seen a hundred TV shows about science and medicine. Could you tell those people one little crucial thing that might save a million and a half lives?'
> 'Boil your water', I'd tell them.
>
> (*White Noise*, p. 148)

39. See Hillman, *Anima*, pp. 18, 47.

40. But despite all the resonance of the 'old house', nothing is immune from the depredations of the estate agent:

> Nothing in this house seemed to stay in the same place.
> 'Just poking around', he said. He had gone up the stairs without us, and I resented his familiarity in my father's house. 'You'll probably get a good price for it'.
> 'I'm not putting it on the market. I'm going to live here'.
>
> (Ackroyd, *House of Doctor Dee*, p. 86)

41. 'Melanie Klein often shows in her work with children that anxiety can be a spur to development, to reparative phantasies and a movement of the libido to higher levels of organisation. Whether it will lead to a fixation or to progress depends on the degree of anxiety. When the anxiety cannot be mastered, a vicious circle results' (Hanna Segal, *Klein* [London, 1989], p. 107).

42. See, e.g., Linda Badley, *Writing Horror and the Body: The Fiction of Stephen King, Clive Barker and Anne Rice* (Westport, Conn., 1996); also Tartt, pp. 467–9; Self, pp. 97ff.; Cooper, pp. 61ff.

43. Cf. Blake, 'The Voice of the Ancient Bard', in *Songs of Innocence* (1789), in *Complete Writings*, p. 126.

44. A phenomenon perhaps most memorably presented by Theodor Adorno in *Philosophy of Modern Music* (1948), trans. Anne G. Mitchell and Wesley V. Blomster (New York, 1973); see pp. 18ff.
45. 'You see, I come from the criminal classes. Yes I do. It's in me, all that, in my blood. Oh, it gets you! Someone like me, I cannot put real distance between myself and prison. I can only put money there. It's in the blood, the blood' (Amis, *Money*, p. 167).
46. Which is in turn to speak of the impossibility of burial and of the interchangeability of surfaces: 'this surface is a skin, the skin of the ego, and it originates in the skin of the other. But if that skin should be missing, anything can be used as a substitute skin; as [Didier] Anzieu demonstrates, words, themselves can be used as a skin' (Laplanche, p. 49).
47. For example, Rudy's house in Gibson's *Count Zero* (see, e.g., pp. 178–94); the phantom scenarios of Self's 'North London Book of the Dead' (*Quantity Theory of Insanity*, pp. 1–15); the many locations of Banville's *Book of Evidence* ('On the harbour there was always a bar, always the same one whatever the island, with a few tables and plastic chairs outside, and crooked sun-umbrellas advertising Stella or Pernod...', p. 10).
48. See various essays in my *Writing the Passions* (forthcoming, London, 1998).
49. '...one could say that the logic of the sublime is not to be confused with either a logic of fiction or a logic of desire, that is... with either a logic of representation (something in the place of something else) or a logic of absence (of the thing that is lacking in its place). Fiction and desire, at least in these classical functions, perhaps always frame and determine aesthetics as such, all aesthetics. And the aesthetics of mere beauty, of the pure self-adequation of presentation, with its incessant sliding into the enjoyment of the self, indeed, arises out of fiction and desire' (Jean-Luc Nancy, 'The Sublime Offering', in Jean-François Courtine *et al.*, *Of the Sublime: Presence in Question*, trans. Jeffrey S. Librett (New York, 1993), p. 37).

Index